D1553956

SHE HUNGERED FOR ADVENTURE, THIRSTED FOR ESCAPE

"I was one of those legions who, in the Sixties, disappeared somewhere between Spain and Pakistan and was not heard from for months. True to Mother's prophecy, I traveled to far places whose every nuance is fixed indelibly in my memory. I recall the scents and sounds of Turkey in the spring; cheap hotel rooms on Paris' Left Bank; the feel of Greek islands on foggy days; the differing cadences of muezzins in Cairo and in Jerusalem; the essence of the Iraqi-Iran border, with trucks lined up twenty miles waiting days to cross, drivers camped alongside in stifling heat with no shade and no bathrooms.

Nearly two years ago I arrived in an oil-rich somnolent land where Kurds galloped the hills and camels plodded the fields. I came to the ancient Persia of Zoroaster and Darius, of Alexander the Great and Omar Khayyám, to a land filled with the promise of figs and honey. And when I left, it was suddenly a land filled with hate, its *joubs* running blood. . . .

LAST FLIGHT FROM IRAN

MARTIE STERLING WITH ROBIN STERLING

Introduction by Leon Uris

This is a true story. However, in order to
protect the privacy of the individuals whose
lives are portrayed in this book, names have
been changed in many instances.

LAST FLIGHT FROM IRAN
A Bantam Book / June 1981

ISBN 0-553-20005-4

Published simultaneously in the United States and Canada

PRINTED IN THE UNITED STATES OF AMERICA

0 9 8 7 6 5 4 3 2 1

DEDICATION

For Lee Uris, who is always there.

And for the American hostages
in Iran who served their country well.
Their fortitude and nobility brought
this nation together. We never forgot them,
and we will always remember.

ACKNOWLEDGMENT

We are very grateful to those who contributed much time and caring during the writing of this book, particularly John Maiorana; to those who unstintingly provided helpful documentation, memorabilia, newspapers and photographs of Iran, especially Jim Liberty; to Dick Wilson of Bell Helicopter International, who provided technical assistance and screened the manuscript for accuracy; to Roddy Burdine, the best editor in town; to the ever-helpful staff of Aspen's Pitkin County Library, who provided their usual cheerful and generous research assistance; and to Dad, who didn't complain when he went hungry.

FOREWORD

My first clear recollection of Arabs and Moslems was in the year 1934. I was ten years old. There was a John Ford film called "The Lost Patrol" starring a lot of golden oldies, since departed. Victor McLaglen, Boris Karloff and Wallace Ford were members of a British patrol that got lost "somewhere in Mesopotamia." The patrol was surrounded and hemmed in by a pack of slithering, unseen Arabs whose sharpshooters picked off the Brits one by one. Blood flowed in the sand of RKO Stage Number Six until we were down to the lone survivor, Victor McLaglen. He digs himself a shallow grave, lies down in it and aims his machine gun at the horizon and waits, just waits for one glimpse at the rotten heathens who were obviously ungrateful that the English had come all the way to Mesopotamia to save them from themselves. Several remakes of "Beau Geste" and a "Casablanca" or two later, I had collected all the standard clichés of this strange and remote part of the world and its strange and remote people. And who will ever forget Boyer and Lamarr traipsing through the casbah in "Algiers"? That was a sort of East meets West parody. Of course Sigmund Romberg's "Desert Song" was the granddaddy of them all and pro-Arab to boot: flowing white robes, gold-banded kiffiyas, super stallions. But the "Desert Song" was before my time.

When I was a kid I remember singing a rouser:

> The sons of the Prophet,
> Were hardy and bold,

vii

And quite unaccustomed to fear,
But the boldest of all,
Is a man, I am told,
Named Abul Abulbul Amir.

Confidentially, I didn't have the foggiest notion who the Prophet was nor did I have any idea I had been an infidel all my life and a Jewish infidel at that.

During the mid-1930's, world communications were conducted at a much more relaxed pace, a cracked, static-filled voice over the radio from London was about our outer reaches. Most Americans had some sort of vague general notion that there was something out there, in an eastern direction, called Islam, but we didn't know very much about them, and frankly, we didn't care. We had a population in those days of around a hundred and twenty-one million Americans, a hundred and twenty million of whom had never seen an Arab or even a Moslem.

In 1937 American geologists discovered that Saudi Arabia was sitting on an ocean of oil. We were edging toward war with the Nazis and it became plain old smart thinking to buddy up to the Arab monarch, a seedy old despot named Ibn Saud. History will record that this modest man was one of the few to name an entire country after himself. I remember that during World War II we felt an engaging need to cement this newly found kinship with nothing less than a state visit. The event was held aboard an American warship in the Persian Gulf and might well have been subtitled, "FDR meets Goatman." Ibn Saud was piped aboard with entourage, tents, goats and wives, in that order. We sophisticates back in America thought it was all quaint as hell. However, the old king and his successors were quickly getting the hang of things, recognizing that there was more to oil than just a lot of decomposed dinosaurs . . . and the world has never been the same since.

By the end of World War II we were already up to our eyeballs in the Moslem world starting to take over the authority of a declining British Empire and establishing an oil blood bank for the nations of the West, courtesy of the oil companies. The action was quiet. Hanky-panky never made the headlines. Through covert moves, the then-potent CIA saved the tail of another modest monarch who referred to himself as merely "The King of Kings." Mohammad Reza Pahlavi was implanted on the "Peacock Throne" which his father, an army sergeant, had seized, and thus we thwarted a possible Soviet takeover of Iran—or Persia, as it was known in the old days. Subsequently we armed the Shah to the teeth and commissioned him to protect the region under our enlightened guidance. The Shah returned the favor by eventually quadrupling the price of our oil and taking leadership in OPEC, the most infamous gang of larcenists in man's entire history.

While the Shah and OPEC were thinking big, we weren't even thinking. As we sunk into quicksands of widening commitments, the general American public had advanced no farther in their knowledge of the Moslem world than "The Lost Patrol." What we didn't know about Moslems was just about everything, and the State Department shared that lack of knowledge with us. We had become a nation of a hundred and seventy-one million people; a hundred and sixty-nine million of whom still had never seen a Moslem.

Although we were the Johnny Come Latelies to the region, in Islamic eyes we were merely a continuation of a thousand years of tugging and hauling and hostility between East and West. In the seventh century, Christian Europe had rallied to stop the mighty Islamic surge at their very gates. From then on there was a never-ending snarl between the two factions until the Crusaders blew the Moslems out of the box.

The Crusaders eventually had to pack up and haul out but the Middle-East was to be subjected to a long and sordid history of Western invasions, occupations and exploitations. Europe had castrated Moslem manhood on the battlefield and showed them to be a technically backward people. They were considered by us to be culturally defunct, not too honest, not too clean but very sneaky. In the past thousand years, every time the West has imposed itself on Moslem turf, which was quite often, we really stuck it to them.

When America entered the arena and inherited the responsibility for safe delivery of oil, we weren't exactly greeted as saviors. The old players in the Middle-East licked their chops as our naivete lit up like the neon in greater downtown Reno.

And then came the State of Israel. America and Europe, using the last of its morality, backed the new state, which, after all, was peopled largely by the survivors of a holocaust instituted on Christian soil. When the Arabs, who live mainly on macho, had their faces rubbed in it by the lowly Jews on the battlefield, it was the crowning insult to Islam. America, Israel's chief supporter, and rightly so, became the infidel of infidels to an enraged Moslem world.

We have groped our way through our relations with Islam with all the clarity of a blind man crossing a low spot in a river on a black night. The Moslem world knew the importance of that black stuff under their sands and the worm turned.

The Orient has been known for its despotism since Biblical times. Rule by assassination, cunning and blackmail are thousands of years old traditions. The instant mob in the street and total illogical behavior of the Moslem has long baffled the Western mind. Things were all right until oil affluence brought Islam and the Arabs out of their ancient lairs and into the West. Unfortunately East and West are all tangled up now, never to be separated again, and the traffic runs in both directions. Bit by bit, like little mouse droppings at first, the Western world was subjected to the ancient rites of the East. Yet, the Arab and Persian invasion of Europe with the introduction of hijackings, assassinations of political opponents, bombings and murder of innocents all seemed a long way from the good old U.S. of A. Oil blackmail on the political fronts of Europe's capitals, financial overkill in the banking markets, the weekly purchase of corporations half the size of General Motors and the bloodletting on European streets still represented a sound of distant drums to most Americans.

Our own very special case, the Iranians or Persians, after all, were not Arabs although they were fellow Moslems. There are differences between Iranians and Arabs, of course, but the similarities outweigh those differences, vastly. The Iranians have been best characterized as Arabs without the Arabs' sense of humor.

The Shah's hundred million dollar extravaganza honoring the birth of an ancient dynasty he had absolutely nothing to do with raised an eyebrow or two, but what the hell, the world loves a big spender, especially one who is on our (or God's) side.

Our two hundred million Americans who had never seen a Moslem before suddenly found them infiltrating our campuses as Iran and oil loaded sheikdoms sold students to needy American universities in lots of a hundred warm bodies, academic ability notwithstanding. The Iranian students in particular did it up brown, first purchasing expensive homes and cars, then setting up as eternal professional students. In order to keep the old pittance coming they got out on the streets and rioted now and then to protest the tyranny of the democracy which hosted them. Otherwise, they have shown little in the way of scholarship and less in the way of inclination to return to their beloved native soil. Even when Iraq attacked their homeland there was something less than a rush to get home and fight.

Our patience and Europe's moral bankruptcy to protect their oil seemed limitless. We've hardly batted an eye as Islam converted the United Nations into an international diplomatic brothel. With the world blowing up and Moslems dropping like flies in Uganda, Afghanistan and Somalia it appears, according to the U.N., that the world's only order of business is the condemnation of Israel. Of course it is one thing for the "Sons of the Prophet" to berate the tiny Jewish nation and another for them to take on the Soviet Union.

Then, one lovely day in the late autumn of 1979 the bubble burst and it was all dumped into America's living room. In the most blatant criminal act of a sovereign nation short of war, the American Embassy in Teheran was seized and fifty-two of our countrymen were held at gunpoint by a gang of two-bit hoodlums. Depending on what stage of "delicate" negotiations were under way they have been variously described as students, militants, revolutionaries and, on very rare occasion, terrorists. We have managed to keep a hush-hush attitude with any possible connection the terrorists have with the PLO because . . . well, hell, we don't want to upset anybody.

What has followed has been a theatre of the ridiculous, a comic-tragic play in which American ignorance, timidity and complete confusion on how to deal with Moslems have held us up to global ridicule. The act has caused us to lose the respect of friend and foe alike, and world leadership as well. We have been putty in the hands of Moslems who have twisted us into pretzels, made us jump through hoops, and sit up and beg like good dogs. Although this is the way Persians have conducted business for centuries our leaders have been totally inept and we in our remote bliss simply view the whole thing with egg on our faces. For despite our deepening involvement with Islam for almost a half-century, we have remained as distant from the Moslem mind as from the stars.

But we have it all now, the hysterical chanting of the faceless mob, the daily blackmail and threats, the flag burnings, the mindless ramblings of a confused and leaderless nation. And the raw, unvarnished hatred against us.

The final icing on the cake came with the outbreak of the Iran-Iraq conflict in which America has been blamed by almost every nation in the Middle-East for starting the war.

So, fellow countrymen, issues just aren't as clean cut as Hitler crossing the Polish border. We have a tremendous amount of catching up to do to understand who we are contending with, why they behave as they do and how we must deal with them. Even though the PLO has put across simplistic slogans like "legitimate rights of the Palestinian people," their notion of "legitimate rights" and our idea of "legitimate rights" are two entirely different things. Islam *is* different in religion, culture, geography, history, values and ethics. We are locked into a strange game with people whose entire existence has been involved in game-playing. The sooner we know them and the more we know about them, the better the chance to avoid violent confrontation.

A book such as "Last Flight from Iran" will go a long way in explaining the unexplainable through the personal adventure of a courageous young American girl suddenly and innocently caught in the bewildering events in Iran. What she has learned and now shares with us is important reading.

I first met the Sterling family when Ken and Martie ran a small madcap ski lodge in Aspen some two decades back. They had five children of their own and were raising two others. Along with the pains and tribulations, love, compassion and a touch of hilarious lunacy were always part of the scene. As a skiing family (young Whit was Junior National Champion and Danny skied the pro-circuit) they owned more Ace bandages and crutches than the Pitkin County Hospital.

Martie, a brilliant wit, has always been a little off the wall and in recent years has written herself into a reputation in the ski world as a sort of poor man's Jean Kerr. Her husband, Ken, also known as Poorken, has gone through all of it with uncommon valor braced with New England Yankee humor of a different kind.

Robin, the oldest of the lot, inherited her mother's fool-hardy spirit, and since her mid-twenties she has spent her life globe-trotting in managerial positions for large American overseas companies. The Iran caper was for Bell Helicopter: Robin arrived just as the monarchy was beginning its swan song. Her experience there continued for two years through the arrival of Khomeini. What happened to this attractive American girl in the middle of someone else's revolution ranges from the ridiculous to the comic to the terror of Savak and the s mobs. It is a wonderful story.

Herein we are given an irreverent view of a mode Western female living in a land where members of her se are sold into marriage for their labor, usually for the price of a few goats. Robin's suitors come and go and vainglorious Iranian male pride is often fractured. The inefficiency of a camel culture trying to go modern has its outrageous incidents. There is also the cold sweat of terrifying events and Robin bore it all with tongue in cheek.

Many of Robin's political perceptions and prophesies have come to pass as the mullahs took over the country and promptly wrecked it. Her insight into the Persian mind is razor sharp and is just the ticket as a primer for Americans to gain some insight into this confounding situation.

In the end, Robin had to flee for her life. In the not so funny scramble to get out of the country, she fortunately remembered to take her diary. In Martie Sterling's hands, the entire scope of her daughter's experiences come marvelously to life in what I believe is one of the funniest and enlightening books in a long, long time. Enjoy!

Leon Uris

PROLOGUE

Monday, 12 February 1979

I am writing on a crude webbed bench in a C-141, a cargo plane of ballroom dimensions that belongs to MAC (Military Airlift Command), United States Air Force. And though we're still in Iran, I already feel as if my feet were safe on American soil. There are more than one hundred passengers waiting for lift-off, most of us slobberingly gay and light-hearted amid dogs, cats, kids and a couple of mild cases of hysterics. Skip Maiorana is here, and Ron Horan and Rod-dey Sherman. A woman on my bench is weeping softly. Joy, I thought; her husband claims it's claustrophobia.

The C-141 has no windows. It also offers no meals, no drinks, no amenities, and no insulation. We huddle on long benches that run lengthwise, from nose to tail. Everyone is burrowed in, and beneath the hubbub there is a steady hum, the sweet sound of contentment. We're going home!

Our BHI (Bell Helicopter International) group left Esfahan three days ago. For any number of reasons it was no longer possible to fly out of Forudgahe Esfahan, and so 120 of us, like a traveling a capella choir, were bused for 290 miles to Teheran. At Iranian, that is, maniacal, rates of speed, the trip takes about six hours; it took us nine.

En route we passed through Qom, religious heart and soul of Iran, the seat of its revolt and stronghold of the Ayatollah Khomeini. No one had to remind us to "keep a low profile."

We made the entire trip with every window closed and curtained, all of us practically prone on the floor.

Any relief we felt at entering Teheran was short-lived. Our driver had never been away from home, and he was hell-bent on seeing all the capital city sights, revolution or no revolution. He spent three hours careening madly around the streets of Teheran, looking for the Hilton Hotel. As he made U-turns in rush-hour traffic, he jovially announced our presence to one and all by shouting, *"Hilton koja? Americae injal"* ("Where is the Hilton? I have Americans here.")

Teheran is a sprawling, disordered city of four million people. Because its shops had been on strike so long, every merchant had moved his wares onto the street curbs. It looked like a gargantuan yard sale. Add to this shoppers scattered all over the avenues and chaotic traffic which is already the worst in the world. (Iran has the highest traffic fatality and accident rate on earth.) Despite this confusion, we acquired the usual Iranian entourage—boys on Mopeds, men in cars, small children running with the speed of sound, and a sizable aggregation of howling, galloping *joub* dogs.

Behind us the baggage truck valiantly kept pace. Eventually we caught sight of Dan Mullins's Great Dane, Killer, thrashing around amid bouncing bags and flying carpets. She had, we learned on arrival, eaten her way out of her cage and through a pilot's entire wardrobe as well as a secretary's cherished collection of Persian miniatures. Poor Mullins was mortified but was unable to make restitution then and there. Like everyone else, he had unloaded most of his worthless Iranian *rials* and had only the forty dollars in American money allotted us by BHI.

Most of us were penniless; you can't write a check on a bombed-out bank. Barry Outcelt, a BHI helicopter mechanic, left Esfahan owing three hundred dollars on a carpet. He tried to find the tradesman to square his account, but Esfahan of late has been no place for a foreigner to roam the bazaar looking for a rug merchant. Barry needn't have worried: His carpet man outraced us to Teheran, found the Hilton, and accosted him in the lobby. Everyone contributed small change, and somehow the man was paid.

Ignoring the spectres of hellfire and damnation, we "Yonky" capitalist warmongers have just spent three deliriously decadent days at the Hilton. We'd been sleeping on

Esfahan floors and eating cold canned goods for so long that we felt like "woodsies" come to town. There was a decidedly carnival atmosphere, like Rome before the Fall. Just to hold our heads up, after months of keeping a low profile, was a blessed relief.

The Hilton is on the northern edge of the city, at the foot of the Elburz Mountains. An Aspen, Colorado, girl, I had determined to ski those mountains this winter. Looking out my hotel window at Mount Damavand, 18,934 feet and rumored to have more snow than Moscow, made me want to weep with frustration. I'll never have another crack at Iran's ski slopes. Khomeini will probably level the mountains as an offering to Muhammad.

The spectacular view of the city is at least one good memory to carry home, a kind of counterpoint to all the bleak ones of the past weeks. Although we didn't dare leave the hotel, we were so distant from the downtown shooting that we felt, for a change, comparatively safe.

We were thoroughly briefed on arrival. The beautiful Royal Gardens Hotel, where I had stayed on arrival in Iran almost two years before, and the Commodore—both former BHI bastions—had been blown up as a little bonus for being hospitable to foreigners. The Hilton was our last "home away from home." Betray the Hilton's trust, warned Security darkly, and the final evacuees would have no place to lay their bloody heads.

Another step BHI took was to separate every man from his weapon. Weaponry had always been verboten, but during the past months nearly all the men I know had *something* up their sleeves. I never saw such a display of Swiss Army knives, kitchen cutlery, lengths of chain and even baseball bats, or so many sheepish faces as weapons were handed over at the Hilton. Only the feeling that we were close to escape, plus Security's dire warnings about last-minute jailings, made everyone surrender their arms.

All of us were sick of trouble, worn-out, fighting nerves, and (typical Americans abroad) juggling too much luggage. At four o'clock this morning we were routed from the heavenly Hilton beds. We'd been briefed the night before: We would leave under heavy Iranian guard and proceed to Mehrabad International Airport before daylight, so as not to attract attention. Naturally Murphy's law was operational, and we spent a long morning in a snafu of forms and papers to be filled out and signed in triplicate. About eleven o'clock we were led single file through crowds of curious and inhospitable Teheranians. I'd been through those paces before, under worse conditions, and I felt fortunate when none of them plucked at my hair or clothes for souvenirs.

While our caravan rumbled across the city, we later learned, downtown mobs finally worked their way to the Hilton. Amidst heavy weapons fire, they took hostages and robbed quaking Americans blind.

MAC's planes have only just gotten permission to land here, and in addition to 250 of us from Bell Helicopter, there are the last tattered survivors from other American companies. We've been standing like sheep on the tarmac, hunkered down among dense clusters of soldiers who alternately try to hide us from view or pretend we don't exist. The temperature is about 48 degrees, with a very nippy wind and everyone is chilled as well as hungry, thirsty, and scared. New rumors whirl like dry leaves: We are not going to be allowed to leave; there aren't enough planes; Khomeini is again threatening to close the airport; we are all prisoners of the carpet cabal.

When C-141s land, their great wings dip toward the ground like a mallard duck's. They are designed this way to give them fast lift-off with enormously heavy loads. On witnessing the first takeoff one of the BHI wives cried, "My God, they're evacuating us in broken planes!"

After watching five of these MAC transports land, load and take off without us, our contingent finally, at four o'clock this afternoon, boarded the last plane leaving today. It was the longest wait of my life.

I could kiss our air force boys. They have been so gallant, look so wholesome, and act so very, very happy to have us aboard. It's been a long time since I've laid eyes on a military man who wasn't a troglodyte.

We've been issued large wads of bubble gum and advised it's not to chew but to stuff in our ears. This is a rough-and-tumble aircraft, and the noise of takeoff will be a mind blower. So, for that matter, will the mere act of flying. We'll all be rendered blessedly deaf and dumb.

There's space to stretch out on the benches if we wish, but I don't wish, thank you. I'm still twanging like a piano wire, and our destination—Athens—is a mere four and one-half hours distant.

Roddey Sherman and Skip, among others, have bared their T-shirted chests. Roddey's reads:

I Came
I Saw
Iran

Others say "Ruhollah Cola" (Ruhollah is the Ayatollah Khomeini's given name, which means the man actually had a mother and did not spring full-blown from a religious tract) and "Iranian War Games Survivor, 1978-79." Skip's reads "Stay and Die with BHI."

Ron Horan has put his handy mechanic's hands to work helping the air force boys serve lemonade, and I haven't heard one complaint, miraculously, about no cold beer. BHI even managed sandwiches for this gargantuan crowd. Wonder bread and mystery meat, but *cordon bleu* to us.

A month ago I was reluctant to leave. Two weeks later I'd begun clawing at the bars. Now that we're airborne and westward bound, I could sob with relief.

Nevertheless, it was a good life, back there. . . .

As I write in a warm cocoon of engine noise, I wonder dazedly what went wrong. Nearly two years ago I arrived in an oil-rich, somnolent land where Kurds galloped the hills and camels plodded the fields. I came to the ancient Persia of Zoroaster and Darius, of Alexander the Great and Omar Khayyám, to a land filled with the promise of figs and honey. And when I left it was suddenly a land filled with hate, its *joubs* running blood.

BOOK I

Monday, 31 July 1978

Summer is half-over, it's nearly *Ramazan,* and I have brucellosis.

Ramazan is the worldwide, month-long Moslem religious observance that commemorates the revealing of the Koran to Muhammad. From one full moon to the next (the date changes yearly, along with the Islamic calendar, and it's no wonder that Moslems have a very imprecise sense of time), there is absolute fasting from sunup to sundown. Hershey bars and Pepsi-Colas gulped behind back fences don't count. When the sun sets at the end of the day, everyone eats, drinks, and gives thanks; it's a time for visiting, hospitality, and if a family has a marriageable offspring, matchmaking. Except that Iranians must have missed the message. Everyone here grows short-tempered and irritable, maybe because there's so much public whipping and self-castigating. We've been hearing plenty from McGaffey lately. David R. Mc-Gaffey, the American consul in Esfahan. He's the one who cautions us *ad nauseum* to "keep a low profile."

The U.S. Consulate communiqués are poorly mimeo'd sheets with lots of typos and a very blurred national crest; they look like a weekly put out by the Sunnyside Middle School in

3

Idlewild, Iowa. Lately they've been trumpeting that Ramazan is a period of very deep religious significance and we are to keep a "very *very* low profile." I can see it. I wouldn't want a lot of outsiders boozing and belching around me while *I* was fasting. I plan to swim quietly in the Kouroush Hotel pool, tiptoe about my business, slip softly into bed at night, and sneak off to the country for an inconspicuous camping trip or two.

As for the brucellosis, I'm not alone with it. Almost everyone in Iran is afflicted. Brucellosis is the generic name for old-fashioned undulant, or milk fever. It comes not only from unpasteurized dairy products but also from cows I suspect have been crossed with camels and are not happy in their work, and the BHI doctors guess that seventy-five percent of Iranians have walking cases of it. It's a devastating disease which, untended, either kills its victims or eventually, in half a lifetime, runs its course. Since I wasn't sure I'd live that long, I sought help. I've been on massive doses of antibiotics for a week.

I also have the other universal disease—worms. I'll admit there are days when health and sanitation concerns make me wonder if Iran is really for me; but after a trip to Egypt last spring, I came back to Esfahan and thought, "It's nice to be home," and found myself signing on for another year.

I first came to Iran in May of 1977, and I've become so fond of this land of cats, carpets, melons, and nomads that I have decided to keep a journal about it.

Iran is a country of anomalies. Though it's sunbaked and drowsy in the south, to the north it has majestic mountains and fine snow for skiing. It is lazy and backward and graft-ridden, yet it is also a busy OPEC country very much in the world's mainstream. And it is *not* Arabic—it's Persian. Although Iranians now use the Arabic alphabet, the Arabs were latecomers here, and barbarians to boot. Iranians speak *Farsi,* an ancient Persian tongue remotely related to Slavic.

These Persian peoples have been catapulted bodily into the twentieth century by their tremendous oil wealth, and there's a tangible unease between them and their new technocracy. Despite the absolute power of the Shah (*shah* is Farsi for king, or emperor), there's also a restlessness, a searching for something I don't pretend to understand.

Americans here know pitifully little about this country or its people. There are few orientation courses after we arrive, and

4

even these are poorly attended. Most of what I've learned I've discovered through feeble gropings. Iranian co-workers, and my own reading. I am also nosy. *"Chetouri, madame?"* I say in the bazaars and *kutches* (alleyways, pronounced *koo-chays*), and hope someone will take the bait and want to be friends and answer my thousands of questions.

Americans as a whole know little about Iran. When my friend Jim Liberty, an engine mechanic from Detroit, announced to his co-workers that he was leaving his job, packing up his wife and two small children, and going to Iran, one of the shopmen looked up and said, "Oh, where's that? On the south side?"

Since last January I have been in personnel with Bell Helicopter International, Inc., a subsidiary of the Textron Corporation. Unofficially, mine is a euphemistic title for answer man and mother confessor to 450 employees on the second shift in BHI's maintenance department.

My "charges" include helicopter mechanics, production control and supply people, sheet-metal workers, painters, welders, engine specialists, avionics and electrical technicians, armament personnel, toolroom clerks, secretaries, timekeepers, and too many supervisors—American-style.

Created specifically to introduce helicopters to Iran, BHI has been here more than five years, under direct contract to the U.S. Department of Defense (hereinafter known as DOD), which in turn is contracted to the government of Iran (known as GOI). The local BHI operation is located largely on the Crown Prince Reza Pahlavi Base, called *Havan-e-Ruz* by Iranians, which is about ten miles south of Esfahan.

Esfahan has a small-town flavor, as though it were still its old oasis-self in the desert; yet there are nearly one million people here—or half as many as there are flies. The city dates back three thousand years, long before the time of Cyrus and Darius the Great. It is on the edge of the *Dasht-e-Lut* (Lut Desert) and has seen the comings and goings of Greeks, Macedonians, Seljuks, Arabs, Mongols, and Turks. In the late sixteenth century, the Shah Abbas, who referred to this lovely oasis as "half my world," made it his capital and built many of its most exquisite mosques, minarets, and *madrasehs* (schools). The name Esfahan is lost in unrecorded time, but is thought to come from the ancient Persian or Greek for warriors or armies. It is no longer an armed camp, thank God.

5

Today it is a marvel of azure, gold and turquoise cupolas, domes and minarets, a sparkling metropolis amid brown crags and foothills and vast expanses of flat, arid land. In the distance, on three sides, rise the Zagros and the Central mountain chains, aloof and snowcapped in winter, sere and sulking through the long, hot summers.

Because Esfahan is watered by the *Zyand-e-Rud* (River of Life), the city itself is green and flowered and dotted with fountains and pools; even the poorest families have gardens planted with vegetables and bursting with peony, rose, petunia and gladiolus blooms. Poinsettias grow wild beside the *joubs* (irrigation ditches); water lilies, lilacs and tulips abound. ("Lilac" is a Farsi word.)

I use the term "watered" loosely; the Zyand-e-Rud isn't very prepossessing to start with, and about forty miles beyond Esfahan it simply peters out in puddles of quicksand. It's full of weeds, catkins and refuse, but in this dry section of the country it is a universal playground. Joub dogs defecate in it, children play in it, and absolutely everyone scrubs carpets, washes clothes, and throws trash in it.

Despite the Shah's educational and agricultural programs, farmers around Esfahan still toil in the old biblical ways, with hand-hewn hoes and plows and the sweat of their brows. Women clean wool for spinning by beating it with heavy sticks in the streams, and they harvest wheat with hand sickles, tossing it high in the air to separate wheat from chaff.

Though flowers are beautiful and profuse, trees are still so precious that each one is lovingly numbered. It's a capital offense to maim or kill one.

Havan-e-Ruz, our army base, is a giant complex of landing fields, helicopter pads, classrooms, dormitories, offices, and an expansive swimming pool that has never been filled. The pool was built on orders from Colonel Shahnaz, our base commander, who thought it would be *très chic* to have a pool like all Americans (at least those in Beverly Hills) and had his men dig a hole 25 feet deep and 175 feet long. Construction was of brick, with very little mortar—exactly like the Iranian home, which tends to buckle in a soft drizzle. When told that the works would collapse under a few buckets of water, the colonel is reputed to have shed many bitter tears. Iranians are pretty emotional.

Shahnaz is tall for a Persian, six feet, and though he considers himself dashing, I think of him as deformed. His nose, immense and bulbous, looks as if it's been broken and badly reset. He is very dark, with piercing, startlingly *blue* eyes, an aberration in this part of the world. When he smiles, his thick lips spread all over that part of his face not already covered by his nose.

The colonel is a minor blight in my life. Though married, with two sons in school in Pennsylvania, he is partial to American women. He has his own phalanx of secretaries, yet once a week he ceremoniously enters my office with a fistful of pencils and watches me while I sharpen them. For some reason this makes me jumpy.

The colonel also insists that I be present at his damnable graduation ceremonies. I fly into my boss Jim Holland's office at regular intervals crying, "I can't, I just *can't* go to another one!" Jim, the manager of maintenance, is a dear, and invariably says, "Go to another wha ... oh, a graduation." There's nothing he can do, of course; he's also a guest in this country. (We are all reminded simperingly, gratuitously, sternly, warningly, or plain matter-of-factly, four or five times a day, of our guest status in this country. Many of our mechanics and technicians do the work of two because, as their soldier counterparts acidly remind them, "You, agha, are the guest in my country." This is one of those continuing irritants we learn to live with, though we yearn to yell, "Oh, drop dead!")

These Iranian graduations occur with sickening frequency. Cadets graduate from pilots' training; Iranian mechanics graduate from mechanics' school; and Iranian students graduate from English-language school so they can attend pilots' or mechanics' schools. All graduations are held in the base auditorium, where an army brass band plays off-key and off-beat and looks very untrim in dreadful, ill-fitting uniforms. On one side of the room sit the graduates; on the other sit the women, with as many Americans as possible to lend the place class. Colonel Shahnaz prefers blondes. I myself am blonde. I am also derelict, for I flee the room the minute Shahnaz's back is turned.

I have to hand it to the colonel. He certainly does *his* part. Each graduate, on hearing his name, leaps up like an activated marionette and goosesteps to the front of the room,

7

stands toe-to-toe and nose-to-nose with Shahnaz and, on receiving his diploma, screams at the top of his lungs, "SHAAAAAAAAAAA-YAAAAAAAAAHH," showering the colonel with spittle. I've never seen the man flinch.

Tuesday, 1 August 1978

For the past few months I have been bunking with Donna Leon, opera buff, malaprop artist, and avid tennis player from Passaic, New Jersey. Donna is built like a small, sturdy oak, has a magnificent crown of coarse black hair and a handsome smile. She has her M.A. in Chaucer, speaks Old English and Italian, and works at Bell's subcontractor, Telemedia, teaching English to reluctant Iranians.

Donna has a Byzantine mind, enormous energy, and is a past master of dialect and pantomime. She is forever "yes'm-Miss-Scarletting" me like Scarlett O'Hara's mush-moufed mammy, and she sticks knives under my bed to cut the pain. She is cheeky and fun and helps keep my head above water at every flood stage.

Donna's house is a beautiful old place in the north end of the city, near the rear entrance to the Royal Bazaar, not far from the *Maidan*, the centuries-old main square and polo field. Esfahan rents are very high, and though we receive housing allowances, they're seldom adequate—except in Donna's part of the city, considered second-class by most Americans. This socially undesirable sector of Esfahan is that half of the city north of the Zyand-e-Rud. The plane trees here are ancient, full-blown, and luxuriant. The streets are a panoply of parks and flower beds and fountains. Just as Shah Abbas called his Esfahan "half the world," so is this half of the city its especial pride. Here are most of the city's two hundred mosques, each with its distinctive charm, architecture, beauty, and history. Here too are the palaces, mausoleums, madrasehs and minarets from which the muezzins call faithful Moslems to prayer.

To the south, beyond the river, in what I consider geographical exile, lie Jolfa (the old Armenian quarter), the Kouroush Hotel, the in-town offices of BHI, the American schools, the British Embassy, the Pepsi-Cola plant, the Nobel Hotel and brothel, ninety percent of the garbage dumps, all

8

new building construction, and The Flats—that ugly, barren housing development so desired by American residents for its up-to-date plumbing. They can have it. I am deliriously happy here in Old Esfahan.

Our rent is eighteen thousand rials a month and shared by a third roommate, Jackie Mason, who labors in BHI tech supply. Jackie is tall and lean, with bones like Verushka's. He is also a thwarted song-and-dance man, fond of boys, and one of the finest, funniest friends I've ever had.

A sum of 18,000 rials (there are 70 rials to one dollar) is a paltry $250, quite a contrast to the average 35,000-rial rent in The Flats.

Here in our northwest corner of paradise the courtyard is aflame with flowers and with the multi-greens of walnut, apricot and cherry trees. We also have two pistachio trees, and one gnarled pomegranate, and a resident nightingale. The plumbing is old but sturdy, and none of us minds our Persian toilet, a porcelain-rimmed hole in the floor with indented porcelain footprints alongside.

I am here for two other reasons: to share expenses, and to avoid direct confrontations with Iranian landlords, who give me bad vibes and a nervous stomach. I moved from my first Esfahan house after giving adequate notice in what I felt was a mannerly American fashion, and my landlord ambushed me from behind a plane tree and punched me in the head. In retrospect, I think he was merely upset over losing a good tenant; I didn't see it that way at the time, and I hit the stinker right back. Since I weigh less than 115 pounds, I doubt that I injured more than his national pride.

I plan to write Gloria Steinem about this place.

It isn't just the landlords. Women are treated like punching bags all over Iran. Though I wear prim, tailored clothes as advised by BHI's handbook, no makeup, and a dignified expression, I have been pinched and grabbed, assaulted and battered without surcease, and I am now spearheading a drive among American girls to fight back.

Wednesday, 2 August 1978

I was the oldest of seven, eight, or nine children, the number varying with Mother's whim and/or state of health.

My mother is an endomorph, a vague and delightful woman who seesaws between being robust and earthy, and glazed around the gills and uncertain about the century. She has great generosity and concocts grandiose, impractical plans that would stymie I. M. Pei and the entire staff of *Geo*.

Certain that Dad or Mammon would provide, Mother, during the years of my childhood, steadily added dogs, cats, horses, kids, and real estate to our burgeoning household. One eight-year-old came to our summer ride-and-swim camp for three weeks and stayed for three years; his father was a navy pilot killed in the Philippines, his mother a dandelion type going to seed in a northern California commune.

Mother invited everyone in for a drink, for dinner, for the weekend, for a year. Sometimes I felt like one of those wizened little child-amahs of the Orient, since I was the one who usually took care of them. I may have had more responsibility and less puppy love than I needed, but I'll say this: It was invaluable training for surviving the rigors of revolutions and interoffice memos.

It's no wonder that I now feel this overweening desire for law and order. Emotionally, I'm a marshmallow. But living in constant chaos at home brought out all that was methodical in me. When I went off to high school at Marymount in Cuernavaca, Mexico, I was very content among the kindly sisters and their gentle, ordered atmosphere of identical uniforms and identical catechism, free of the petty tyrannies of cashmere sweater sets and matched, single strand pearls. Our Marymount life had a certain canned, assembly line banality, a flavor that may not have been gourmandish—but neither was it unpredictable. Eventually Marymount grew too tame for my expanding tastes, but it was a comforting haven at a time I needed it.

Dad is one of those extroverted, witty men who should have been a politician but had neither the stomach nor the need for it. He was a father who nuzzled and cuddled his babies and changed diapers with aplomb.

When we became thinking, snarling, talkative, talk-back children, Dad grew hurt and bewildered. He was a termagant with his first teenagers, Victorian and severe. But the sixties, Beatles, abortion, and the strong, sweet smell of pot eventually rounded off his more straitlaced edges and made him, like millions of other fathers, a reluctant participant in a feckless

10

new world. Today he's very giving and forgiving—and still one of the funniest men I've ever met.

Although our parents had Marx Brothers personalities, not one of us children was born with a well-developed sense of humor; for years we considered Mother and Dad a cross we had to bear. I am happy to report that eventually we all developed kindred streaks of lunacy.

We moved to Aspen as children after Mother went on a quiz program and won a lot of money. Uncle Whit, Mother's physician-brother who couldn't find kindly house-keepers for his own young children, simply sent them along. Eventually Uncle Whit joined us too, and we became a noisome gaggle of seven kids and three parents.

Mother, between sinking spells, had already donated ten thousand hours to the Junior League and the United Fund and felt her tour of duty in civilization was done. She took to the West like Cattle Kate and, after helping Dad clear the land for our ski lodge, reverted to eastern ways only to remove snakes and moss rocks placed in her bathtub by my brothers so she could sink into clouds of bubble bath and complete the Sunday *Times* crossword and the *Saturday Review* double crostic. Meanwhile, she imbued her children with a strong sense of drama and an unhealthy desire to be different.

One of my childhood memories is of us kids, very small and fat, sitting around the dinner table while Mother, starry-eyed, announced, "And you, Robbie dear, are going to be another Margaret Bourke-White."

"Who's Margaret Boork-what's-her-name?" I sniffed suspiciously.

"She's a wonderful woman who straps a pack on her back and hikes into parlous places to take pictures: to the high Himalayas in search of the Yeti, to the Amazon to track jaguar, to Baja to live with the Seri Indians."

This made me wail piteously, "But I j-just w-wanna be a m-mother!"

I have wondered, in passing, what in God's name finally possessed me to strap a pack on my back and cross the Sinai on the heels of the '67 War with tanks still smoldering in the sand; to crawl through dense jungle to Monte Alban before it even hit *National Geographic;* to book myself on the farewell journey of the Orient Express. By the time I was twenty-two, I had left college, lived on a kibbutz in Israel, become

11

enamored of Greece and spent two months camped in the Acropolis parking lot, crewed a 48-foot ketch from Southampton to Palm Beach, and remodeled a Victorian hotel in Sag Harbor. I refuse to believe in auto-suggestion and can only suspect Mother knew us better than we knew ourselves.

Wearying as it often was, I was a happy and fulfilled member of our devout family. We children welcomed outsiders on a trial basis, but more often it was the clan against the world. Dad says that the seven of us, aged three to thirteen, were real show-stoppers, skiing the mountain single file, picks and shovels on our shoulders, family dogs galloping at our heels, like the seven dwarfs headed for a mine. Actually we were constructing ski jumps, a pastime that ended abruptly when Whipple Van Ness Jones, the owner of the ski area across the road, unexpectedly hit one of our newer molehills and broke his arm in two places.

Today Aspen has changed hands, but in the fifties and early sixties it was a wonderful, hospitable, neighborly small town. Silver mining was only for small change, valley ranchers lived from bank loan to bank loan, tycoon Walter Paepcke's dream of a great ski resort and cultural center had not yet caught on, and we all starved cozily, together, and most of the time. The Aspen of those days was innocent of pill pushers, Werner Erhard, Cher Bono, Saudi money, and Hollywood-Miami entrepreneurs. We were just a flavorsome small stew bubbling on a back burner, seasoned with dashes of cowboy, sheepherder, Trappist monk, retired generals, bewildered poets, and world-weary thinkers. The mixture was eclectic but very tasty.

One of Mother's better ideas was our twice-weekly summertime chuck wagon suppers. These were held in the Lower Forty, our euphemistic term for the two-acre area of corrals and tack rooms down the hill from the lodge, adjacent to tumbling Maroon Creek. In addition to our lodge guests and the college kids who wrangled horses and made beds, Mother and Dad invited anyone they ran into at the post office or grocery store. The guest list could, and did, include oil drillers, Austrian pastry chefs, our milkman, the Basque who broke our horses, occasional aging ballet stars, minor European royalty, our schoolteachers, the sheriff, ski patrolmen and instructors, and a lady who levitated people in her living room.

Ours was a noisy, hectic childhood peopled with hundreds

12

of strangers who became lifelong friends. I suppose it's not surprising that I've reached maturity alternately needing to be as surrounded as a queen bee in a swarm—or seeking solitude as frantically as a nesting bird.

When I was twelve and growing faintly restive, Mother drove me to Grand Junction to visit a psychologist who announced, "This child must have a room of her own." Since this was patently impossible (all our money had gone into the guest rooms, and we kids were crammed into two CCC-style barracks—bunk rooms with approximately fifteen inches of closet space per child), Mother shed tears of quiet desperation and compromised by moving each of us into our very own guest room in the spring and fall off-seasons. This took a terrible toll on the guest rooms. But for half the year we were able to stretch our limbs and psyches to the limit, only to be crunched together like accordions when the next season began. I used to yearn for one of those ruffled, blue and white, French Provincial bedrooms boasted by several of my friends. What with one thing and another, I never did have my own room until I was twenty-five, and today I could live happily in a downtown bus depot.

Mother's brainstorms led directly to my love of sailing and of painting. The sailing occurred when she had a little talk with a nice Minnesota family who owned a summer sailing camp, after which I went to their camp and developed an insatiable love of life before the mast, and they came to our lodge and broke all their legs skiing. Then Mother ran afoul of and hired a young artist who looked like John the Baptist and was quietly starving to death—first to paint the lodge rooms and then to give me instruction in oils. The lodge rooms took on a very rakish air, and it was incidentally discovered that I possessed artistic talent. I won a number of prizes and one juried show, but unfortunately became involved with horse breeding and manure shoveling to the detriment of cleaning paintbrushes and scraping palettes.

Of my childhood I remember working like stevedores trailering horses, pitching hay, shoveling snow, making beds, mucking out toilets, and, oh God, folding guest towels that flowed in an endless stream from our giant gas clothes dryer, feeling like the mother who has never in her married life gotten to the bottom of the ironing basket and promising myself when I grew up to be rich and employ three full-time laundresses; entering small potato, country horse shows where

13

Mother hung our costume changes on clotheslines in the back of the station wagon and Dad stood ready with the next change of tack: One kid would race a horse around the barrels, gallop from the ring like a maddened Cossack, and whip off chaps and boots while Dad wiped down the lathered horse and buckled him (the horse, not the kid) into English saddle, girth, and snaffle bit; the next child, attired nattily in rat-catcher shirt and one of our three hardhats, would then jump aboard the beleaguered animal and trot sedately into the ring for an English horsemanship event. Each of us garnered bouquets of ribbons that Mother still preserves, faded and fly-specked.

And over everything, like a thick, warm quilt, was the comforting blanket of family solidarity. We were bound together by blood, bread, close quarters, and the absolute necessity for sharing. My brothers and sisters often infuriate me, but when one of them calls, I fly home from the ends of the earth. In my friends' families, everyone is either dead or in Australia. In our family we manage one hundred percent turnouts for holidays, birthdays, and airport arrivals and departures; these are tribal rites, and we observe them.

I have no particular recollection of passing from childhood into young womanhood, except that it happened unobtrusively. After two years at a gargantuan state university crawling with preoccupied students, I decided this was not my métier and, with a small inheritance, set out to see the world and locate my immortal soul. I was one of those legions who, in the sixties, disappeared somewhere between Spain and Pakistan and was not heard from for months. I had retained the same sturdy-legged, small-bosomed, size-eight body that I had as a child and still have today—built for backpacking, cleating sails, and talking my way past suspicious border guards.

True to Mother's prophecy, I traveled to far places whose every nuance is fixed indelibly in my memory. I recall the scents and sounds of Turkey in the spring; the feel of Greek islands on foggy days; the differing cadences of muezzins in Cairo and Jerusalem; the essence of the Iraqi-Iran border, with trucks lined up twenty miles waiting days to cross, drivers camped alongside in stifling heat with no shade and no bathrooms; cheap hotel rooms on Paris's Left Bank.

It was during this period that Grandmother Whitcomb took to meeting me at eastern airports with a voluminous

14

trench coat. Bitter experience had taught her that I might appear wearing a tattered Nomad dress and the remnants of thong sandals, or a patched Canadian flag, or the national costume of some foreign country neither she nor any of her friends had read about in their Baedekers. She therefore stood ready to swaddle me in the coat and rush me straight to Peck & Peck or Sears Roebuck, whichever was nearer. Once she ushered me in and out of a neighboring department store, newly attired in blazer, flannel skirt, hosiery, and stacked-heel pumps, my cast-off clothes deposited in a handy trash barrel —in a record forty-five minutes flat.

Without all that travel for training, and the family humor for armor, I'm not certain I'd survive the vagaries and quandaries of life in Iran. Here where East meets West, often head-on, I've witnessed plenty of crack-ups, near-misses, and emotional traffic jams. Our cultures, religions, and thinking are so different that it's difficult for us to find common ground or a place for our minds to meet.

Take the Ruhis. The Ruhis are my Iranian neighbors and friends. I break a lot of bread and eat plenty of kebab with them, but that doesn't mean I understand them.

There are Mama and Papa (pronounced with the accent on the last syllable), their daughter Guity and her husband, Jahan, and Guity and Jahan's baby, Tina, who is eight months old.

Papa works at Iranian Customs and so does his daughter Guity, who belongs to the new school of modern Iranians. Guity named Tina for an unclaimed American package in Customs. She loved the way it sounded, and it was American, which made it eminently desirable and appealing in her eyes. (Jahan had no say in the matter.)

Papa is upper-middle class, and he bought Mama a proper modern house, which they now share with Jahan, Guity and Tina. Each family has two rooms, and they keep their possessions scrupulously divided. There are two refrigerators, two charcoal braziers, two stoves, two space heaters, etcetera.

None of the Ruhis speaks English except Guity, and her English is on a par with my Swahili. But I spend a great deal of time with them practicing my Farsi, and we communicate just fine. They are a warm and wonderful family, and I've learned much about the Persian art of hospitality from them.

Mama is typical of older Iranian women, her whole life

15

devoted to her husband and her small family. She is very content just to care for them and has never even left her neighborhood.

Also typical of her generation, Mama still cooks on the floor. She insists I share their meals with them when I am there. We eat on the floor amid a splendor of heaped Persian carpets. For although Guity's two rooms are jam packed with Western furniture (which runs to tapestried pieces featuring gamboling unicorns and plumed knights, and chandeliers dripping with gilt chains and crystal bobs), her parents' wealth and most of their furnishings are those magnificent carpets on which they sit, lounge, eat, and presumably die. The Western rooms are rarely used except for display. Sleeping is done on pallets stacked at the back of the house during the day and brought forth at night.

This afternoon I baked quiche for the Ruhis, and they made a great to-do over it. Alas, I know from experience that only Guity, gallant girl, will make an effort to eat the stuff. My cuisine is simply too alien for their tastes.

Because my first house in Esfahan was nearby, I've known the Ruhis for more than a year. When I spent last Christmas in Abadan, I gave them the key to my house. I returned to find they had made me a Christmas—from pictures in magazines! They themselves had never seen a Christmas, but they found a tree, made decorations, strung crepe paper from floor to ceiling, and bought and wrapped me all sorts of presents. Though it was dreary and drizzling outside, it was one of the very nicest, and the prettiest, Christmases I've ever had.

In the Ruhis' household I learned that there's more to the inscrutable Mideast than first meets the eye. It took me awhile to realize the great importance of a man's "face"—his pride—and of saving it at all costs. This turns into a kind of tyranny that rules everyone's lives. An Iranian will go to improbable lengths to prevent friends or family from suspecting he has a care in the world; thus day-to-day lying about things great and small becomes an integral part of his personality. But, though an Arab or Persian might die to save face in public, he rarely suffers guilt in his own mind. Pay your money and take your choice, folks: The convoluted face-saving measures of the East, or the guilt-ridden neuroses of the West. I wonder what Sigmund would have to say about it all?

I find it impossible to equate Jahan or Papa or my other

Iranian friends with your average man in the street. If Jahan or Papa suddenly popped up on Char Bagh and gave me a hefty pinch, I think I'd faint from shock. Actually men here don't settle for a pinch, or even a good hard gouge: They swoop down on their bikes or motorcycles, grab a girl by the crotch, and launch her five feet into the air. This hurts not only your dignity but also your crotch.

When I am on foot and hear the distant farting of Mopeds and Iranians, I quickly back up to the nearest wall and ready my weapon. A weapon can be a rock, horsewhip, can of Mace, or hat pin; none of us girls ever goes forth empty-handed. I have stopped carrying Mace or spray paint, however, as the wind blows constantly and I end being hoisted on my own petard. I ruined a perfectly good gabardine suit with pea-green paint in a sudden wind shift.

Iranian women accept their mauling without a whimper, but we Yankees are making our mark. Last week Barbara Bushby raised a cast-iron frying pan over her head and destroyed a man's bicycle when he had the bad judgment to come by for a second pass. We treated her to lunch at the Shah Abbas and awarded her a Bronze Star with fig-leaf cluster.

I find it fascinating that when American women fight back, the Iranian male goes into a kind of startled trance. One man, when I caught his hand up my skirt, stood patiently while I held his necktie and smacked him repeatedly across the face, all the while asking me in an emotionless voice for directions to Shah Square.

In May I was walking down Char Bagh with a bag of tomatoes when a deranged cretin on a motorcycle jumped one of the joubs and ran me down. I found myself sprawled on the sidewalk in a purée of tomatoes, my right leg peeled neatly as a grape, and my right hand broken. Shortly afterward I bought Jack Jyanne (pronounced *Gee-on*), my fine little Iranian car that resembles a mustard-colored toad.

Thursday, 3 August 1978

The janitors are all mine!

Yesterday when no one had the time or talent to repair our office cooler, I called the *haji,* and he came galloping. Though

17

Iranians are notoriously unmechanical, he had it fixed in no time. There was a Kleenex in it. This haji and his cohorts also fill our coolers with water four times every hour just to keep them purring. Jim Holland says, "If it weren't for you, Robin, nothing would run and we'd be roasted like cashews."

I think it's because I speak Farsi. Well, not quite that, either. But enough of a facsimile so that Iranians appreciate my valiant though misguided efforts.

I'm the first to admit there have been tense moments. One bright day when Guity and Mama gave me some *saebsi* seeds for my garden, I asked in humble Farsi (with Jahan standing immediately to my right), "When do you plant the seed?" Mama nearly choked on her *shirini,* Guity collapsed in gales of laughter, and Jahan retreated, scarlet-faced, from the room. Apparently I had asked the question in terms so delicate they're relegated strictly to the marital bed.

"Xaeste nabashid," I say to the garden workmen as I pass, and they fall all over each other picking up my handkerchief. *Xaeste nabashid* is a universally used nicety that means, literally, "Don't be tired—don't work too hard." We Americans also say bitchy *nabashid,* mad *nabashid,* sad *nabashid, ad infinitum.*

"Chetouri, madame—hale shoma chetouri?" (How are you?), they answer, and we discuss families, children, and general health in the manner of friends and neighbors everywhere.

Haji janitor, like our haji gardener, has made the pilgrimage to Mecca and is thus entitled to wear a beard and be called haji.

Farsi is fun. It is remotely related to Urdu (Pakistani) and to Armenian. I am sorry to relate that, beyond kitchen vocabularies, few Americans trouble to speak it.

Since the translation of Farsi into English is very inexact, there are many different ways of spelling any given word. Some simple examples: Esfahan/Isfahan; Teheran/Tehran; Savak/Savac; Mohammed/Muhammad/Mohammet. The city of Qom might be spelled Qum, Ghom, or Kum.

I attended two semesters of Farsi classes at the Iran-American Society, where my teacher, Manucher Abazani, became a good friend. Manucher is now at the University of Iowa, and my most attentive teacher at present is Guity Ruhi (we rarely use her married name). With her help, my vocabulary grows like a schoolgirl's. Also, the gurgle in the back of my throat sounds even more groovy. Those months of studying Hebrew at Mishmar Ha'emek in Israel a few years back were invaluable training. Same throaty gargle, and words like Qom/Qum are almost visibly cast out in a deep gong sound.

Among my favorite Farsi expressions are *Chesh-meh* (Step on my eyes), meaning, improbably, "What can I do for you?" as asked by a waiter; and *Otafucu's* (pronounced *Oughta-fuck-you's*), the brand name for a widely worn Iranian plastic shoe; and *chosiefeel,* which means "elephant fart" but is also the idiom for popcorn. Like plenty of foreign idioms, it causes more trouble than it's worth. The last time I asked for popcorn in a kutche store in my most maidenly voice, I placed an iota of emphasis on the wrong syllable, and naturally the proprietor thought I called him a fart. It required so many heartfelt explanations to extricate myself that I have given up popcorn forever.

I am also pretty fond of *barf,* which means snow. I plan to go home to Aspen, Colorado, and fling barf around like confetti. Or popcorn.

Persians are great lovers of poetry. Since they receive their educations by rote and memorize at length and for years, they can quote from their great national poets at the drop of a doggerel. I am sampling a little Sadaki, Rumi, and Daqiqi. But it's the dog-eared Fitzgerald translation of the *Rubaiyat* that sits by my bed at night.

This evening I quoted some Khayyám to Skip Maiorana over dinner at the Shah Abbas Hotel. Skip is a charmer with an ear for Omar, so I guess I'll let myself fall a little in love with him.

> Oh, come with old Khayyám and leave the wise
> to talk; one thing is certain, life flies. . . .

Friday, 4 August 1978

Today is the Sabbath, and tomorrow marks the start of Ramazan. Jackie and I have laid by enough food for the Siege of Masada. Donna lives on yoghurt and Puccini and doesn't count for much in our long-range dietary plans.

I paid a pre-Ramazan visit to the Ruhis, and we chatted

amid the chirping of their parakeets. Every Iranian household has canaries, parakeets or parrots, and for a very practical reason. If the birds die, people know their kerosene heaters are malfunctioning. There's a profitable trade in birds in Iran.

Mama Ruhi is very fat and has had breast cancer. If there are no men about, she again shows me her mastectomy scar; then I know it is my turn to exhibit my appendectomy incision, and a good time is invariably had by all.

Papa Ruhi eats pork. As do many Iranians, who also smoke, drink, sodomize, and otherwise flout Islamic law. (Only the *mullahs,* the Muhammadan priests, seem to observe Moslem religious tenets.) Jahan drinks, and Papa smokes. Since Papa invariably falls asleep with a cigarette in his hand, the family has devised a kind of shield to surround his pallet so he won't burn up the carpets, the house, the birds, and his loved ones.

I have been reading *Daniel Martin* and enduring the heat. It is no hotter than last year, but that's small consolation. We move in large clouds of dust like Pigpen in *Peanuts,* and there is dust in our teeth, nostrils, eyes, ears, lungs and pores. We stay fairly cool at home, where the walls are thick, and we have our courtyard pool and fountain. The fountain is a mixed blessing: At the same time it is cooling us off, it is also attracting great armies of mosquitoes, which form and attack in squadrons.

Between the noisy and wily old rooster abiding at the Hamazes next door, and Donna's recording of Victoria de los Angeles singing *La Bohème,* I wonder that we harbor insects *or* birds. It's the butterflies and nightingales that are frightened away, and the crows and mosquitoes that are wholly tone-deaf and forever with us.

Jackie and I have constructed a scarecrow for our garden. It looks like someone's bewhiskered maiden aunt in a print housedress and frightful straw hat trimmed with a drooping calla lily, and does nothing to frighten away the crows, who are the size of bald eagles and as heartless as contract killers. They terrify me. They swoop down and attack fat-tailed sheep and small children in the kutches.

Donna is singing along with Frederica Von Stade, her current operatic idol. She performs at three hundred decibels, under the mistaken impression that she is dispensing culture among our underprivileged Iranian neighbors. I keep telling her it will get us murdered in our beds. Thank heaven tomorrow is the beginning of Ramazan, when by custom *all* extraneous noise must cease. This may even give Jackie and me one more excuse to stalk, and hopefully strangle, the Hamaze rooster.

Peace, Allah, and God bless. May the crows migrate to Oman, and all the chickens perish of religious root-rot.

Tomorrow I plan to dawdle in and around the Kouroush Hotel swimming pool. But softly, softly. *Allah Akhbar.*

Saturday, 5 August 1978

I don't know about the Iranian celebrants of Ramazan, but the heat is making me crotchety. The air is so heavy it struggles sluggishly in and out of one's lungs. The Zyand-e-Rud pulses with half-naked bodies, bank to bank and morning till night. Everyone suffers in silence, too spent to do more than wet parched lips and mop fevered brows.

There are no windows in my office. Also no air conditioners. It's been 115 degrees during the day, which is one of the reasons I elected to work at night.

We in administration work in shifts like the helicopter crews, and I've been a lyrically happy volunteer on the four P.M. to one A.M. shift. I don't see Donna or Jackie much, but I have a sports membership at the Kouroush Hotel, where I swim and shade-bathe daily. I have lunch dates, and lots of daylight to do my batiking, at which I am mediocre but happy. (Batik is the art of wax-resist fabric design and, since it is messy and requires plenty of space and water, is an ideal craft for Iranian courtyards.)

My most frequent date of late has been Skip Maiorana: straight A's, prelaw, University of Arizona. He's a tall Italian nobleman with limpid black eyes, handlebar mustaches, and the kind of wry wit I adore.

Skip reached his present unlikely status of helicopter mechanic via the circuitous route of Vietnam. After graduating from college, he found himself drafted and door-gunning on a Bell 205 helicopter. The war over, as much for a lark as to escape limbo, he applied with some friends for an overseas job with BHI. On the basis of a six-months' acquaintanceship with helicopters so trifling he did nothing more than apply a squirt of grease, refuel, and wipe down windshields, he was hired at an astronomical salary. He's been in Iran two years and, because he's bright and quick, has been promoted faster than a battlefield survivor. At this rate he'll accumulate enough money to purchase downtown Tucson.

I prefer Skip to the pilots I've dated, who are largely Steve Canyon–Foreign Legion–paid mercenary types with Panatellos dangling from the corners of their mouths and that old I-am-the-world's-greatest-lover look in their eyes. They are absolutely brilliant fliers, with brooding personalities and the morals of goats.

Skip has an endearing quality of otherworldliness and he spends a lot of time with his mind away from home. It's nice being around a man who is civilized, creative, and behaves something like a Thurber dog. The only thing is, I can scarcely abide the name "Skip," which I consider in a class with "Buddy," "Junior," and "Spot." He, on the other hand, is crazy about my baptismal name, Robinson, and is the only person who has ever addressed me as Robinson at all times and in all places.

Monday, 7 August 1978

Despite orientation lectures to the contrary, I'm going to kill an Iranian: Lieutenant Arbob.

Yesterday in the office (since the Iranian Sabbath is on Friday, their weekend, and therefore ours is on Thursday and Friday, thus making Saturday and Sunday ordinary workdays), the lieutenant asked me, one more time, "Excuse me, miss, do you shave your pussy?"

As I may possibly have implied, most Iranian men are afflicted with satyriasis. Because they marry late, and unmarried girls are heavily chaperoned, they are often bisexual. On our base they're after each other (and us women) in every dark corner, toolroom, broom closet, helicopter hold, field and foyer. I believe a lot of my affinity for Iranian women stems from the thought of the poor things on their wedding nights.

Lieutenant Arbob has been to Oklahoma and considers himself worldly. In truth he is fat, unwashed, married, and from Mashad—Iran's second holiest city. When the lieutenant was wed, he pulled the fingernail from his little finger, in the custom of Mashad, to pledge eternal fidelity to his bride. I would cheerfully pluck out the rest for him (as well as his eyes and all the hairs of his head) if I thought it would keep him home with his wife.

He's been courting me for months. Mostly I considered him boring and harmless, though lately he's taken to ringing me from across the street and breathing heavily into the phone. In addition, the tenor of his questions has sunk so low I wouldn't dream of committing them to paper.

Yesterday, nearly plunging headlong down my dress front, Arbob insisted I supply him with particulars about positions. I was a tad hasty shoving him out the door, and when I slammed it I smashed his finger, the one missing the fidelity nail.

What a mess! Arbob has gone to his commanding officers, insisting he have my job. He just may, too. "Face" must be served and saved. Damn! I don't *want* to leave Iran....

Wednesday, 9 August 1978

Today I ate crow. Iranian crow. I made a public apology in front of forty of Arbob's assembled fellow-officers. They stood at rapt attention like a flock of vindictive, psalm-singing old biddies and listened to me read a speech about ". . . your selfless devotion to duty, Lieutenant Arbob, your noble bearing and courtly demeanor in face of all adversity . . . have made you a paragon among men, an apotheosis for our times. . . . Your virtues and your . . . blah blah blah . . ." I felt just like George Patton.

The Iranians were pretty impressed. But watching Jim Holland cracking up in the back of the room didn't help my composure. The officers looked very solemn and clapped enthusiastically at the finish. I think they liked my style.

Jim, who's manager of Bell's maintenance, looks like a young version of Saint Nicholas, replete with twinkles. He is wonderful to work for. If he hadn't saved my skin, I'd be winging my way home.

Arbob's commanding officers had simply sneered at the weighty report I worked up. So Jim invited the lieutenant in for a little chat. He assured him, very soothingly, that of course the proper thing was to have me fired. But did

Lieutenant Arbob understand that before I left, as a matter of procedure, I would present my report and corroborative evidence of Arbob's unenlightened behavior to the base commander (i.e., Colonel Shahnaz) at a formal hearing? And although *certainly* no one would believe a word of it, still there would be a number of ranking officers present, and just possibly there might be planted some seeds of doubt. Did he, asked Jim, feel absolutely certain that he wanted to chance such seeds sprouting? And so on, and so on. With promotion in mind, Arbob opted for the public apology.

The pillorying was at five this afternoon. My tongue may have been in my cheek, but my knees are still rattling in their sockets. I begged off work, came home, and poured myself a stiff drink.

Thursday, 10 August 1978

The streets are teeming with demonstrators, and there are many planned parades. A little violent, some of them; there's been gunfire, and people have taken to insulting the government. I didn't think that was allowed.

We've heard and glimpsed Ramazan celebrants in the evenings before sundown. They're rather in the style of the world's longest funeral procession, with none of the color of a Polish-American or a St. Patrick's Day parade. The parade participants are joined in spirit, and sometimes in voice, by our Iranian neighbors on their rooftops. Everyone lives on his roof in the summer heat, and the interchange between street marchers and rooftoppers sometimes gives me an eerie feeling of Romeo and Juliet in a dark and offbeat balcony scene.

I've heard shouting and howling for the past hour and presume it is one more procession of flagellants whipping themselves into a frenzy. I wonder what they're rioting about. Maybe they need a good meal, and this is turning into a counter-hunger strike. Or an anti-American demonstration?

Except for brown eyes, I don't look the least Levantine. As it's difficult to disguise blonde hair, a fair complexion and pug nose in this part of the world, now is scarcely the time to parade my phiz along the main streets of the city.

I'm too young and tenderhearted to be strung up on the

24

See-oh-Say Pol (Thirty-three-Arch Bridge), or whatever it is they do with infidels, so I believe I'll steer clear of the *Chehel Setun* teahouse and my friend Akhbar Abarjani's cozy carpet corner for a while.

We're close to the *maidan* (*may-dahn*) here, and the maidan is the heart and soul of Esfahan. It's the royal square which dates back to pre-Christian times; but the legendary Shah Abbas was the one who, in the seventeenth century, created the maidan as it stands today. He made it the scene of public fêtes and festivities, as well as of the royal polo games. (The marble markers that marked his polo field still stand.) The Royal and other lesser bazaars surround the maidan as well as such famous landmarks as the magnificent King's Mosque, the smaller and very exquisite *Shaikh Lutfallah* Mosque, and the unique *Ali Qapu*, a combination six-story building and portal plus enormous balcony reviewing stand used for centuries by shahs and their families to watch everything from games to feast days to mass executions.

The mosques in this city are breathtaking: At the right time of the day the whole of Esfahan seems a blaze of turquoise, azure, violet, gold, and silver. At other times, it looks like nothing so much as an oversized, dust-colored pile of dung.

With our food stockpile, Donna's new recording of *Il Travatore,* and my latest tape of Hank Williams, our creature and cultural comforts are cared for, and we'll just hunker down till the end of Ramazan.

I'm content here, rereading most of Dickens, and I'm going to tackle all the Russians on days they don't make me suicidal.

Friday, 11 August 1978

While I nattered on, Esfahan erupted like an angry she-bear. The nitty gritty is that we've been placed under martial law, the *only city* in Iran to be so distinguished! We're to have nightly curfew, 8:00 P.M. to 6:00 A.M., just like dear old Camp Soangetaha.

A haji messenger arrived at my gate smiling toothlessly and exclaiming *"Lutfan, Meesus, farda; Shambe,* you work *no."* Which means I'm to report for work at nine o'clock Monday

25

morning (tomorrow, Saturday) just like back in the emporium in Peabody, Kansas. I'll return to my old sizzling-griddle hours, 9:00 A.M. to 6:00 P.M. daily, right at the height of the heat. No more sweet, velvety hours of the night, and when I get home from the base I'll have about ninety minutes to shower, dress, savor a leisurely dinner with drinks and wine, and stampede back to the house so my date can bolt across town doing eighty to reach his own quarters before curfew drops with a thud.

Curfew? Martial law? The whole city is seething with martial guards, and we're assured they mean business. If we're caught out a minute after curfew, we don't give them our most endearing smiles and a lot of broken Farsi, mealy-mouthed excuses. We keep our mouths shut and pray we aren't rushed straight to the *Savak* (secret police) chambers to have our heads shaved and our tonsils torn out.

No one seems certain of the reasons for all this. Rumors and directives and dire warnings fly like grapeshot. Ordinarily we don't watch TV and rarely listen to the radio. At Ramazan the programming is mostly exhortations from the Koran, and readings from the Imam Ali, and uplifting nature programs. Today we kept turning the dial, trolling for news, and I *did* notice that the religious material was a little inflammatory. There was lots of talk about "I shall water the flower garden of religion with my blood." I hope they're not planning to hemorrhage all over the city parks and flower beds.

Donna and Jackie and I went to the Ruhis' to listen to NIRT, the English-language TV channel; the toll from yesterday's bazaar rioting—all that wailing and shouting I heard from here—was four rioters dead, forty-five policemen and fourteen firemen injured, and the Shah Abbas Hotel bombed from eight different sides. Most of the troublemakers were thought to be young boys, street gangs. *"Xaeli bade,"* (It is very bad), growled Mama Ruhi. The little brutes managed to blow some pretty definitive holes in that beautiful old caravanserai.

The Shah Abbas was once, around the time of Christ, an overnight inn for desert caravans. Eventually Shah Abbas, the same Savafid emperor who made Esfahan the pearl of Persia, transformed the caravanserai into a magnificent guest hostelry. Its original two-story camel stalls open off courtyards the size of a football field that are bowers of roses and rare blooms, of fountains and trickling pools, of date palms and

26

flowering trees. The rooms are decorated with opulent Persian rugs and mirror and faience work, and it is the most breathtaking hotel I've ever laid eyes on.

Now why would anyone want to destroy a beautiful old monument with so much historical significance? Ramazan? Ill humor? Shortsightedness? Tired blood?

Papa Ruhi and Jahan talked a mile a minute this evening, arguing recklessly about politics, the *Majlis* (parliament), and the general unrest. I've never heard them do much more than grunt, belch, and complain about prices and the heat. Guity tells me there is hard feeling, this Ramazan, about *baksheesh*—the graft. I thought she looked a little troubled when she gazed at Papa. I'll just bet that wily old chainsmoker has been on the take. When Guity and Jahan got married, he bought them a *Peykan*, which is the Cadillac of Iranian cars and costs a cool $5500. Not exactly peanuts for a humble Customs official. Papa himself drives a Yamaha bedecked with gadgets, gewgaws, plastic hyacinths, baby shoes, ball fringe, satin tassels, and a windscreen as flared as a Valentino nostril. He's a sight to behold when he sets out in full panoply to purchase groceries or to begin his day at the Customs offices.

I have never seen Mama on the Yamaha or even in the Peykan.

After tonight's TV news, we took part in another Ruhi ritual. While Mama readied the *chie* for sundown, Guity brought forth "The Wardrobe."

As a Customs clerk, Guity, like her father, does not pay import duty. Therefore she orders extensively from stores and outfitters abroad. She is the proud possessor of catalogues I have obtained for her from: Sears Roebuck, J. C. Penney, L. L. Bean, Neiman-Marcus, and the Horchow Collection.

Though baby Tina is only eight months old, Guity has purchased all of her wardrobes, winter and summer, from now until the kid reaches postpubescence. There are complete outfits for every year of the child's life from kindergarten through high school: Little skirts and blazers; sweaters and blouses; patent leather shoes from Mary Janes to Springalator pumps; party dresses from taffeta to tulle; all progressing in orderly fashion from child to preteen to junior sizes, each lovingly encased in plastic. It's the most heartbreaking exhibition of a young woman's desire to be westernized I've ever beheld. Foolhardy or not, I love Guity for it, and I never fail to marvel and exclaim, no matter how often I see the damn-fool clothes. So what if they *are* rendered obsolete, will never be the correct size, become moth-eaten, or Lord knows, even subversive? To Guity they represent everything that is American and wondrous and unattainable.

Jackie was touched nearly to tears by Guity's fashion show. Donna simply adopted her snootiest Philadelphia drawl and said, "Daaaaaahling, I rayally think the child shouldn't wear those tweeds with her diamonds. So stickery in this ghastly heat, you know." Even at eight o'clock at night it was about 99 degrees, so Jackie and I avenged Guity by pushing the rotten snob into the fountain, fully clothed. Then we jumped in after her.

Saturday, 12 August 1978

I'm not happy without my afternoon sherry and the cool waters of the Kouroush. It's still hotter than a two-dollar pistol, and our haji kept filling my water cooler at five-minute intervals, looking like he was ready for heat prostration himself. I finally made him lie down while I put cool cloths on his head.

With all three office shifts condensed into one, courtesy of curfew, we now have six people working in a space designed for one undersized troll. The only idyllic aspect of it all is that I'm in a corner office in the main hangar with an actual *window,* a window, what's more, that overlooks the Great Tar Pit. Not wholly inspirational, but it *is* a view of the outside world.

The Great Tar Pit is one more manifestation of Howe's law, "Every man has a scheme that will not work." Again the inestimable Colonel Mohammed Shahnaz. Although there are literally thousands of parking spaces scattered around his giant installation, the colonel decided we feckless Americans should be herded together, car-wise, in one great big hyper-inefficient morass. To this end, he had his soldiery construct a large, lumpy parking lot in a field of gluey red clay, spray it with an amorphous mixture of tar and resin, and voilà! The upshot is that Americans park together in the Tar Pit, walk as much as a mile to their respective posts, and are subsequently robbed blind. Since they can no longer keep a weather eye on their vehicles, an endless parade of jacks, windshield wipers, spare tires, tools, and extraneous car parts disappears into the Iranian sunset.

Our entire installation is about the size of a thirty-six-hole golf course. "On the line" (meaning out on the airfield, not in the hangars for repairs or servicing), there are close to two hundred helicopters worth approximately $280 million. With parts and auxiliary equipment, make that monetary value around one billion, not including those ships and parts in the FASC units at the far end of the base.

The FASC units are Forward Air Support Commands, special units in charge of going into remote, uncivilized areas to set up virgin bases. FASC employees on new frontiers receive twenty-five percent higher pay because of hardship, danger, and a notable lack of common sense.

These *heelos,* as they are known to Iranians, or ships to Americans, are obviously a whopping investment in money, manpower, and maintenance.

The Bell ships in Esfahan are AH-IJs, attack helicopters also known as Cobras; Jetrangers, the 206s used by many U.S. sheriff's departments; and the 205 Hueys that we see making spectacular hook-and-cable rescues on TV.

The Shah is a bug on defense, the armaments godfather of the Near East, and his personal favorite back in 1973 was the Bell 205. But he wanted a heelo with newer technology, one that was heavier, more full-bodied, with a greater carrying capacity and a longer range than any ship the company had manufactured to date. (Security note: When I speak of the Shah, especially in these touchy matters, I'm really referring to *Fred.* Immediately upon arrival here, we're taken aside and warned that every fourth man may be a Savak spy. "No funny stories about our leader," warned my secretary after hearing a few of my jokes. "For safety's sake we all call the man 'Fred,'" is the way Frank Light explained it. Feeling slightly subversive, I try to call the Shah Fred like everyone else.) ... Ahem. So Fred personally supplied the cash for research and development of the 214, designed and then mass-produced at Bell's plants in Texas. Present price: $1.3 million per ship.

The humane and practical uses for a fleet of first-class helicopters are virtually endless. Yet I've never seen our ships, in my time here, used for any missions of mercy. This may *possibly* be excusable on the grounds that this is a

29

training base where Iranian pilots and mechanics have been painfully slow to train. After all this time, we have only certified eighty Iranian pilots and every man is sorely needed to instruct.

Supporting this Iranian juggernaut and struggling to counteract what we call the camel culture is an American task force which, on its own, could probably take over the Horn of Africa.

Starting with twenty centuries of wildly differing cultures, we Americans have great difficulty getting Iranian trainees to submit to the tyrannies of time and mechanization. Most Moslems are not interested in ordering their lives according to time schedules or precision standards. They have kept few written histories, do not use a set calendar, and seldom glance at a clock. It's my theory that they don't win wars because they can't synchronize their watches. Nor is it surprising that we have so much difficulty teaching them mechanization when their entire heritage is geared to nonspecifics. (And who's to decide which is the better way? I'd leave it to old Khayyám.)

> Ah, fill the cup; what boots it to repeat
> How time is slipping underneath our feet;
> Unborn tomorrow and dead yesterday,
> Why fret about them if today be sweet?

The BHI complement in Esfahan, with dependents, is about three thousand people. (Teheran has another 3500.) Since many of us have Iranian counterparts—Iranian Army people we are training to take over our jobs—that number, in combination with regular Iranian Army personnel, is more than doubled.

Not only is BHI organized along the lines of the U.S. Army and manned in the main by retired generals, colonels, captains, and top sergeants, we also use army training manuals. Our maintenance forms are the same as the army's, and we employ army service designations and the same promotional procedures. There are days, faced with mountains of GI paper work, when I long bitterly to go AWOL.

We BHI helots are assigned to four principal divisions, or countries, each with its own ruler, prime minister, and flag: Department of Support (DOS), Headquarters, Department of Instruction (DOI), and Employee Relations (ER).

30

Also, downtown, across the city from ER, are the BHI Clinic, our warehouse, the Teen Center, and Bell Family Services (BFS). The clinic operates twenty-four hours a day, or did before curfew, with a staff of one American and three Iranian doctors and twelve nurses and lab technicians. At BFS, slackening morale is tightened with swimming lessons, pre-ski clinics, doily weaving, volleyball competitions, and instruction in Serbian folk dancing.

Last Monday I attended my first meeting of the Bell Belles, a homey group of company women whose principal social function is stapling together issues of the *Whirly Bird,* our company newspaper. These women also sing homemade songs and pass out little blue beads to newcomers. Blue beads, like all things blue in Islam, ward off evil spirits. I went to Monday's meeting to hear a man present a history of Thai jewelry. Afterward I made a mental note to avoid future meetings of the Bell Belles at all costs.

The physical plant of Havan-e-Ruz is a sprawling complex of hangars, offices, barracks, mess halls, supply depots, Telemedia classrooms and auditoriums, and FASC units—all the accouterments of a typical military installation. Except that this one is Iranian, which means it looks like a Bangkok klong and operates like a Chinese fire drill.

My office and others like it have been constructed of welded sheet metal along the sides and down the center of the large main heelo hangar. The clatter of typewriters, adding machines, drills, and generators bouncing off these metal sound conductors is as deafening as a city block of Jabberwocky jackhammers.

There are days when the myriad initials and army designations and secret codes and remembering to call the Shah "Fred" and the fraternal handshakes make me want to reach for my Buck Rogers' code ring and tap out an SOS to outer space.

All of Havan-e-Ruz is heavily fenced and guarded and rather awe-inspiring. Without one's great big baby-blue BHI pass, one might as well turn right around and toddle on home. The place is supersecret, supertough, and superstick-lish about passwords and procedures.

But nothing, they say, compared to BHI's first FASC installation at Kermanshah amid thousands of howling Kurdish tribesmen. The Kurds despise their Iranian masters even more than the Iraqis dislike Iranians as neighbors. As soon as

31

I get up the gumption, I plan to run over there and peer around.

The crowning touch to Havan-e-Ruz is Colonel Shahnaz's Great Wall of Iran. After seeing the Great Wall of China in an astronaut's space shot, our beloved colonel decided to use his coolie labor (once again the lowly Iranian enlisted man) to construct a fifty-foot-high wall that's five feet thick and winds around in serpentine and unpicturesque fashion and off into the desert headed for Afghanistan. This quixotic structure doesn't even circle the base and is pointless as defense. I don't know, maybe Shahnaz has a Cheops complex. It's my idea that he is a frustrated building contractor who should be retired outside the country with a lifetime supply of Play Dough.

Another of Shahnaz's babies is a playground bristling with swings, seesaws, and rickety carousels. None of us has ever decided what this rigamarole is for, except possibly to keep the soldiers entertained. They do use it, many of them, although soccer is the sport of preference. Iranians are marvelous soccer players and here on the base, as everywhere in the country, they get a game going at the flick of a pants leg. Off come the uniforms, and into the playground or the parking lots go the soldiery in their pajamas.

Your ordinary Iranian wears full-time pajamas under all outer clothing, mufti or military. This readies him at a moment's notice for sporting events, dalliance, or bed.

American employees of BHI *are requested* to wear uniforms. Since this isn't an out-and-out order, I have chosen not to comply. The BHI uniform consists of charcoal slacks or skirt in polyester with elastic waistband. (Given a list of ten things I loathe, polyester would rank number one, and elastic waistbands possibly number five.) Also light-blue nylon shirts which, in warm weather, cling to the skin like napalm. And a navy-blue blazer with the BHI logo in red, navy, and royal blue perched neatly over the left ventricle. It was this bull's-eye logo location that made me balk.

When I arrived in Iran, the very first thing I heard about was a group of gaily uniformed Americans who'd been killed en route to work the month before. The story must have been true, as I was chauffeured to my job by different routes, and at different hours, every day, and the U.S. Consulate in Esfahan (very circumspectly) does *not* advise uniforms. That's plenty for me, folks.

32

Since the world may possibly wait with bated breath for a listing of BHI's job ranks, I include a sampling, as follows: An A-2 is on the lowest rung of the company ladder. These are clerks who make $680 a month, with no extras, and are mostly captive wives of BHI men.

Jumping to A-14, we have supervisors such as my good buddy David Burdick of Sanford, Florida, home of the auto-train. In addition to supervising at $60,000-plus per year, David is writing another in a line of Great American Novels. I am his mentor and editor.

The pilots are A-14s; mechanics, A-9s.

Starting with A-5, employees receive housing allowances, transportation allowances, cost-of-living allowances, differential money, year-end bonuses, and home-leave allowances. (It all adds up.)

I have a salary, after seven months with BHI, that could make a girl learn to live in, and love, Nordvik, Siberia.

At the top of our corporate pile up are the executives and those with particular expertise in their fields (all *men*), all making $100,000-plus per year.

Countless Americans become "contract junkies," hipped on overseas life and the plush pay. Very few take advantage of the art, manner, culture, language, and mores of the country they've invaded economically. The vast majority live, eat, breathe, sleep, and fornicate in American compounds like Esfahan's Shahinshahr, which is Main Street in Missoula transplanted lock, stock, and appliances from the States. This insular existence in a foreign land does little to endear us to the countries where we are "guests," and I don't think it's a dynamite idea.

> That inverted bowl they call the Sky
> Whereunder Crawling Cooped we live and die....

That's us, folks: cockroaches, crows, flies, and anthropoids —"crawling cooped."

Sunday, 13 August 1978

My friend Rocky Guthrie, marine ace and sometime helicopter pilot, tells me that one-third of all the trainees at Pensacola Air Station in Florida are Iranians and Yemenites.

33

And that it's as painful there as here trying to work instant mechanization on men whose direct antecedents would have been baffled by a John Deere combine. Some Iranian pilots, despite Bedouin backgrounds, do very well. Many, going through pilot's training on extravagant allowances from home, spend their days goofing off and pinching girls on the Pensacola streets.

There are several recurring problems with your Iranian pilot. The first is that he's prone to falling asleep at the switch. Rocky has actually flown pursuit trying to wigwag an Iranian (who'd put himself on automatic pilot and settled back for a sound sleep) awake. Another bugbear is freezing at the controls.

I once made a test flight with an Iranian instructor pilot and his student in a helicopter without radios. The student pilot froze at the switch, and the two men screamed and fought each other for control through the entire trip. Alighting from that little excursion, I tottered into the hangar and signed a blood oath never to "Fly Iranian" again.

Since it is BHI's job to modernize, civilize, mechanize, and "aero-nize" this nation of nomads, we do our damnedest. But it takes a lot out of all of us.

Overnight Esfahan is an armed camp. There are tanks, tank drivers, machine guns and bazooka men everywhere. Jackie just flew into the house, flattened himself against a wall, and howled, "There's a German half-track out there with the gun muzzle pointed straight at our gate!" Donna and I went to investigate, and sure enough, there it was—and still is.

What I'd like to know is where they acquired this heavy hardware? Thirty-seven-ton tanks don't exactly materialize out of morning vapor, and they can't hurtle down the highway from Teheran in less than a month or six weeks. For the life of us we can't figure where they came from. It's Jackie's theory that they'd hidden them in the *qanats* and have just now winched them to the surface.

The qanats are the very ancient system of wells and underground canals covering much of the Iranian and Afghani deserts. There are hundreds of miles of qanats around Esfahan alone, and we suspect there's a whole hidden population down there—mostly Moonies and Hare Krishnas—preparing to take over the world. Look at the tanks. First there were none, and now there are thousands. They're parked along Char Bagh, in the maidan, at every traffic circle, in the flower beds, anyplace they can crush shrubbery and trees.

Just before curfew Jackie and I drove furtively around the city, and the place looks more like Entebbe or Brazzaville than the most beautiful pearl in all Persia.

> Ah love! Could thou and I with Fate conspire
> To grasp this sorry scheme of things entire,
> Would not we shatter it to bits—and then
> Remold it nearer to the heart's desire!

Monday, 14 August 1978

Bicycles are the most widely used form of transportation in Iran, and they swarm everywhere, thick and tricky as hornets. Made mostly in Taiwan or Hungary, they have great balloon tires and fat, cumbersome bodies.

What astounds me is the native agility on these poorly designed bikes, trikes, and *taxi-barghs* (a kind of three-wheeled, motorized, outsized wheelbarrow). Rarely do you see any machine with a single rider. With an élan that could only come from circus ancestry, a biker will carry two passengers behind, one on the handlebars, another on the crossbar, and a moppet weaving atop his shoulders. I've seen a Moped with three riders stop to pick up two more people. And a taxi-bargh sail along loaded with three stepladders, four mattresses, a six-drawer bureau, a refrigerator, and a crystal chandelier. On a memorable morning in Esfahan I witnessed a man riding by with an orangutang on his handlebars.

The entire, city-wide donnybrook is an exercise in balance, foolhardiness and mass fratricide. This is the only country I've known where men constantly exceed the speed limit in reverse. No one owns a helmet (or a muffler). Offhand, I'd warrant the only ones safe on our streets are the men crouched in those tanks.

Since I've been badly battered on foot, it looks like I'm firmly committed to Jack Jyanne, my little car, and the lesser perils of traffic. My nerves may suffer, but I won't be torn limb from limb.

Jack is your typical Iranian car. He has front-wheel drive and will go through sand, sleet, mud, or snow. His manly little two-cylinder engine requires one litre of gas every fifty-five miles. A Jyanne's speed is scarcely roadrunner class, and I've never tried to push him over eighty kilometers (forty-eight miles) per hour.

The Jyanne is modeled along the lines of a French Citroen, but without a Citroen's sturdiness. I love the boy, but I'll be the first to admit he's not physically strong. Sitting on a Jyanne chassis dents it deeply, and BHI men swear the body is molded of recycled beer cans. Mine is a pseudo–station wagon model, which means it has a sheet-metal rear end that makes it look like a squat and inadequate pickup truck. There's no insulation or interior finish, and there's just space enough for two people to ride in front, with camping gear stowed to the roof in the rear.

Tonight I staggered into the house beset by prickly heat and self-doubt. When Skip arrived to escort me on a wildly venturous dinner date between the hours of 6:30 and 8:00 P.M., I was submerged in the fountain, hair plastered flat as a water rat's, eyes glazed with heat, ill humor and sangria, mournfully absorbed in Donna's symphonic sound. (As there is no testing and little schooling during Ramazan, Donna is on summer vacation. After an early morning tennis game, she writes novels and wallows in classical music.)

We finally struggled through a haze of heat to Little Mexico, a surprisingly good Mexican restaurant where the tortillas are made by Thai women. (In this part of the world nobody gives a hoot about culinary experience, racial origins, sexual preferences, or—except for the more spiteful Shi'ites —religious persuasions.) Outside the entrance two mullahs were exhorting a crowd about something or other. No thanks to these so-called holy men, xenophobia grows by leaps and bounds. Even the *Kayhan,* Iran's English-language newspaper, has taken a stand and said to the mullahs, "Hey, fellahs, cool it!"

Skip insists we must eat in every foreign restaurant in a big tearing hurry, as he believes they'll soon be bombed into oblivion. Yes, bombed. Explosives multiply like the loaves and the fishes, and there are puffs of smoke and firecracker bangs on every side.

Tuesday, 15 August 1978

All civil service (postal, Customs, teachers) and other government employees have gone on strike. I trotted over to the Ruhis' to hear what they had to say about it, and Papa Ruhi just looked sullen and chainsmoked English cigarettes. Guity says anyone not on strike will have his home firebombed in retaliation. "But what is everyone striking *for*?" I asked querulously.

"I do not know, Ro-been," she said, shaking her head sadly. "Our people are angry with the Shahinshah and his advisers. They are also angry with their superiors, with the *Majlis,* with the tax men, their neighbors, and each other."

"What about Savak?" I asked, and could have bitten out my big fat tongue. Every face in the room blanched at the mention of the Shah's hated secret police. I apologized and artfully changed the subject from politics to religion. "Is the anger because of Ramazan?" I asked, and Guity answered sadly, "I fear it is much more. . . . And that the world will not be quiet soon again."

I also asked Guity if their Customs salaries would cease, which of course she said they would. Jahan teaches in an auto mechanics school which, though government-operated, is not on strike. As nearly as I can figure, their combined family income, sans strike, is about twelve thousand dollars a year plus whatever Papa can steal. Pretty hefty for a newly industrialized nation—and family.

Mama's mother, Guity's grandmother, was a *Qashqai* (*Gosh-gah-ee*) nomad who moved across the desert from water hole to water hole. A tribal family's income in hard cash is rarely more than a few dollars a year, so Mama and Guity have come a long way indeed.

I do not mention my salary to the Ruhis. I'd be ashamed to have them know how very rich I, mere woman and humble chattel, really am.

There is still a strong caste system in the Arab-Persian world. If the father is a tile maker, his sons are tile makers. If a father collects garbage, so do the sons. The only way to break out of this insidious familial pattern is through schooling. Every schoolroom contains its share of eager young men and women struggling for an education. Jahan was one of these. His father is a farmer, and he had to work very hard to educate himself as a mechanic.

Far more usual are the rabble-rousers who raise hell and disrupt classes and don't give a fig for being educated or upwardly mobile—such as the gangs of vicious kids who're dying to take over the country and loot the shops. The monsters should be trussed to their desks ten hours a day till they're big enough and old enough to work on the Great Wall of Iran.

Skip's friend, Jim Norris, a gentle man who teaches helicopter fundamentals, finds it tiresome to reach the high point of a lecture only to have one of his students pipe up with a leer, "Would you care to accompany me to the water closet, Aghaye Nor-rees?" (Iranians are very partial to toilet trysts.)

Jackie, Donna, Skip, and I, along with interested passersby and drop-in guests, conduct an ongoing debate about the merits and demerits of a Moslem education. We don't understand why the thousands of Iranians, Egyptians, Saudis, and others who are educated in Western universities don't come home and do something about the quality of their own education.

In the eighth century, the Islamic world had the finest universities in the world: Great learning centers throve in Fez, Cairo, Baghdad, and Istanbul. The Islamic edge on world education was tremendous. Yet Islam has not evolved or progressed much from that day to this. Young scholars in Mideast countries can be seen pacing like caged polar bears in parks and courtyards and *madrasehs*, memorizing by rote like the scholars of centuries ago. And their principal textbook is still the Koran.

With such strictured teaching, a student doesn't learn to question, to analyze, or to reason. And an Irani student becomes beet-red and boiling mad when someone like me—alien, female, and insolent—dares to question anything he's said. To question is to insult. It causes loss of face and is an affront to honor.

How are we supposed to work out treaties with such people? That's what I asked Donna tonight, when I came home from the Ruhis'.

Donna did not care to discuss the question. In correcting test papers, it's understood she's to turn a blind eye on many an error and allow a calculated percentage of "flunkees" to slip through her noose. She has tough moral fiber and a big stubborn streak, and this grates on her like nails on a blackboard. Her strong Etruscan face grows dark with righteous indignation as we sweetly remind her that she is, after all, a guest in this country.

Me, I secretly think Fred may have educated himself out of a job. He's built more than two hundred colleges and universities—up from a grand total of one at the start of his reign. Nowadays it seems like every third Iranian is a student, working or nonworking, and that their favorite extracurricular activity is marching and demonstrating. Maybe they ought to initiate fraternities and freshman hazing, and I'd be only too happy to introduce the idea at Esfahan University early this afternoon.

Wednesday, 16 August 1978

Now they've gone and blown up the Park Pol Restaurant. The food wasn't *that* bad, for God's sake. Skip invited me there for dinner tonight, naturally for an early date, and when we arrived the place was a sad, smoldering heap, like a pile of autumn leaves and offal. The bombing happened about three o'clock this afternoon, during siesta. Siesta occurs daily from one until four, which is plenty of time to electrify the city *and* the country.

The Park Pol was operated by Koreans who served pseudo-American dishes such as pork chops, french fries, and something that nearly passed for apple pie. Americans liked it, except me, and many of the bachelors on base ate there twice a day. It was a favorite watering spot and feeding trough and on weekends (Wednesday and Thursday nights) the Marz Band played an emasculated version of hard rock which even the A-21s turned out to hear.

When Skip and I reached the scene, crowds of BHI pilots, mechanics, and instructors were standing around the rubble like Cub Scouts staring at blackened marshmallows and charred hotdogs. They were stunned. Absolutely crushed.

Skip and I returned to the old southern manse, where we lighted candles and ate leftover *gormeh saebsi* with Jackie. Donna lives largely on yoghurt; she has developed permanent

39

antibrucellosis bacilla all her own. The National Health Service could probably use her for antitoxins.

Our manse is quite spacious. Jackie occupies the far corner bedroom, since it has a small latched gate leading into the back kutche. He entertains his companion for a night, usually a comely Iranian lad, and then escorts him right into the street. Jackie is pretty discreet about his pickups, and the only time we're aware of them is at three o'clock in the morning when they invariably set up a howl about being turned out into the night. Jackie just grumbles that he won't have any "sand niggers" robbing *our* house, and out they all go. I have ambivalent feelings about whether he's spreading love—or dissension—throughout this city. In any case, with curfew he, like the rest of us, is reduced to near-celibacy.

Tonight we all sat around the courtyard, sprayed each other with Pif Paf, and listened to the crowds shout *"Allah Akhbar!"* to the rooftoppers, who wailed back, *"Inshallah!"* It was one of the highlights of our summer social season.

Thursday, 17 August 1978

This is the weekend of the Great American Softball Play-offs at the Carr School baseball diamond. The stands will be jam packed with frenzied fans. Skip plays first base for the Choirboys, and today marks the quarter finals between his team and the Desert Rats, plus two more men's play-offs and one between the Bad News Babes and the Eager Beavers. Jim Liberty's wife, Judy, pitches for the Bad News Babes. I haven't played because of my former nighttime work schedule and because I am on crutches. So I am cheerleader for the Crabby Little Girls.

The only men players we cheer are Skip and Roddey Sherman. Roddey is Skip's newest crew member, a shy and ingenuous young man who played the banjo while his grades sank, flunked out of Penn, was disowned by his family, and fled to Iran. He got his mechanical start racing cars and working in the pits. He's a born ballplayer and looks more like a male model than a grease monkey.

I am on crutches because of last spring's contretemps with the delinquent on the motorcycle. It seems that, all unsuspecting, I lost my media meniscus in the fray. This causes my

40

knee to buckle at discommodious moments: When I am attempting a sedate entrance, moving toward speaker's platform, preparing to curtsey to the queen, etcetera. I am a disgruntled and unwilling cripple, perfect material for the Crabby Little Girls.

The softball delirium is composed of two parts homesickness, one part alienation, and one part fed-up-with-Ramazan frustrations. The *Whirly Bird* is grinding out special editions with scores, batting averages, game schedules, and player biographies. When a lead-off batter honks into his bandana it makes headlines.

The wives bake carloads of cookies and cakes for sale, beer is dispensed by clean-living Boy Scouts, players and spectators get falling-down drunk in the heat, and lifelong enmities are made and made up in a day.

Iranians are not allowed near the American ball park. One of them, in the heat of the game, might be killed or beat up, dragged down, and stomped on. Then the army would call out the troops, there'd be an international incident, and *the games would be called off*.

There are thirty-seven men's and six women's teams in Esfahan alone. Heaven knows how many haunt the rest of Iran. Give an American a bat and a mitt, and a team is born.

The games are behind schedule, as some of the play-offs had to defer to martial law, curfew, and the old low profile. I'm writing these notes early in the morning so I can pack a picnic and chug out the Shahinshahr Highway by nine sharp, saddle shoes and megaphone at the ready.

Later: I got to the field about nine-thirty; the players scheduled for later games never made it. Gangs of hoodlums blew up the back road leading to Shahinshahr (and the baseball field) in four different places. Gerry Husung, the hottest pitcher on the Miracle Workers, was trapped between two fire bombings and had to run over some Iranian toughs to get his car through. Things went right on downhill from there. Roads, parks, fences, everything in sight went up in smoke; the ballplayers are livid; mothers with small children are frantic; and there are Iranians all over highways and byways screaming, "Yonky go home!" I sat in the stands just stunned, a bedraggled cheerleader with a wilted pompom, bum knee, and downcast heart.

As for poor Skip, his team took him downtown to the BHI

Clinic with three broken ribs. When the mobs started turning cars over, they pushed a (fortunately small) Jyanne on top of him.

I have him stretched flat on some carpets borrowed from the Ruhis, and I am gently spooning my most expensive Scotch down his throat. His ribs creak audibly when he takes a deep breath, and he's hopping mad because the Choirboys had the play-offs in the bag, and they'll never be able to prove it.

I guess we just didn't keep the old profile low like we should have.

Friday, 18 August 1978

Today dawned particularly bright and beautiful—perfect, alas, for a ball game. The turquoise sky was a match for the turquoise dome of the Friday Mosque. And our nightingale was back trilling rapturously in the pomegranate tree, the one with the crooked trunk. Between carnivorous crows and thousands of guano-producing pigeons, we rarely get to hear an honest-to-Allah Persian songbird. I tiptoed into the courtyard and caught a glimpse of him, his throat swelling mightily, through thick-leaved branches.

With the games canceled and the boys glum, I took matters in hand and went to the gendarmerie station to register an out-of-town trip. Since the start of martial law we've been required to announce our whereabouts at all times. So I duly informed the cops that four BHI employees would be driving to Shahrekord, that we would return before nightfall, and that we trusted in them to insure our safety. I suspect theirs is the newest technique for spying on *xaerigi*—with us doing all the work ourselves; so I smile sweetly and sign their dozens of papers "Susan B. Anthony."

I drove over to Skip's, notified him and roommates Roddey and John Gannon of my plans, and told them to stand by.

John Gannon is a cocky Celt with a Jack Benny sense of humor, a jackstraw fuse, and a wallet so tight we suspect he seals it with epoxy. All three of these guys would make great end men in a minstrel show, and there are times I long for my tap shoes, straw hat, cane, and sound knee.

The boys thought the whole idea of touring the countryside

42

without *raison* or destination infinitely boring; they said it reminded them of the Sunday drives their parents made them take when they were little.

Ignoring the lot of them, I packed a picnic starting with whole wheat bread warm from the Arj oven (whose temperature is regulated by opening and closing the door and either fanning or banking its loathesome little flame). I sliced some good strong German cheese, washed fresh cucumbers and melons, and added hard-boiled eggs and plenty of Château Rezaye—a fruity and very pleasant white wine. By the time I brought out the homemade sugar cookies and brownies with pistachio nuts, all three doom sayers were standing by the car panting like puppies.

Donna the Recluse was staked out in the manse working on one or both of her two novels. The first is set in the international world of grand opera and features two prima donnas, both contraltos. The other is about a double kidnapping in a Swiss boarding school. She needs a lot of peace and quiet to keep all her characters and subplots sorted out.

Around ten o'clock we headed south on the Shiraz Highway with some vague notion of shopping for pottery and exploring a new road into the Zagros Mountains. I wanted to find the weaving factory in Shahreza, a kind of carpet co-op where everyone works together while professional readers recite aloud from the great epic poets, Sa'adi or Rumi. Everything was tightly shuttered for the Sabbath except the bazaar, which was of that unappealing variety featuring live chickens, dirty eggs, rhinestone jewelry, plastic hair combs, and piles of virulent pink *Otafucu's* (plastic shoes).

When we headed west toward Shahrekord, a very primitive town of mud and wattle huts that are worn and wind-beaten and look as though a heavy rain would bring them down, I spied a clutch of black Bedouin tents far on the horizon, and squealed to Skip, *"Turn!"*

It was so hot we were limp as chiffon scarves, except for Skip, whose ribs were taped too tight to let him slump, and John Gannon croaked in disbelief, *"Here?"*

Skip said hoarsely, "If you think I'm calling on any nutty natives at 120 degrees in the shade, you're crazy."

"Listen, you guys, it's *my* trip, *my* lunch, and *my* car."

"Female supremacist," sneered Skip.

The tents were more than five miles beyond the main road. We arrived shortly after noon, with a young woman and two small children shyly watching our approach. While the boys hunched down in the car, I approached the woman and her children, hand over my heart. *"Salaam, xanum . . . shoma chetouri?"* (Hello, Miss. How are you?) I said, smiling and rocking back and forth in the Iranian fashion. *"Xahesh mikonaem"* (Please excuse the interruption).

She beamed broadly, assuring me, *"Befarmaid, befarmaid"* (Be my guest). Guiding my arm, she ushered me into her tent and insisted I occupy the place of honor on her carpets.

Those incipient cowards, Skip, John, and Roddey, cowed by a lone woman and two helpless infants, cringed in the hot car moaning audibly. "Excuse me, madam," I said in Farsi. "I have friends, very big strong men who quake with fright. . . ." She laughed merrily, her voice like the sound of strong bells. She shouted, *"Bia inja!"* (Come here!) to the boys, who at last slunk out of the car and into the tent to huddle disconsolately under my wings.

The woman and her people were Bakhtiari, Bedouins from the Zard-Koub Mountains south of Esfahan.

Her name was Marhamet, and she told me her husband and the other families were in the foothills with their flocks. She was tending the tents and hoped in the coming weeks to meet her Qashqai cousins.

I found it impossible to explain where I was from, beyond saying, like a character out of "Hiawatha," "far over the water." She'd heard of the Persian Gulf, and of Esfahan, but she had never heard of Teheran. Her world was completely circumscribed by the traditional paths of the sheep and goats and the location of the water holes.

Marhamet thought she was about eighteen years old. She looked thirty but was very striking. Her figure was more willowy than a city Persian's, and she wore a pride of rustling silk, satin, and organdy petticoats, and a long-sleeved pink shirt topped by a gauzy *chador* which resembled a filmy wedding veil instead of the bulky, sheetlike chador of the towns. She did not cover her face.

The baby Michi was about nine months old and the little boy Reza perhaps three years, and both were in layers of colorful, embroidered, very heavy clothing. When I asked why they wore so many clothes in the intense heat, she assured me this was what kept them cool. I translated this for the boys and Skip inquired wanly, "What kind of thermodynamics are these? Both those kids look like they have a chill, and I'm sitting here in a T-shirt sweating like a condemned man."

Marhamet scurried about making preparations for chie, as John Gannon muttered, "Christ, not today. I already have a fever of 101 degrees."

I assured Marhamet that chie was not necessary and that we understood about the feast of Ramazan; she just shrugged and indicated Michi—mothers with suckling babes are exempt from such foolishness.

She dug carefully into a pit and unearthed coals of dried dung that, after very brief blowing, blazed into a small, efficient fire. Tea is as much a ceremony here as elsewhere, and this was to be a special, shared experience among friends.

The tent was a large, longhouse affair of typical Bedouin fabric, a kind of sturdy but gauzy burlap woven of goat hair—very strong and black, supported by rough, peeled-wood poles. Even at midday it was almost cool inside.

I was impressed with the order and sense to Marhamet's housekeeping. Her family's personal effects were located in sacks about the floor or tied to the tent posts. In neatly ordered goatskins with the legs tied off were her water, her yoghurt, and her milk. Other skins held goat cheeses, and tucked in a large stack of napkins was the flat, unleavened bread she'd baked that day over her fire.

The spectres of botulism and brucellosis loomed everywhere.

While Marhamet prepared a meal, I launched into a very long and very sad tale explaining the vile instability of the unworthy American stomach. Moaning and rolling my eyes like the Madwoman of Chaillot, I demonstrated the agony of my daily shots. All this produced mild hysterics in the males, which only added to the confusion, and finally both children began to scream. I interrupted one of the great dramatic pantomimes of the decade to threaten Skip, John, and Roddey acidly, "If you guys don't pipe down, I'm going to dump you at the nearest oasis."

I dispatched Skip to the Jyanne to bring the picnic so our hostess might share *our* food. The children, though at first suspicious of my cookies, were soon eating them as eagerly as

45

the potato chips and melons. Marhamet was pretty doubtful about the propriety *and* the food, but her curiosity won us the opening round.

Iranian tea is excellent, although I am not able to drink it with the heavy amounts of rock candy sugar Iranians prefer. Marhamet insisted, breaking off big chunks of the jagged, unrefined stuff which we then held between our teeth while we sipped the hot tea. She had no idea where the sugar came from. She said her husband traded for it.

We visited most of the afternoon and eventually felt so intimate that Marhamet proudly displayed her front tooth with the gold cap which, since her teeth were otherwise white and perfect, must have been purely decorative; her few gold bracelets; and her many petticoats. She was patently poor, but nonetheless proud of her dowry.

Then it was gift time, and I said I would be honored if she would accept the striped silk scarf on my head. I tied it on her, showed her how fine she looked in my compact mirror, and she was so excited she laughed and stamped her feet. Though she refused our offers of money, the boys and I gave all our coins, about ten dollars' worth, to the children. I capped the occasion by pressing on Marhamet a large bottle of Vaseline Intensive Care (her work-worn hands were cracked and bloody) and demonstrated how to use the lotion effectively but not extravagantly. At this she took my hand and offered me my choice of her finest possessions—carpets, copperware, petticoats, gold. I selected a small enamel pot that might sell for eighty-nine cents in Denver and prayed fervently it wasn't something she cherished.

Late in the afternoon Marhamet rose, went outside, and uttered a strange, piercing call. From over the horizon, as if on cue, appeared a very distinguished-looking gentleman. She gave me to understand that he was the resident guru and wise man. He was very tall for an Iranian, about six feet three inches, and appeared to be between 98 and 120 years old. He wore robes and a rounded felt hat that vaguely resembled ancient Ottoman headgear.

The old man smoked a kind of rank, home-rolled cigarette that smelled like hashish and was very pleased with the boys' gift of a pack of Winstons.

We'd lingered because we were not only fascinated by Marhamet and the tribal seer but also in hopes of seeing the rest of the Bakhtiari group. Queen Soraya, the Shah's first wife, whom he's reputed to have loved very much but eventually divorced because she was childless, is the daughter of a Bakhtiari *khan* (chieftain).

Eventually it grew so late that Marhamet, who had never interrupted our visit for so much as a token bow toward Mecca, whipped out a breast and began nursing Michi. This mortified our softball champions, who gulped and stared moodily off at the skyline.

As we bade our Bakhtiari friends an affectionate *"Hoda hafez!"* (Goodbye) I clasped Marhamet's hands and said *"Dust-e-maen"* (my good friend), knowing somehow that indeed she was. When we bounced back onto the main road I could still see her straight, proud figure against the harsh and desolate skyline.

Saturday, 19 August 1978

Another Monday, another week in the Wasteland. Lawrence of Arabia was tougher than I thought. A stifling haze hangs everywhere, caking the insides of one's mouth and nostrils and lurking between the toes. At home we keep it at bay with the garden hose, spraying constantly to lay the dust and coax our geraniums to half-mast. We seem to have water, but the Zyand-e-Rud is sadly shriveled, and the city is brown and sere. Mix with a little blood in the streets, and you have Esfahan and Ramazan, August, 1978.

On their way to the manse to pick me up yesterday, John, Skip, and Roddey passed large coagulating pools of blood alive with flies and swarming with crows. They didn't want to spoil my day and never said a word, but today I myself drove past the bloody pools still not cleaned up. There's a terrible pause on seeing blood spilled in the streets, whether from a sacrificial animal or a sacrificial human. A life has waned, and it is an ugly, unnatural, and dehumanizing sight.

My office remains crowded and abominably hot. If I breathe too deeply I nearly hyperventilate—and am referred to caustically as the corner tire pump. Mechanics on the line suffer dreadfully and a man without a hat is a man about to die, like someone out of *Mombasa*.

47

Sunday, 20 August 1978

The *Khayhan International* headlines hit us like circus broadsides; "Holocaust!" they screamed, and the tiredest blood screeched to a stop in its veins.

Terrorists of some ugly stripe set Abadan's Cinema Rex on fire and 377 people were burned alive. Women, children, small babies, and old men died, and it's so unspeakable even the awful heat doesn't kill the chill. People don't seem to know if it was the *Tudeh* (the Iranian Communist party); or religious fanatics; or angry mullahs who felt people weren't being obsequious enough for Ramazan; or Savak, who thought they *were*.

The fire started at ten o'clock last night, and fire fighters were still putting the last of it out and extricating corpses at ten this morning. Thousands of bystanders listened in horror as people inside screamed for help, and now a mob is gathered in front of the police station, demanding that the arsonists be punished. I doubt that anyone will ever know who planned the crime, or even if those who planned it imagined the gruesome cost in lives; the doors were locked and barred, and no one could get out.

Though there have been increasing cases of arson and fire bombing around the country, there's been nothing like this, and everyone is stunned and shocked.

Abadan, the site of the fire, is on the Persian Gulf, at sea level, where it's *really* hot—the kind of place that causes even Englishmen to run about croaking, "The heat, the heat! Oh my God, the heat!" I know oil men who've worked there, lasted only six months, but still have come away with eighteen thousand dollars in profit. A great place to turn a sow's ear into a silk purse if you've got pigskin hide and a high boiling point.

The British set up oil refineries in Abadan at the turn of the century, the first in Persia, and the place has grown, along with Kharq Island, into one of the most important oil refining and shipping points in the world. I went there last winter with my friend Frank Light to visit Ruthie and Dave Huff, who teach English to NIOC (National Iranian Oil Company) technicians. The turn-of-the-century homes of the British are lovely Edwardian ladies with flounced verandas and lacy fichus and pale, lavenderish coloring, their elegance enhanced by gay flower beds and sweeping trains of velvety lawn.

The city is located on a once-attractive island at the confluence of the Karun and the Shat-el-Abab Rivers, the ~~Shat-el-Abab being the body of reluctant water in which the~~ Tigris and Euphrates unite further north in Iraq. Nowadays, thick black smoke and noxious fumes from the refineries pollute the air like tubercular old men, and the delicate Edwardian ladies are reduced to hiding decorously behind voluminous handkerchief curtains.

When we sailed, we sailed around tankers, oil slicks, derrick platforms and cumbersome loading docks. Abadan's pristine face has grown pocked and very dirty, and old-timers say seeing her is a shock—like coming upon a dignified maiden aunt out hustling on the docks.

On leaving Abadan, I had my first run-in with Savak, the Shah's notorious "Skinny Ties."

Because of its many foreign oil technicians, Abadan has company stores that carry the largest selection of American goods in the country. When I stepped into Dave Huff's store, I felt like one of those contest winners who's given a cart and three minutes after the guy with the stopwatch shouts *"Go!"* My cart was piled high in a jiffy, but the finest, most fulfilling prize of all was two priceless cans of Crisco. Unobtainable in Esfahan, Crisco meant fried chicken and chocolate cake and tollhouse cookies and apple pie. It meant home, the flag, and motherhood. It meant . . . oh well, you get the idea.

I believe I have mentioned that Iran's International Customs inspections are as full of holes as a fishnet sweater. But I may have neglected to add that internal, or domestic, inspections are inexplicably stuffy. This was my first experience of just *how* stuffy. I started to board Pars Air with my precious cans of Crisco clutched in a paper bag—and the battle was joined.

Within seconds several airline executives and at least two Savakers—whom I identified by their five o'clock shadows, Sidney Greenstreet eyes, and skinny ties—were crowded beside me on the retractable and inadequate steps of the Pars plane. For reasons that were unclear to me, these supercilious men were trying to wrest twelve pounds of cooking fat from

49

me, a mere woman. I regret to say that we all began shouting, with the exception of Frank, who only pled piteously, "For God's sake, Robin, give them the Crisco!"

One of the Savak men smiled grimly (he had ill-fitting teeth and a very unstable grin) and again pointed out that "there ees space for gun eenside thee Creesco." I showed him the unbroken seals, talked about motherhood and apple pie, especially apple pie, and I clung to that Crisco like an infant to its pacifier. One of the Savakers finally gave me his solemn promise that if I would permit "thee Creesco" to travel in the cargo hold, he personally would accompany the luggage and carry it in his lap for safekeeping the entire trip. I said, "Weeeeeeellllll . . ." as Frank danced agitatedly around in the background trying to pantomime the rigors of life in an Iranian dungeon. Nearly in tears, I finally relinquished the damned stuff.

No one was more surprised than I when a very rumpled, nearly heat-prostrated Savak man emerged from the cargo hold at the other end and proudly delivered my Crisco. Frank was visibly shaken and unable to eat apple or any other kind of pie for months afterward.

Monday, 21 August 1978

Tonight we hosed the house down for an hour, thereby lowering the temperature to an endurable 96 degrees.

People are staggering around in the heat and the after shock of the Abadan fire. Some of our Iranian officers had friends and relatives die in the Cinema Rex and are taking the whole ugly business very hard.

It's good to have tough-fibered friends to come home to. Jackie is unshaken by spilled blood, dirty diatribes, outright sedition, or downright destruction. In addition, he claims to know every hidey hole and secret exit in the city qanat system, and if civil war breaks out will spirit us away through the joub culverts of his underground railway.

I'm not so sure about Donna, who talks a lot tougher than she really is.

But I know I can count on the family dog. We have a joub dog named *Pichi* (Kitty Kat), whom Jackie barely tolerates. Kitty Kat came with the house, which is part of her territory.

Jackie has known her since he arrived in Esfahan over two years ago, but their relationship is guarded at best. It was love at first sight for Kitty and me, and naturally Jackie is irritated when Kitty Kat comes galloping across the courtyard to smother me with kisses at the end of a tiring day.

It's Jackie's own fault. He thinks all joub dogs are lower than sewer rats and nothing but typhus and rabies carriers, while I know good and well they're too smart to harbor germs, worms, or rabid blood. Street dogs must be Disraelis just to survive around here.

Kitty Kat, so named because she is confused about her species and meows like a Siamese cat when excited, is extremely independent and roams the city on her own much of the day; but by evening she's always at the courtyard gate to greet and accompany me ceremoniously to the fountain.

When I flew to Egypt on vacation, I had to walk eight blocks to the taxi stand at 4:00 A.M. to catch a cab to Forudaghe Esfahan. Kitty Kat escorted me, fighting for her life and mine every inch of the way. She was infringing on other joub dogs' territories and taking her life in her paws, and she knew it. But she was far too faithful and protective to have me make that hazard-fraught trip alone. She also accompanies me on shopping trips to the bazaar, where she displays a marked distrust of Iranian business ethics. If the shop owner asks too many rials, she curls her lip and snarls, and the appalled merchant invariably lowers his price.

Kitty Kat sleeps in our courtyard on an old quilt and wouldn't dream of setting foot in the house proper. I brush and groom her, and she allows me to give her a bath although she is terrified of water. Like most joub dogs I have known, she is affectionate, faithful, and fiercely individualistic. If it costs my last cent, that dog is going back to America with me.

Shortly after six o'clock Skip and John Gannon went with me to the Mir Street Liquor Store where we purchased half of their imported stock. The reason we purchased half their stock, or enough hooch for a convention of American Legionnaires, is that the small liquor store on Nazar was blown sky-high yesterday, and word of this disaster spread like a case of hives. We decided someone had better buy out Mir Street before it too goes up in smoke.

Particularly in the heat of summer and softball, Americans here drink vast amounts of beer which they purchase from the two "Western" liquor stores or from John Moffitt's Boy Scouts. Some available brands are Heineken, Lucky Lager, and Schlitz Malt Liquor, all roughly equivalent in price to *Bal de Versailles* by the ounce. Our men insist Iranian beer tastes as if it's bottled when the Zyand-e-Rud is high and go to unbelievable lengths to find American or German brands at two or three dollars a bottle. If you ask me, they can't taste the local beer through the foam in their mouths. There's an Iranian brand called *Star* which, like Mexican beer, is really excellent.

We can buy almost anything we pine for in the Mir Street and Nazar liquor stores—if we're willing to pay the price and they haven't been blown out of business. Chivas Regal is around thirty dollars a fifth, although Iranian vodka is both cheap and good. When Anthony Quinn was filming *Caravans* in Esfahan, I watched him buy sixty- and seventy-dollar bottles of imported French wines like a housewife stocking up on twenty-seven flavors of Jello. I used this as minor inspiration tonight when I forked over half my month's salary for demon rum.

Using a combination of Donna's, Jackie's, Skip's, John's, and my bad guesses, we have just finished mixing and consuming: Harvey Wallbangers, Sidecars, Pink Ladies, Rusty Nails, and a bastard version of something called a Black Russian. Donna is now singing the farewell aria from *Madame Butterfly* lying face down in our haji's favorite geranium bed. John and Skip are running across the rooftops trying to catch and strangle the Hamaze rooster. And I—I am writing double-entendres.

Wednesday, 23 August 1978

I can honestly admit that along with your average Iranian I've contributed nothing to Ramazan. I am further disappointed in the good Moslems of this community who have not entered into Ramazan in a spirit I could admire. It should have been a time of devout concerns and contemplative prayer. Instead, it has turned into a let's-tear-the-place-to-pieces, Inshallah free-for-all.

Between the mildly hysterical U.S. Consulate communiqués,

orders from BHI headquarters, and the step-up of Molotov cocktail parties, we foreigners seem to be the ones doing most of the praying—for our own necks.

We drive straight out of the city to the Crown Prince Reza Pahlavi Base in the mornings, make our appointed rounds, and come directly home at night. I have not been to a discotheque, gambling den, movie house, public debate, or doily-tatting class this entire month. And our single excursion has been into deserted countryside.

The Iranians at Havan-e-Ruz have conducted themselves through Ramazan like all peoples in all times and places. Some are sincere in their religious observances. Others (the majority) snack sneakily through the day and then stagger into my office, backs of hands held limply against their foreheads, gasping that they're too weakened by starvation to work.

Though Islam does seem more a part of its peoples' daily lives than other religions, I don't get the general impression that Iranians are very devout. Maybe the true believers are congregated in holy cities like Qom and Mashad. It sure seems as if Esfahan is bursting with infidels.

The muezzins, recorded on cassettes, call their people to prayer five times a day. The faithful throw down prayer rugs, slip out of their shoes, wash, face Mecca, and pray dutifully. But the vast multitudes go about their affairs ignoring muezzins, Mecca, their Prophet and Islam. They may believe, but they do not abide.

I've often been in the Ruhi home during the muezzins' calls to prayer—at 5:00 A.M., nine, 1:00 P.M., five, and nine. Mama Ruhi throws a wimple over her head and herself to the floor in the manner of a four-man tent collapsing in a crumpled heap. She is genuinely devout, and I bow my head in respect for Mama and her God. Women do not pray in the streets as the men do.

There seems to be a Koran in every home, but I haven't had the cheek to ask the Ruhis or Hamazes or Abarjanis how often they read it, or on what occasions. (Before the Shah's father came to power, the illiteracy rate in this country was ninety-eight percent.) The Koran is the irrefutable guidebook by which Islam lives. It contains specific instructions for every form of behavior from ritual prayers, to which side of a camel to walk on, to who gets to draw water first, to what is a fair price for a five by six foot Turkoman rug, to how to choose a wife, to the manner of conducting business with a stranger in the marketplace.

Unfortunately much of Islamic practice—such as the subjugation of women—goes back to the pre-Islamic bards, who were out-and-out heathens. Even today an Iranian mother may caterwaul like a damned Druid and blacken her face in despair should she bear a girl baby. It was again the Shah's father, Reza Pahlavi, who outlawed the widespread practice of infanticide of female children, and good Lord, that seems like only yesterday or the day before. These boneheads still haven't gotten the message that it's the *father's* genes that decide the sex of a child. (I know a few American provincials who aren't convinced of the fact either.) If we tried to prove it, they'd only accuse us of Yankee imperialist lies.

Because neither Islam nor its Koran has evolved like the theology of other religions, the result is a lot of ironclad dogma that's tightened a scriptural noose around its followers' necks, women who are relegated to the same third class status they held in the fifth century, and children who receive their sole educations from an honorable but outdated book. Imagine teaching kids in the Bronx and South Philadelphia and Aspen their ABC's from Exodus and Leviticus.

It's my idea that Moslems need a born-again Islam and a spanking new J. C. Penney version of the Koran to bring everything up to date in Constantinople, Cairo, Riyadh, and Rabat.

Thursday, 24 August 1978

In ancient times the qanats tapped great underground water tables much as artesian wells do today. Qanats were constructed by sinking shafts to the necessary depth to strike water—anywhere from twenty to three hundred feet—and leaving the shaft openings surrounded by beehives of dirt and sand brought up in the excavating. Canals were then dug to carry the water along underground so it wouldn't evaporate in the blistering sun. These great networks of wells and canals brought life to the deserts of ancient Iraq, Palestine, Persia, China, and Afghanistan.

In the Esfahani countryside the well diggers and tenders

are called *moqanis,* and theirs is another of the traditional jobs passed down from father to son. They know every inch of their sections, keep the conduits free of debris, prevent and repair cave-ins, dig out wild animal burrows, maintain smooth water flow, and probe for new, deeper water tables; the beehive entrances must also be kept open, as one of their purposes is to catch precious rainwater and channel it into the waterways below.

One of Frank Light's jobs in the Afghani Peace Corps was to work underground with the moqanis. Not being born to the qanats, he found the bats, owls, foxes, snakes, spiders, cave-ins, and dank, treacherous earth not to his liking. Next to probing mine fields in Vietnam, he ranks it as the most demoralizing period in his life. He has given up all thought of spelunking, and he plans to spend the rest of his days sitting behind consular desks in three-piece suits breathing the impure, sulphurous air aboveground.

It is nearly impossible to take an afternoon stroll and fall *down* a qanat—you have to climb *up* first. However, Captain Ardashir of headquarters did just that last month. Actually his was more a midnight than a teatime caper, as the captain was out baying at the moon when it happened. (He was rumored to be on a monumental toot in preparation for the rigors of Ramazan.) His faint cries were heard the next morning by a wandering haji, and he was finally located cater-wonker across the bottom of a qanat shaft, his head nearly submerged in water. The moqanis weren't able to extricate him and climbed out to inform a gathering of some fifty Iranian Army officers, several dozen BHI officials, and more than a thousand onlookers that one of the captain's legs was broken.

The captain was finally pulled out by a Bell 214 with the aid of a grapple hook and a very foolhardy BHI Medevac team. It was quite an operation, as there were three sizable cave-ins during the proceedings.

Poor Captain Ardashir. *Both* legs are broken, as well as his sixth vertebra. Shahnaz had planned to execute him before a firing squad as an example to his fellow-officers, but the poor devil didn't have a leg to stand on. They would have had to nail him up to shoot him, and even Shahnaz isn't *that* callous.

Friday, 25 August 1978

This is a three-day weekend, a national holiday that arrived just in time to relieve tensions and keep the BHI pressure cooker from blowing.

Explosions are rife as it is. Esfahan's total to date: twenty-nine movie houses, fifteen restaurants, four nightclubs, and one liquor store.

BHI artfully suggested we get out of town, so to speak.

Our motley crew is now two hours west of the city in a world so different we could almost be on the Great Lakes. Skip and Terry Alexander and John Gannon and Roddey are here; also Jackie; and Jim and Judy Liberty, our friends from Detroit; Rose Fazio, my Montessori-teaching pal; and sundry other orphaned souls from the storm. The Libertys brought their dog, Kid, and their children, Dawn and Jimmy, Jr. I tried to entice Kitty Kat and Donna along, but Kitty Kat has another litter hidden away and her poor swollen dugs are dangling around her ankles. Donna is going great guns on the last chapter of the kidnapping saga and didn't want to quit while she was ahead.

We are at the Shah Abbas Dam and Lake, and it's late and I've been lying in my sleeping bag savoring the 60 degree chill and the sound of jackals coughing in the hills and the sight of stars turning off as the moon fills the night sky.

The Shah Abbas Dam is an enormous construction that provides Esfahan's water supply and its hydroelectric power, and it's been a popular Iranian spa since the day of its completion. The mere fact of so much water in the midst of vast desert is enough to draw the inevitable crowds. Although it's in the Zagros Mountains, which are snow-covered into April, there's not enough runoff to grow more than mesquite and buckbrush. Again the country is like Arizona or Nevada, little more than rock and barren sand.

I'm writing in this journal by flashlight, as I try to do when everyone else is busy, asleep, or drink-dazed. Otherwise I'm referred to as Swiss Family Robinson or Sam Pepys and accused of tearing off secret reports for Savak and the CIA.

These men will eat their hearts out when I'm elected the first woman governor of Colorado. Or the next queen of Tasmania.

Iranian and American tourists are segregated here. I wish it weren't so, but there's the omnipresent and unhappy fact that Iranians congregate at the flash of a beach towel or the flip of a bathing hat. Let an American girl take off the sweat shirt over her bathing suit, or American kids throw a beach ball, or an American housewife swim a few laps, and there they are—Iranian mobs spectating from planes, cars, bicycles, water wings, and paddle boats. It's the single most maddening aspect of life in Iran.

I myself find it difficult to concentrate on my reading when five hundred heads swivel every time I turn a page; it makes me feel like I'm on center court at Wimbledon. And being surrounded by spectators while you brush your teeth, comb your hair, chew your food, and kiss your lover gets pretty tiresome. It's either segregation—or the loony bin.

The Iranian Army boys who're in charge of policing camp sites find their own morbid ways of invading our hard-won privacy. They drive their trucks pell-mell through tent enclaves, merrily pulling out pegs and sending camp gear flying. A truck driver nearly drove over me in my sleeping bag under the mistaken impression I was a red sand dune in the sunset. One soldier, pitter-pattering in to do a little night peeping, almost lost his manhood to Dan Mullins's Great Dane, Killer. Killer is so named because ordinarily she's as bland as a two-toed sloth. We were all pretty pleased and proud when she bit the front of the soldier's pants out.

Today everyone water-skied behind Inspector General Pemberton's boat for hours. I tried wind surfing on my one good leg, was dumped ignominiously in the drink, and gave up that tricky sport forever.

Jim and Judy Liberty are among my favorite Americans. Judy is a hyperkinetic, American Beauty housewife who dotes on her husband and children. The kids, Dawn and Jimmy, Jr., are blond, furry, well-behaved, and have very high IQs. On my list of beloved people they rank number one and number two. Jim Liberty is the small fungus of the base. He knows who drinks and who uses dope and who shacks up with whom, and he reports on everyone. He is the head rumor monger, information gatherer, and tale-teller of BHI. He can

57

also tell you, and will at the drop of a wrench, what's wrong with Iran, the United States, his congressman, the Ayatollahs, the IRS, the GOP, BHI, Europe, China, Russia, and Ramazan. He's a male chauvinist pig, a wonderful husband, and a loving father. I adore him.

Judy Liberty, bless her old-fashioned, homemaker's soul, fixed a picnic with everything from potato salad to pickled eggs and beets and even whipped up a spectacular coconut layer cake. Rose Fazio, a teacher I met on a tour to Persepolis last fall, brought an antipasto that ranked right up there with a Dubuffet still life.

After dinner we gathered around the fire and sang college songs and camp and football songs plus a few tug-in-the-throat spirituals. We were so grateful to be free of curfew and gathered together that there wasn't a dry eye in the place. Jackie danced and sang a rendition of "Minnie the Moocher" that brought down the house.

I love my friends, and I love Americans, but I can see why Iranians think of us as an eccentric subspecies to be observed carefully under glass.

Sunday, 27 August 1978

We returned to find the Liberty house vandalized in the most despicable way!

The thieves left untouched: The TV, the stereo, the camera and movie equipment, the furniture, and the appliances.

They stole: Little Dawn's costume jewelry, the children's piggy banks, all of Liberty's *Penthouses* and *Playboys* (a heartrending loss), his flight jacket, and his tennis shoes.

In the center of the house the thieves poured the following in a mountainous dump: Judy's Tampax and Kotex (shredded like top secret papers), all the Tide, Clorox, breakfast cereal, children's toys, mechanics' tools, dishes, bowls of fruit, dog food, pots and pans, kerosene, checkbooks, bank books, records, receipts, bills, house plants, and the children's goldfish, still merrily swimming around in about an inch of water.

There were filthy black fingerprints and hand marks on the walls, and there was human excrement all over the courtyard.

Judy Liberty, a housekeeper to put Mrs. Marylebone to shame, sat in her hammock and wept piteously.

It's taken us hours of combined forces to achieve order and mop the place out, and Judy is still shaken to the core.

Jim, who is not known for tact or patience, shoved one hairy hand through the front door in a fury and can still be heard howling in the wilderness, "Those fucking *Rags*! Those goddamn stinkies! I'll get those murdering, shit-eating assholes if it's the last thing I ever do!" *I mean,* that Liberty has a way with words.

I'm sure the perpetrators have fled to Kerman, cackling over their silly loot and petty little triumph; I kept begging Judy to shut Jim up or at least quiet him down. He may get himself salted away in solitary in the Esfahani Tombs.

"I can't do anything with him, Robin," whispered Judy in a quaking voice. "I've never seen him this way before. It's all I can do to keep him locked in the courtyard and not out in the streets punching strangers."

When the gendarmerie came to inspect the mess, they were so casual and unconcerned that Liberty roared at them too, calling them ass-holes. We're terrified he'll be dragged off for a head shaving if he doesn't shut up.

While our faces were to the lake breezes somebody also blew up the Mir Street Liquor Store and most of the banks in Esfahan. Apparently we foreigners are to be condemned to a life of lemonade and Master Charge. It's OK by me, we've stockpiled plenty of spirits, and my credit's good.

With payday three days away, rumors fly like flapjacks. Will the government shore up its currency? Print fresh rials on toilet paper seconds? Reinstitute the barter system? Tune in this same time tomorrow, soap lovers, and hear the latest episode in *As Iran Turns*.

Monday, 28 August 1978

Those holed up in the city over the weekends, like Donna Leon, child-novelist, said the street howling has increased daily, as have the hand-painted banners with defiant religious slogans and growing anti-American sentiment. Ramazan or no Ramazan, Donna turned up her phonograph volume in sheer self-defense. She had to. The crows and the Hamaze rooster were going bananas. Roddey and I are going to sneak over the wall and assassinate that old bird for sure. We've made elaborate plans to lasso him from behind.

Donna had a horrifying experience while we were gone. Crossing the Khaju Bridge onto Kamil-Esmail, not far from here, she passed a dead body (human) being eaten by a flock of crows. She made frantic inquiries of our kutche cop, but he didn't seem to know if the person was an accident victim or someone shot by martial guards. "Well for God's sake, go clean her up!" shrieked Donna and stalked away. It was a woman, or at least the body was wearing a chador. Poor Donna acts like she's living a Hitchcock movie and darts about staring furtively over her shoulder and bumping into furniture.

I hate to say it, but I think both Judy and Donna are marked for life.

Tuesday, 29 August 1978

All the principal hotels and restaurants are closed for four days as a placatory gesture from Fred, who is rumored to be pretty upset by the trouble and travail. I'll just bet the man will breathe a sigh of relief when this whole big happy "holiday" is over.

Even the gambling casinos are closed.

There are eight or nine gambling hells scattered around the country of Iran. The one in Esfahan is near the Carr School baseball park and features a rotten restaurant, a mediocre discotheque, blackjack tables, baccarat, crapshooting, and roulette wheels. It also requires a jacket and a tie. I've been there for dinner, which immediately ruined my appetite for anything further, especially high rolling.

Most of Iran's posh resorts and elaborate casinos are in the Caspian area in the north. The Caspian coastal towns are the Newports and Palm Beaches of the Iranian affluent. The very high class hotels *cum* casinos are owned by the Shah, the Shah's family, or the Pahlavi Foundation, whose sole purpose is undoubtedly funneling money into Swiss bank accounts and the hell with the Iranian Girl Scouts.

I've been to the Caspian only once, and it's as different as

Iraq is from Nepal. The seaside country (actually the Caspian is not a sea at all, but the world's largest landlocked salt lake) is high and green and mountainous and semitropical. It holds most of Iran's population outside the major cities.

The Caspian is full of rice paddies and cotton plantations and barley fields and grows most of the staples for the rest of the country. There are also tea and sugar beet plantations, sturgeon-caviar fisheries, and extensive walnut groves.

This is the land of the mighty Elburz Mountains, a continuation of the Hindu Kush and the Himalayas to the east. It is magnificently contradictory country containing both palm trees and great stands of black timber and is fine for mountain climbing, trekking, and big game hunting. It abounds with wild boar, ibex, mountain sheep, snow leopards, and, it's rumored, tigers.

During this hottest part of the summer the Caspian resorts are jam packed with Teherani upper-crusters, probably all hopping mad because their caviar, champagne, rosewater, income, and gambling have been shut off for the weekend. Tiresome, old things, but one must muddle through, mustn't one?

Wednesday, 30 August 1978

Today the Eagle shat.

On the next-to-last day of every month we are paid. Or as these louts I work with express it, "The Eagle shits." The U.S. flag and the bird get no more respect than poor Rodney Dangerfield.

Apparently the bombing of the Bank Melli (the Iranian National Bank) did not affect the principal gold supply. Maybe the crown jewels were used as collateral. In any case, we were paid, and Monte Carlo Night will not have to be canceled for lack of interest. Or funds.

Monte Carlo Nights in Esfahan are a post payday tradition; they take place at the Old American Club and are owned and operated by Smokey Hayden, a would-be Amarillo Slim. He's currently doubling his bets so he can go home with a stake big enough to open his own Atlantic City poker parlor or Reno, Nevada, Laundromat. Smokey is a semiprofessional gambler who only incidentally works in BHI Tech Supply. I am exceedingly fond of the California Kid, though he tells me to my face I have as much card sense as Alice in Wonderland.

Smokey got in a big game with an Iranian businessman who, when he was down $2500, scoffingly refused to pay Smokey. He said Smokey was "only a guest in this country." After trying every recourse in Iranian law, Smokey resorted to some time-tested, extralegal tactics; he got three of the boys in his outfit to work over the man's Mercedes. They slashed tires, metal-set the locks in his doors, and ruined a brand-new paint job. The Iranian got off lucky. In good, old-fashioned, highly civilized America, he might have been planted six feet under. Iranians may not understand about not welching on a bet, but now there's one who does. He got the message, and he paid Smokey what he owed him.

Thursday, 31 August 1978

The BHI communiqués of yesterday said there have been increasing incidents on the highways, including some casual little roadblocks and juggling of fire bombs. And the gunfire in the streets increases daily.

The martial law troops are largely from Kermanshah and, outside of the Palace Guard, are Fred's most elite corps—the Iranian Green Berets. I am impressed with everything about them but their trigger fingers, which twitch a lot. They're a far cry from the slovenly recruits stationed at Havan-e-Ruz: tall, immaculate, with a razor-sharp press in the pants, their eyes straight ahead, always at attention. They're the cream of anyone's crop, and I've seen a number who turn me on to the point where I almost sidled up and asked them home for "coffee, chie, or me."

It's those ugly, deadly guns that depress me: Machine guns, bazookas, turret tank-guns, small cannon. And they point them at everybody.

Sometimes I have an incandescent feeling about this entire month, as though it were all a marshmallow disturbance in an alabaster mirage with little toy death machines darting about like something in a Magritte painting. Then, with a sudden, shuddering start, I realize the sound of gunfire is *real*, and the bitter sulphurous smell of cordite is not a figment of my unwholesome imagination.

62

BOOK II

Friday, 1 September 1978

Ramazan, with its pushing, shoving, and shouting, has about five days to go. It's like coming down the stretch in a horse race.

Today was the quietest Sabbath in weeks. I dyed fabrics in the courtyard with Pat Johnson, who's been my batiking buddy since early summer. Pat is tall, stunning, chic, and has the same artistic bents I do. She is an ex-highway patrolwoman from Huntington Beach, California, and when she gives me a sample of professional tough talk out of the corner of her mouth, I'm appalled—it *can't* be the same woman. She also practices tai-kwan-do, manages the BFS swimming pool, and teaches at the American grade school.

While Pat and I were up to our elbows in wax and dyes, Mama Ruhi and Guity came bearing a kettle of the special holiday soup which is eaten every evening after the muezzin sounds the end of fasting.

They also bore news: Two boys shot on Abbas Abad close to the Iran-American Society; one old man dead of the stroke and religious frenzy on the far side of Sheik Bahai; a small exchange of fire involving martial guards and unknowns between the American Consulate and the Esfahan Hotel, no one hurt. Mama Ruhi kept making the standard Iranian "no" sign—tsk-tsking, throwing the head back, and curling the upper lip (I do it rather well myself)—to portray her consummate disgust with the whole disorderly business.

Later Skip and Roddey showed up looking like they'd been backyard barbecued, visions in black face. Chuck Low's house and car were fire-bombed last night, and the boys spent hours hauling furniture to safety, moving Chuck's family to Shahinshahr, and cleaning up soot and water. Skip's broken ribs ache and I can't even hug him. Well, not very hard.

Pat said, "They don't look good in that color."

I poured both of them what I hoped was a double Cuba Libre made with Iranian Pepsis. They needed a drink, but not *that* bad. They finally held their noses and chugalugged the things. I simply have to find a bartender's book somewhere.

A fire bomb is pretty much like a Molotov cocktail, homemade, usually as simple as an empty liquor bottle filled with kerosene, with a rag for a wick: All that's required to turn a house, car, or human being into a roaring inferno in five seconds flat.

Chuck Low is a maintenance chief, A-16, who lived with his wife, children and dachshund on Bozorg Mehr on the other side of the Royal Bazaar. His house was in an area of many historic old mosques and a religious community of hard-nosed zealots. Not a friendly milieu with the natives feeling fitful.

Chuck phoned the base shouting that his house and car were on fire and that he was probably under siege; word spread, and our men rushed over to pound out the flames and hold off the Saracens. Iranians had rolled two fire bombs off a neighboring roof. One tumbled into his front hallway and exploded, and the other hit the back of his car, gutting the rear end. There was so much smoke and flame he actually thought we were at war.

This made Pat and Donna and me feel mildly morose. We *all* have neighboring rooftops, and they're *all* flat and accessible. Half of Esfahani life is lived above tree and roof line. Every block of houses is connected from kutche to kutche by adjoining courtyard walls, and homes meander in and out for a quarter of a mile. (I don't know how in the devil anyone surveys a property line.)

Esfahan rooftops are like combined summer gardens *cum* block parties. On hot nights mamas, papas, grandmothers, small babies and young marriageables sit up there, everyone visiting back and forth except the young marriageables, who are expected to eye each other appreciatively but keep their distance. People sing, gossip, dance, and swap chie and ghand.

I used to hop the rooftops when I wished to take a short cut to Guity's, evade curfew, or talk shop with Akhbar Abarjani. But, besides being crutch-ridden, I don't have my old carefree feeling about it anymore. Jack Jyanne has been tucked away in the courtyard and was, I felt, as safe as in church. I know in my heart that the Nazires, the Shirazes, the Naderis, the Hamazes, and the Mostafis would throttle a stranger who appeared overhead with a funny-looking bottle. But they are my friends, not my keepers. And they can't stand guard the night through. Suddenly I feel very vulnerable, for me and my friends and for my little unarmored car.

I sent Pat off with a pail of Ruhi soup and a warning to watch her skyline.

Sunday, 3 September 1978

As Ramazan nears its end our political seminars gather momentum. Increasingly Skip, Roddey, John, Terry Alexander, Ben Roche, the Libertys and a Busby Berkeley chorus of men from the base gather in this courtyard after work to drink my supply of Scotch, gin, vodka, and Iranian wines and beer; to play backgammon, gin, and rummy; to discuss the undercurrents boiling beneath rebellious Iran; and to attract a whole lot of unwelcome attention to *my* house. Also to arm wrestle.

Donna is bitter over this running beer party and sports forum, as she wishes only to listen to the death throes of *Rigoletto*. I am powerless to do a thing about it.

Anyway, the Kouroush pool is closed, I am no longer able to swim or walk or bicycle, and I like the company.

The consensus of the backyard consortium to date:

1. Local businessmen and minor government officials are sick of paying baksheesh to the boss, to Savak, and to Fred's

67

hundreds of grasping relatives and in-laws. (Mexico, Argentina, and Saudi Arabia, please take note.) Truckling is widespread and has to go.

2. Nepotism is worse. It's awful watching a neighbor with the mind of a musk ox shoot up the ladder of success because his cousin is a city official.

3. People are sick of seeing Savak haul away a family friend or aged uncle because he inadvertently insulted a government clerk in a public park.

4. On the other hand, there *are* plenty of *Tudeh* (young Communists), and they're the ones who're adept at playing cat and mouse with the Savak. There's a deep-seated hatred and mistrust of the Russians in this country, and it goes back centuries. Peter the Great and Ivan the Terrible wanted Iran's saltwater ports, and Brezhnev the Bully is no different. What bothers us (and our thinking Iranian friends) is how cleverly these Tudeh kids shift all propaganda blame for everything that's amiss onto these bloody, bowed, and oh-so-stupid American shoulders.

5. The typical blind mistakes, misuses of power, and petty abuses of an absolute monarchy are starting to get on the Iranians' nerves.

6. Back to the Tudehs, those young Johnny-on-the-spot Communists for whom the Shah's university programs are made-to-order forums and who have been infiltrating campuses as fast as he and the *Shahbanu* can found them: They are sowing wild oats that this country is going to reap in bitter harvest. I just hate myself for seeing red-hot Communists on every corner. But this isn't Berkeley or Boston College, by God. And these Communist kids are the kind who only go to class to plan airport attacks, hostage holdups, and how to take over governments in ten easy steps. Fred may have his shortcomings, but I believe he's right about them at least. They don't give a fig for Iran, not unless she's dogging the footsteps of Mother Russia.

(During points one through five, Jim Liberty continues to pace the courtyard, beer in hand, roaring about those "shithead Savaks," "sand nigger Commies," and other obscenities ignored by all.)

7. *My* point was—and I raised my voice an octave to get it across—that we Americans are doing the Persians no more good than the Communists. This was greeted by boos and

catcalls, and I was doused with a barrel of dirty fountain water and retired to the showers.

Not all Americans are bad guests of this country. The Jack Massey family dropped in to join the forum last Sunday, and they're a fine group who are my idea of beautiful Americans abroad: Jack, his wife, Jo, and their teenagers, Dana, Gerry, and Beth, all love Iran. They've been here four and one-half years and have put 100,000 kilometers on a rebuilt Mercedes visiting every corner of the country. The children have many Iranian friends and don't isolate themselves among American schoolmates. Jack Massey is a top BHI executive who thinks me marvelously efficient and innovative at my job, and I therefore consider him a corporate genius and a man of many parts. He and his family are from Panama City, Florida.

Jack and Jo Massey have finally stopped traveling. They've been caught in three major riots, had a soldier use their car to aim and fire into a crowd of women, and Jo was trapped head-on in a volley of gunfire that singed her hair. They contribute a great deal to discussions of what the hell is going on here.

I have a fine, private corner by the chimney pot where I can retreat to oversee Jack Jyanne, the kutche, our pistachio trees, and the breathtaking view of the Queen's Crown in full flower. The Queen's Crown is an enormous butte topped with a large, vulgar simulation of the royal tiara done in Christmas tree lights of red, green, and white, the colors of the Iranian flag. This outdoor monstrosity is lit up for special occasions— invariably when a fine sickle moon's on the rise, or the Milky Way's crossing the sky, or Orion is raising his sword aloft.

We have platoons and squadrons of men, headed by Jim Liberty, who have sworn, before leaving Esfahan, to shoot every last light out of that harebrained, oleaginous display.

I've only seen the real queen once, when she came on an inspection tour of the base and we women threw bushel baskets of rose petals in her path. I felt just like a toddler dancing around a maypole. The Shahbanu, who's very attractive, and reportedly very intelligent, smiled graciously throughout. Frankly, she reminded me of an iron butterfly. Nor do I have a helluva lot of affection for a dame who'll permit the mutilation of thousands of rose bushes and one perfectly good mountaintop.

Fred and Farah Diba's marriage was arranged, just like

the common folks'. As were his several divorces, on the ostensible grounds the ladies couldn't bear him sons. (Hah!) Even the most westernized and affluent people in this country have brokered marriages, although with some degree of approval from both bride and groom. Guity and Jahan never even held a conversation until after they were married.

Listen, I'm not knocking it. We Americans, with our divorce rate and shattered hopes and dreams, aren't doing such a swell job on our own. We'd probably do better using Dolly Levy than the family minister.

I have this funny hunch that your average Iranian female, who is plain, ugly, or mustachioed, wants to hide safely behind her chador until she's married off. This naturally does not apply to the Teherani sophisticates who wear sleek Valentinos and Diors and Mary McFaddens. But how about your plain Jane who uses the chador as a cheap and very handy vehicle for coquetries and is able to leave plenty to the unsuspecting man's imagination?

What's more, if electrolysis were introduced nation-wide, and Nair became a best seller, I believe the chador would disappear with the facial hair.

On the other hand, I can think of any number of women in the States who would have led fuller lives in the blessed sanctity of the chador. . . .

These flights of fancy can only lead to further culture shock. Why don't you pipe down, Robinson, and try drifting off into a deep, untroubled sleep?

Monday, 4 September 1978

Our Pony Express haji appeared at the crack of dawn with another cheery message. Most of us are served by these messenger hajis because only a very few elitists have telephones. (You must buy your own, for the same price you'd pay for a good secondhand car.) We're not to work today, as the government is in a state of flux, flux being a euphemistic term for total bedlam.

All hell has broken loose, and the country is a cauldron of riots, demonstrations, marchings, and howlings; it's like a giant camp meeting of Whirling Dervishes.

Later Pat Johnson sent her own haji who announced,

"Madame say no work, you like bateek?" Skip was still here from having spent the night.

"It's all right, we're engaged." I grinned at Pat when she arrived. (Plenty of people have taken to sleeping over, and not entirely due to the *Playboy Adviser*. Seven-thirty on a summer evening is just too all-fired early for normal, red-blooded Americans to head for bed.)

While Pat and I mucked around with wet tapa cloth, Skip sat under the pistachio tree drinking Turkish coffee and fuming about the known particulars of the Abadan fire. He, Skip, is ordinarily cheerful at all hours, but this morning he was a dour and pensive Sherlock Holmes.

"Why wouldn't an oil city as strategic as Abadan have a finger on all its terrorist groups?" he pondered. "You know, I wouldn't put it past Savak to start a bonfire just to blame the mullahs or the students."

"Watch it," warned Pat, "you're referring to the law enforcement body we all know and hate."

"You, baby, have a law enforcement body I could learn to love," grinned Skip wolfishly.

"I don't know," I said pensively, "I don't think Savak is that damned clever. If they can't cope with a can of Crisco, how can they plan a reign of terror?" Then I yelled, "Skip, you're spilling coffee on our batik!"

"Maybe this isn't a good day for pursuing the arts," Pat said.

"Try explaining this!" cried Skip, splashing more coffee. "First it takes the firemen half an hour to get to the fire; then all the theatre doors are locked; and finally, none of the fire hydrants are working."

"But that's just good old Iran, Skipper. No Savak plots required. *Nothing* ever works."

"Ah, but you are wrong, Madam. The Iranian sex drive works full throttle twenty-four hours a day, seven days a week, fifty-two weeks in the year. . . ."

"Oh dry up, you drip!" This from Pat.

Pacing the courtyard in his go-aheads and Moorean pareu Skip looked more like Don Ho than Holmes: brown, wholesome, and unjaded. "You know what I think?" He paused expectantly. "It was definitely the moqanis. They're going to burn down everything aboveground so the underground can take over."

Pat and I threw cutlery and copperware, and Skip made a

71

dash for the pomegranate tree and fell backwards into the fountain. A fitting finish for old Holmes.

Eventually we dispatched the world's greatest detective to Bonsi Pars to find some fish for dinner while we spread our dripping cloth from one end of the courtyard to the other. Skip took Kitty Kat with him; though she's extremely fastidious, she doesn't quite comprehend the matter of footprints on fabrics, especially when they're on the ground where any intelligent dog knows they don't belong.

Pat and I talked about Fred and the government. We're ashamed to admit none of us has taken the interest we should have: Changes in cabinet offices and governmental ministries under an absolute monarchy are as flat as old soda, with none of the savory salt of electioneering and political infighting and dirty tricks that we're accustomed to back home. Ah, but how things have changed. Nowadays Iran is an incendiary blend of a fired-up town meeting and the Spartacus uprising.

Fred started off with some great ideas. His redistribution of land was important: He took the mullahs' and the wealthy landowners' properties and passed them along to thousands of virtual slave workers and sharecroppers. What's more, he organized volunteer teams to go into the deserts and highlands and teach basics from simple addition and subtraction on an abacus to reading, writing, and crop rotation.

"But," said Pat, "he tromped on a lot of big, important toes along the way."

"And," I added, "graft and greed reared their ugly heads . . ."

". . . and messed up the whole glorious giveaway," finished Pat.

Almost hourly, it seems, there are more daring criticisms of the Shah. This was so unheard of a few months ago that it's like watching the Kremlin tumble down. His pictures are being removed, even defaced. He is called, sneeringly, the western Shah, the American Shah—the vilest insult that people can hurl.

"I don't even know the man, let alone love him!" I protest.

"Neither do the Brothers Karamazov over at the Russian Embassy," Pat sniffs. "But you can bet they're paying their little Persian cousins to spread the rumor that we're the bad guys."

"Listen," I said, "I know we aren't always the most gracious guests, but neither do I understand why every last thing that goes wrong is credited to the American account."

"Simple, my friend. We're not Moslems. Once a Moslem gets cranked up, he'll turn all his frustrations and furies on the handiest infidels—and that's usually us."

We decided that, here or in Watts or at Berkeley, there's an incipient ugliness in crowds: They so easily lose self-control, develop mob mentalities having little to do with the decency of the individual. Mobs are ravening beasts with hallucinogenic frenzies that are terrifying.

"This is the twentieth century, Pat. Demonstrations are here to stay. But palace intrigues? I thought they were gone forever. I can't believe the Persians are really going to depose their king."

"Wait long enough and every style comes back," she said grimly.

"Listen, you'll never convince me that the high and mighty Shah Mohammed Reza Pahlavi, with his tons of tanks and Kermanshah troops and squadrons of heelos is going to let a passel of teenage rowdies take over his country."

"I'd be happy to give you odds, honey, but I can just hardly stand to take candy from a baby," Pat said softly.

Tuesday, 5 September 1978

We've had another curfew change, this one for the better, from 10:00 P.M. to 5:00 A.M. I don't know why, no one earned any lollipops or merit badges.

I crutched across the bazaar this evening to talk to Akhbar about carpets and politics and play some backgammon.

Akhbar Abarjani has good breath and a clean mind and is one of my favorite Iranian men. He has enormous brown eyes, a beatific smile, and displays such undisguised delight on seeing me that I feel like an ambassadress to the king's court.

Akhbar is not only minty-breathed, intelligent, politically savvy, and above petty street pinching, he is also a good (i.e., honest) rug merchant.

I have touted him to all my friends, and even the helicopter mechanics are buying Persian carpets. Skip and

John Gannon originally treated the idea as if I'd suggested they invest in phony bridge shares. When Mother sent me articles from the *New York Times* and the *Wall Street Journal* stating that the best hedges against inflation, and very big money-makers, have been real estate and Oriental rugs, they choked on their own pooh-poohs. I ran those little tidbits past the BHI nonbelievers and really started the carpet train rolling. The final clincher was: When I shipped my first gift carpet home to Dad for his offices, a four by six foot Turkoman Four Seasons silk beauty that was an Akhbar bargain at $720, Mother took it to Mr. Arabajian in Denver to be appraised for insurance purposes, and Mr. Arabajian got all starry-eyed and said it was worth $6500 at *least*. Mother sent a Xerox copy of his written appraisal, along with his offer to buy, and I posted them prominently on my office bulletin board.

"Well, I'll be dipped in shit," said David Beekman in awed tones as he surveyed the board. Ray Hogan, nattily attired in plaid pants and polka dot shirt, the picture of taste and decorum, answered, "Jesus H. Christ, can you believe all that money for a damned Farsi rug runner?" Ed Thorpe shifted his cigar to the other side of his mouth and said, "Listen, Ray, I think I'll just pick me up a rug come payday." By now there's a well-worn BHI pathway to Akhbar's door.

I myself am interested in weaving to the point of lunacy and did intensive reading on Oriental carpets before leaving home. And it's Akhbar who's given me my on-the-job training. Over a samovar of steaming hot chie and a platter of melon, biscuits, *pesteh,* and watermelon seeds (eaten by Persians to mend jangled nerves), we settle down on luxuriant, silken piles of Baluchis, Kirghiz, Turkomans, Kachlis, Souhbulags, Bijars, and Feraghans. Then Akhbar tells me tales of his carpets, the evolution of the designs serving to recount Persia's history, tribal customs, and legends.

Advanced seminars are conducted in the countryside, where I walk into homes, factories, bedrooms, and sheds—any place I spy a loom—introduce myself to the woman weavers, tell them of my own four-harness jack loom made in faraway Littleton, Colorado, and am invariably welcomed with warmth and delight. After I have been offered the inevitable chie, I'm persuaded to sit in to try a few knots of my own. Me knotting the lilliputian threads of a Persian carpet is akin to a dock walloper threading a fine needle. The

74

weavers try not to titter openly at Old Fumble Fingers, and our ladies' auxiliary settles down to a blissful afternoon of whistle-while-we-weave.

Home weavers in Iran use a vertical, two-harness, warp-weighted loom which is the most simple and easily constructed loom in the world, nearly identical to those of the Navajos half a world away.

A prayer rug approximately three by six feet requires two women from six months to two years to make. It was the present Shah who made it illegal for weavers to work more than four hours at a stretch; he did it to prevent the blindness which traditionally struck most of these women in young middle age. The mullahs, I hear, would like to return the ladies to their knots and shuttles on the old twelve-hour-a-day shifts. "Getting back to our basic values," they call it. A Persian carpet averages 120,000 to 240,000 knots per square yard, and by heaven I'd like to see these mullahs condemned to tie knots for five or ten years apiece—and without a single coffee break.

Tonight I told Akhbar I wished to buy a carpet for Polly and my Uncle Whit, and I gave him the color scheme of their new house and my budget limitations. Since Uncle Whit cured Akhbar's outbreak of warts at a distance of eleven thousand miles, Akhbar considers him a Great Swami and immediately allotted me a thirty percent discount.

Akhbar is very generous with that precious commodity, his time, and he thoughtfully mused aloud over possibilities. Some rugs he returned to his stockpiles as inferior, overpriced, or of poor-quality dyestuffs, these to be reserved for tourists. He explained why one Baluchi was a particularly fine buy, another was not, and apologized for the expense of a third, while explaining that this was the coloration we sought and if I attended carefully I would see that the same coloring and quality were to be found in the Cabestan, the one on the back wall. The less expensive model, carried into the twilight, had the look of jewels afire on a translucent rose and violet sea. I said, with a lusty sigh, that neither could I afford that one. We are not actually bargaining: Akhbar reserves his no-holds-barred theatrics for rich and elderly tourists who can afford them. But he pats my hand gently and says for the great Docktor Whit he will take off an additional fifteen percent and further reassures me, "It is all right, my friend, I'll carry you."

Rug merchants are Esfahan's street bankers. They carry us xaerigi peons from payday to payday at no interest charge. After my proselytizing, half the men at BHI are in hock to their eyeballs and being "carried" by Akhbar and his friends.

Tonight I visited Akhbar to talk turkey instead of carpets. "Akhbar," I said, "can we speak of politics over backgammon?"

"Yes, but softly, my friend."

"Who are the Ayatollahs we hear more and more about? Sharietmadari and Khomeini?"

Akhbar shook the dice and threw a double six. "They are very wise men, very holy."

"What do they wish of the Shah?"

"Sharietmadari wishes justice to be served. In an Islamic nation justice *must* be served."

"And Khomeini?" I took my turn.

"He has been in exile fifteen years, since he led the mullah revolt. He also wishes justice to be served, and he wants the Shah tried and punished for his sins."

"What sins, for Lord's sake?"

Akhbar rolled his eyes and the dice. "Only Allah knows for certain."

"Why did Khomeini lead a revolt?" I asked, throwing a one and a four.

"Because the Shahinshah challenged the holy men, stripped them of their wealth."

"Is this Khomeini a wealthy man?"

Akhbar threw doubles again, this time fours, and said quietly, "I believe he is truly a holy man, this Ayatollah. He lives like the poor, speaks sometimes like a saint, sometimes like a devil, and he cares nothing for the material things of this world."

I threw a one and a two, Akhbar doubled, and I surrendered. No one, me least of all, can beat a Persian playing backgammon.

Curfew was nearly upon us. We blew out the lamps and said good night, two old and good and slightly disheartened friends who trust each other.

Wednesday, 6 September 1978

That old migraine special, Ramazan, is done and gone. I've never been so glad to kiss a holiday goodbye in my life. I hate being a bad sport, but I've decided I can live forever without these emotional religious celebrations. This one left me limper than a wet dish rag. I'll take the twenty-four-hour, red, white and blue variety any time: Arbor Day, the Fourth of July, Halloween. Anyone notice how happy and *congenial* they all are? None of this weeping, wailing, and gnashing of teeth in the jovial U.S. of A. If we can't enjoy it, we don't throw the party.

I regret to say that I am feeling anti-Persian this morning. These people are not required by their government or their Prophet to blow up cars, shoot children, maim young girls, or pull out the hairs of their own muddled heads. One wonders if they have a very good opinion of themselves or their Islamic world.

Last night Akhbar explained the revolt of 1963, when the mullahs were madder than wet hens at losing their land, and Khomeini led armed men through the streets. Khomeini was jailed by the Shah and then exiled to Iraq, which was delighted to harbor any enemy of Iran's. There he muttered threats and incantations until they too tired of him and shipped him off to France.

I don't like the man's looks, and I don't trust his motives.

Despite Iran's decadent management and wallowing, pigsty bureaucracy, the technology, education and modernization of Persia have made tremendous forward strides under the Shah.

"Why on earth," I asked Akhbar, "do your people want to bite the hand that betters them?"

"The Persian people, through history, do not see the forest for trees."

"That's a rotten comparison, Akhbar, when you have hardly any trees and not a forest in sight."

"But my friend, you know whereof I speak. . . . Here each man has his own small trouble: a son is underpaid . . . a brother arrested for making speeches in the park . . . a young cousin is hurt in traffic on Shah Square."

He continued, "A Persian, you see, expects his Shahinshah

77

to come down from his throne, appear at his courtyard gate, and make wise judgments in the manner of the ancient khans. When he does not, a small anger begins, is added to the anger of his neighbor, and together they grow larger."

"And what are *your* feelings, Akhbar?"

"I think it is time for a change. We too would like to taste your democracy. This land does not belong to the Shah Reza, a man whose father comes from dirt, who used the army to seize Peacock Throne for himself. The son of that father has grown rich. His is a greedy family. His Shahbanu travels the world in diamonds and sables. They move, with their children and many servants, from palace to palace. They spend our money among xaerigi. I myself wish to see our land back in the hands of the mullahs, of holy men who care for us."

I felt like he'd told me there was no tooth fairy. "But Akhbar," I wailed. "It never works to mix church and state. The poor will lose their land, universities will close, your women—they'll go back to polygamy and the harem and the veil."

"I do not think so," said Akhbar solemnly. "Much good the Shah has done will live on."

"How can you be so sure?" I could have bawled.

"I know one sure thing, my friend. Already I have been promised a position on the National Carpet Council in the new government."

"Oh boy. Ohboyohboy . . . the tree in front of the forest, Akhbar?" He had the good grace to grow red in the face.

It's conversations like this that give me that tired blood feeling of late.

Thursday, 7 September 1978

Iran has a new prime minister. The discarded one, Hamshid Amousegar, was supposedly a genius at industrialization and efficiency engineering. But his heart wasn't in the right place, not for these times; it was in turbines and core drills and stock issues.

The new premier is Jaafar Sharif-Ememi, about whom I know little. Except that he kowtows to the mullahs, has more than one wife, and prays from morning till night.

The government must be pretty shaky for Fred to change

premiers at a time like this. Somehow I doubt if Sharif-Ememi will do much to shore it up. He's only a bone to throw to the mullahs and to hell with the state of the nation. The following hideous changes have already been made:

One: We are returning to the old Islamic calendar, which moves up eleven days each year and means none of us will ever again know the hour of the day, the day of the week, or the time of our lives.

Two: Press censorship has been lifted for the first time in fifteen years. The *Kayhan* announced this in banner headlines and then proceeded to feature exactly the same old canned items that are written any time from June to December. The Ayatollah Sharietmadari, that comforting voice for moderation, did say in an interview that "We have no intention of implementing the traditional Islamic criminal codes such as cutting off thieves' hands or stoning adulterers to death. We don't want another Saudi Arabia or another Libya." Well thank you, Ayatollah Sharietmadari.

Three: They've abolished the post of Minister of State for Women's Affairs. That cowardly Fred and his villainous advisers have made the usual sneaky concessions and sent three decades of reform down the joubs!

In the proper spirit of a good guest, I have long had large, hand-tinted portraits of the Shah and his Empress tacked conspicuously in our front entrance hall. Donna almost had an attack when I first put them up. Well, she can rest easy. I just ripped them off the wall and into shreds. If that's all the faith you have in us girls, Fred, then the same to you, fellah!

The Pahlavi family is on display everywhere—in gas stations, public buildings, kutche stores, private homes, post offices, Customs houses, banks, supermarkets, and bordellos. At Havan-e-Ruz the janitors weekly distribute fresh portraits, most of them looking like they'd been photographed postmortem. Skip and his roommates use them for dart boards, as Fred's nose makes a dandy bull's-eye.

Akhbar and his cousin and Mike Conrad and the Libertys came over last night. We all argued crackerbarrel style about the methods and motives of the new premier.

We bought melons on the corner, located the traveling shirini man and purchased pastries, and heated up a pot of my *kuku saebsi* from yesterday. I also broke out the last case of Château Sardasht, a good local wine. There were eleven

79

for dinner, and we toasted the passing of the sixth of September and Ramazan. Then we prayed for and drank to the end of martial law, revolutionary zeal, curfew, and all Skinny Ties.

Akhbar downed more wine than the rest of us put together. Afterwards he announced that he regrets it but the revolution is here to stay and not to worry, all of us will be safe from harm as we are his good American friends and very best customers.

I went to bed feeling, for some reason, inordinately depressed.

Friday, 8 September 1978

Despite my prowess as a planner, we came down to the Ramazan wire with a cupboard as bare as Mother Hubbard's. After stocking up at our kutche store, I stopped at Guity and Mama's for chie, and they pressed their usual Roman banquet on me. They conspire constantly to fatten me to a decent Iranian standard, and the shirini today was a mouth-watering concoction of pistachios, honey, nectar and ambrosia. I threatened darkly, "Mama, I shall not return to this happy house if you make me fat."

"But Rob-een, sweet one, you have no meat which a man may grasp in love."

"I have been grasped, entirely without love, every time I turned a corner in your country." This last elicited hoots of laughter, for though Mama doesn't go out much, I believe she considers it the height of flattery to have her crotch grabbed in her kutche. No man could ever get his hands on anything worthwhile anyway, not with all those layers of fat and chadors between him and his target.

When I asked Guity if she minded awfully losing her Minister for Women's Affairs she looked at me nonplussed, as if I'd asked something as improbable as, "Do you miss your pimp?"

When I left I reluctantly accepted a small kettle of *abgusht*, or "slimy soup," an Iranian staple I loathe. Mama also gave me a big bowl of *mosamma bedemjan*, eggplant and chicken stew—a delicacy Donna and Jackie and I could exist on through all eternity.

80

Kitty Kat escorted me to the Ruhis' and then daintily escorted me back home before returning to her litter down by the joub. She is an extremely busy dog. I gave her the abgusht for her trouble.

With adjustments in seasonings, Iranian food is quite tasty. Kebab is the equivalent of the American hamburger. Other staples are: lamb; chicken; every size, kind, and color of beans and lentils; rice; the basic *saebsi* (dried or fresh herbs); nuts of all sorts; and of course yoghurt, the principal national dish and repository of brucellosis bacillae.

Fruits and vegetables aren't readily available in winter, so over our long spring-through-fall season we Americans slurp up local eggplant, zucchini, limes, spinach, tomatoes, and of course the glorious Persian melons. Esfahan has twenty varieties of melon, most of them unlike anything we eat at home and all delicious.

Ninety percent of the world's pistachios are grown in Iran. Walnuts, almonds, and sunflower seeds are universally eaten here. BHI mechanics turn the air blue because Iranian pilots fill their flight suit pockets with nuts and seeds and merrily toss aside shells which filter down into the delicate heelo machinery and gum it up like glue.

We have our regular nut man on the kutche corner, and we patronize him frequently. He faded into the Ramazan moonlight but just the other day knocked timidly on the gate to tell us he would be making his rounds again. He looked pretty peaked, which led us to believe he's a good Moslem who fasted himself to near-starvation.

Vendors also sell delicious pomegranates, common as melons, and hot beets, a specialty during the cool winter months.

Under Mama Ruhi's tutelage I've learned to make a number of Persian dishes. I'm the only one in my circle who cooks, as Donna would starve to the bone before lighting a stove, and all the men I know would rather eat Korean than crack an egg. One of my current specialties is Mama's *kuku saebsi*, a kind of egg soufflé featuring fenugreek, dill, fennel, and other local weeds.

Although breathing garlic on one's friends is considered a terrible breach of decency, Iranians are nevertheless addicted to it. The trick is to turn one's face delicately to the side while conversing. This is patently ridiculous, with garlic rising in clouds black and thick enough to cause a solar eclipse.

Farming is big in Iran and so is fertilizer. All around

Esfahan are ancient, fortresslike pigeon towers that resemble the old Moorish watchtowers standing sentinel along the Mediterranean coast. When it was discovered centuries ago that *guano* made superior fertilizer for Persia's sere and sandy soil, pigeon towers were here to stay. The towers are very picturesque and supply enough guano to fertilize Yemen, Saudi Arabia, Iraq, Turkey, Austro-Hungary, Poland, and most of East Germany. Would somebody please tell me why this scenic and simple solution has not been applied in other backwoods farming areas of the world?

Saturday, 9 September 1978

All hell broke loose again yesterday—the newspapers are calling it Black Friday. Apparently everything exploded late in the afternoon after the newspapers and radio stations announced that martial law and curfew were to become permanent fixtures in the cities. People from Teheran and Esfahan took umbrage at this, although I thought the curfew change to 10:00 P.M.–5:00 A.M. was at least endurable.

There were bitter, ugly confrontations between citizens and soldiery. Those in Esfahan took place from the Shah's statue on Mojasamay Circle, up Char Bagh, across the See-oh-Say Pol to the British Consulate.

What infuriates me is that the crowds pushed women with babes in arms to the forefront to face the soldiers. And, holding their babies at arms' length, those women walked right at the creeps carrying guns, crying, "We are your mothers, your sisters, your friends." There were so many of them that the soldiers, *not* Kermanshah troops, but local army and air force, grew panicky and tried to fire above their heads. With the kind of training and attention *they* get, naturally they hit somebody.

Guess who got shot? Women and children only—about forty-seven of them, according to newspaper accounts.

Iranian men are poltroons and pigs. I rained blows of fury all over Skip's quivering, bandaged ribs.

Sunday, 10 September 1978

I stay glued to the crutches like a nine-legged sea anemone, ignoring suggestions that I hire myself a monkey, organ, and tin cup.

A bum knee, like an albino complexion, does not fit graciously into the Persian world. I have had to work out impossibly convoluted gyrations just to keep the soles of my shoes hidden from sensitive Irani eyes. And then of course there are the toilets.

The toilets of this land, as in most of the Mideast, consist of holes in the floor which empty into the purling sewer stream directly below. I am in no condition to do one-legged knee bends lowering myself to the usual Persian level. Nevertheless I manage.

When I catch myself wrinkling my nose at what I consider unsanitary practices here, I try to remember the disgust of an Indian friend when she asked how we Americans could wallow about in our own dirty bath water.

Monday, 11 September 1978

We didn't go to work yesterday or today because of continuing street clashes and warnings from the U.S. Consulate to lie low.

Bored, frustrated, and piqued, I ignored Jackie's and Donna's warnings and set off on my crutches down Dirbande, a small kutche between Ferdowsi and the King's Mosque. It's a shortcut to the bazaar that I've often used.

Kitty Kat did not escort me, one of her puppies had colic. I was irritated with Iran, bored with the caprices of armies, and so sick of politics I was ready to scream. I intended to buy some dyestuffs in the bazaar and just possibly cheat the wily Akhbar at backgammon. In the midst of this self-induced snit, I suddenly became aware of a band of teenage rowdies taunting a young girl. She was wearing a Western-style school uniform of pleated skirt and simple cotton blouse, probably on her way to a tutorial since school is still not in session.

Without a second thought I turned tail to flee, on the grounds that there are always hundreds of natives to rush into the breach. (The BHI handbook sternly warns: When in doubt do *nothing*. At the first sign of trouble, depart on the double!)

Then I heard a heart-stopping scream. And another. And I turned to see those big, bold bullies disappearing like rats down a sewer.

I paused a mini-second. The girl was on the ground, writhing in pain. No natives appeared. One small boy seemed to be trying to help. I waited. Not even a group of two gathered. Since I knew in my bones she'd been knifed or kneed or worse, I gave up and went to her side. She was clawing at her face, and when I forced her hands away the flesh of her cheek was raw and actually *smoldering*.

The usual cast of thousands was slow in gathering. Several men cowered in their kutche shop doorways, and I bellowed at them, *"Bimaristan, bimaristan! Ambulanceh, ambulanceh!"* Meanwhile, I had a grip of steel on the small boy while I questioned him.

"Bale, madame, bale!" (Yes, Mrs., yes) he cried. Yes, he was sure the bad ones had thrown acid in the girl's face, acid from the battery of a "mah-sheen."

Between the girl's pitiful cries, the boy's sobbing, and the increasing crowd cacophony, it was the noisiest nightmare of my life. I have never longed to flee as I did then, but I gulped hard and hung on. I knew if the kutche women got their hands on the girl, they'd apply chicken fat, sheep dip, or goat urine—something that would do irreparable damage. I shouted, *"Ab ab AB!,"* a few men began running for nearby spigots, and suddenly people appeared from everywhere, bearing buckets and pans of water.

Acid burns, *eats* its way through flesh and tissue. Already it appeared there might be damage to an eye.

I implored the still-shrieking girl, *"Lutfan,* please. I am your *düst,* your friend."

Several men helped me to pour pitchers of water over her face. Then someone appeared with a garden hose, and/we gently flushed the burns until we were crouching in puddles of water. The girl was so convulsed with pain that I was afraid she would go into shock, if she wasn't already there, and instructed some of the women to elevate her feet and cover her with their chadors.

A seeming life span—possibly five minutes—later, a Sepahan Hospital ambulance arrived. One of the attendants spoke good English and was apparently a kind of resident physician; when he questioned me, I explained about the battery acid, my voice creaking like an old bedspring.

Iranian hospitals, ambulances, and physicians' offices do not dispense drugs. They must be provided and paid for by the patient. "Please give her morphine. I will pay," I begged.

An ampoule and a hypodermic appeared magically, as if from a coat sleeve. (Who knows, maybe they *came* from a coat sleeve.) "She's in terrible pain, she must be in shock," I said. His only reply: "I must ask you to accompany the patient to the hospital, missus. This is a most grave matter." I thought "grave" a pretty poor choice of words but was too spent to say so.

During the trip to Sepahan I prayed I hadn't botched up my first aid. Then I prayed for the girl, who was at last mercifully quiet. And finally I prayed that both of us would live to see another dawn.

At the hospital the girl was rushed off to surgery and I was ushered into a small, overheated cubbyhole. I was not allowed a phone call and couldn't think of the names of anyone I knew anyway. I could scarcely remember my own. I cowered in a corner wishing my mother were there.

Eventually two men in blue business suits, sincere, skinny ties and dark glasses appeared and asked me for my driver's license, passport, resident permit and BHI base pass.

When I inquired about the patient, they eyed me with weary disdain, as if I'd asked them for their job résumés. After that I kept quiet. I also stopped shivering. I was damned if any clammy-eyed Savakers were going to make *me* quiver and quake.

At length we were joined by the young ambulance doctor and an older man in a white coat, stethoscope, and beard who looked a lot like Louis Pasteur. The five of us filled the cubbyhole wall-to-wall, and the blue serge suits smelled, at close quarters, like sour washcloths.

"You are Miss Robinson Sterling?" asked Louis Pasteur, who was obviously Chief of Surgery and General Inquisition.

"Yessir," I said firmly.

He cleared his throat. "We have ascertained that the patient was attacked by terrorists and that a sizable amount of sulphur acid was thrown into her face. She is a young woman sixteen years of age with a strong heart and very able constitution. She should recover well."

I gulped and waited.

"Your actions, Miss Sterling, undoubtedly saved Miss Mazhari from serious complications." Then he added, "I have attended medical school at your Syracuse University in the state of New York."

I was too dazed to decide whether to thank God the patient was all right or congratulate the doctor on his medical degree.

Dr. Pasteur continued, "Miss Mazhari will retain the sight in one eye for a certainty. Also, plastic surgery will be of tremendous asset. Her parents wish very much to have converse with you, properly to express their sentiments."

With a start I noticed the blue business suits grinning paternally at me. They assisted me to my feet and bore me bodily out to meet Miss Mazhari's parents. They astounded me further by chauffeuring me home. As an American and a female, I would ordinarily have been dumped on the hospital steps to find my own way out, crutches or no crutches.

The blue suits were Savak all right, and they've already paid me a return visit. (Their appearance caused Jackie to take to his bed, and Donna, for once, to be rendered speechless.) They tell me the attack on the pretty Mazhari girl was ordered by mullahs, because she was not wearing a chador. Well, that's what they tell me.

Wednesday, 13 September 1978

Miss Elena Mazhari is the daughter of a senator and her uncle is territorial adviser to the Shah. Her parents have flown her to the American Hospital in Teheran, and from there she will go to a special clinic in Switzerland.

The reason I am so well informed is that Colonel Shahnaz "assembled" me in his office with a cadre of disapproving officers, and notified me of the girl's position, background, geneaology, political connections, and current health. He also (looking as if he had a mouthful of alum) told me that on Wednesday next I will be awarded a commendation at a full-dress ceremony in the auditorium.

I nearly died. The pompous ass passes out beribboned scrolls for minor helicopter heroics like they were bubble gum cards, and the BHI mechanics get thoroughly ticked off because they must dress up in suits and neckties and stand at attention. I can hear the howls of protest now.

I informed the colonel that I appreciated the gesture but I did not wish to receive a commendation nor even a small pat on the head. He just barked, "You have nothing to say in the matter!"

Thursday, 14 September 1978

Last night all of Esfahan was on the rooftops baying at the moon.

It suddenly occurred to these mad Moslems that Ramazan is over and all's right with their world. There have been picnics in the parks. Celebrations. Flowers. Kites. Peace. Love. Goodwill. The loudest noises today were the burping of taxi-barghs and Persians.

Tanks still abound, a stern imprint of the Shah's firm hand, but there's a marked improvement in the emotional climate.

Three representatives of the Mazhari family called on me last evening, in a Mercedes-Benz that must have cost a cool $150,000. They were utterly charming, spoke beautiful English, and were very much at ease socializing with a Western woman. We compared notes on Penn Hall, Mercersburg, Mexico City, Marymount, Harvard and Cambridge like a gaggle of girls at a tea pouring.

They apologized at great length, explaining that in ordinary circumstances I would have been invited to the Mazhari home; but since no one is in residence at present (the family's en route to Switzerland with Elena), they hoped I would understand and forgive them the social breach.

It was around seven o'clock, so I mixed drinks (Scotch), and we sipped and chewed the fat until we ran out of conversational fodder. We'd all been to Wimbledon, Gstaad, Palm Beach, and the Riviera, but we hadn't stayed in any of the same places; I slept on some beach or crashed on a friend's floor, while they stopped at the Ritz or the Palace.

Donna was so impressed she almost peed her pants right in

the courtyard. I'm surprised she didn't rush out and find someone in livery to serve the hors d'oeuvres. Jackie was his most charming, and I think one of the uncles has taken a shine to him.

Thus endeth the late-Girl-Scout, early-Nightingale period of Robinson's sojourn in Iran.

Skip and crew, recalling our Bakhtiari visit with a lot more pleasure than they felt at the time, are planning an expedition to Persepolis for the weekend, starting now. I've been there twice, but look forward to going again. The boys have even done the grocery shopping. We may suffer malnutrition, but for better or worse we leave on the hour.

"We'll take care of everything," they insisted.

"You've had more hassles than Tillie the Toiler," they said.

It's nice to be cosseted and comforted.

Saturday, 16 September 1978

Persepolis: We stayed in a motel last night, one of the very few in Iran. Cheap, draughty as an outhouse, but clean. It resembled those 1930's roadside cabins in the U.S., the kind cunningly named Dew Drop Inn. Mustard-toned stucco trimmed in a winsome brindle brown.

The site at Persepolis is the largest royal compound in antiquity, although its glory was unhappily short-lived. After the Persians pillaged Greece and burned the first Parthenon to the ground, it seemed only fair that Alexander the Great come to Persia and return the gesture. He razed Persepolis like it was a neighborhood slum. As I keep telling everyone, this ridiculous waste of good antiquities has got to stop.

We are high here, on the great, god-touched plain of *Marv Dasht,* which is why the temperature dropped like a stone at sundown. It was out-and-out *cold* after the scorching days and sullen nights of Esfahan's summer, and we were happy to sleep indoors out of the wind, away from the icy gropings of Aechemenid ghosts.

Behind the *Takht-e-Jamshid,* the Persian name for Persepolis, rises the Mount of Mercy, a stark and baleful peak that sets off the site of the city like a Metropolitan

Opera backdrop. Its swirling curtains of sand were dramatic but did not serve as much of a windbreaker.

Persepolis is awe-inspiring and moves me greatly. You come upon it suddenly and inauspiciously along the highway, amid roadside junk reminiscent of the Gettysburg battlefield. But soon, out of your car and walking the mighty boulevards of kings and courtiers, all memory of trash is discarded among the litter of forgotten time.

A mighty stairway leads upward from the lower plain, serving as entrance to palaces and halls and giving faint concept of bygone grandeur. Guarding the stairway are two colossal stone bulls. To the right of the main gateway, which would admit with ease a Concorde SST, Antony and Cleopatra's armies, and the grand finale of the Ringling Brothers, Barnum and Bailey Circus, stand the remains of the *apadana*, the great audience hall where ambassadors came to call from every corner of the known world. Though the apadana was a minute part of the whole, it was about 195 feet square, with a wooden roof supported by 72 stone columns. After 2500 years, 13 of these columns still stand.

An astonishing number of relief sculptures, such as the likenesses of envoys from subject nations bringing New Year's gifts to their emperor, are still here. . . . There are hundreds of "remains," and about 1400 archeological dig sites on the plain. One could explore for months and still come upon startling, revelatory discoveries.

My personal favorites are the inscriptions. Great numbers of cuneiform documents, tablets and carvings have been found to date. A typical inscription that sends icy fingers up and down my spine: "Says Xerxes the King: By the will of Ahura Mazda, these are the lands outside of Fars over which I was King. . . ."

(Reading a thing like that from a far-off time before Christ makes me go goose bumps all over.)

. . . I ruled over them; they brought me tribute; what was ordered them by me, that they did; my law held them: Media, Elam, Arashosia, Armenia, Drangiana, Parthia, Aria, Bactria, Sogdia, Chorasmia, Babylonia, Assyria, Sattagydia, Cardis, Egypt, the Ionians that dwell in the sea and those that dwell beyond the sea, the people of Make, Arabia, Gandara, the Indus Land,

Cappadocia, the Dahae, the Amyrgian Scythians, the Pointed-Capped Scythians, Skudra, the people of Akaufaka, the Putites, the Carians, and the Cushites.

So many people, in so many long-dead lands, so little remembered. And who in the *hell* were the Pointed-Capped Scythians, I wonder half-frantically as I search my historical memory in vain.

The Persepolis court spawned Zoroaster, or Zarathustra, as he is often called, the first true genius among Aryan thinkers, prophets, mathematicians. He was also first among the Persians to promulgate the concept of monotheism. His single god, worshipped by the ancient Persians and some present Iranians, plus the Parsees of India, was Ahura-Mazda, the benevolent god of fire and light and goodness. The exact origins of Mazda worship are lost in antiquity, but it's believed that oil seepage from the great gas and oil fields caught fire and burned for centuries, thus leading to the fire cult.

It was an exemplary religion. Its practitioners abjured the then-commonplace practice of human sacrifice and like monstrosities. And Zoroaster was an astonishingly farsighted man who believed in universal brotherhood, the equality of man, peaceful coexistence, benevolence, and the pursuit of art and learning.

Gazing up at the great pink fire temples of the Mazda worshippers, their majestic doorways now twenty-five feet in the air, I wish that these marvelous granite and marble remains, and the wisdom they signify, could live another thirty thousand years.

Persepolis somehow makes me proud of my humanity.

Sunday, 17 September 1978

I thought, despite Bloody Friday, that Ramazan had acted as a kind of national catharsis for a constipated country, and that after everyone dumped his accumulated hostilities, we could go back to scattering rose petals for the queen. I am *so* naive.

Three-fourths of Iran's teenagers are collectively asserting their jingoist adolescence instead of studying the Koran.

There's still no school. Too bad Esfahan schools don't feature wilderness survival like those in Aspen. Every kid here should be supplied with one match, a single blanket, a hunk of jerky, and sent alone into the desert to commune with Allah and his conscience. A few nature boy exercises might bring them closer to Muhammad, where they belong.

Juvenile delinquency has condemned us to further eight o'clock curfews. Eight o'clock, and aaaaaaaaaaaaalll's well! We *should* be well—veritable pictures of blooming good health—we're getting enough sleep to last us into the middle of next year.

Jackie's love life is piteously curtailed. He finds it impossible to make assignations under the See-oh-Say Pol at five o'clock in the afternoon. "Lord God," he says to me, "when I see them in full daylight, my fires aren't only banked, they're *doused.*"

Iranian men are, on the whole, far handsomer than the women. For one thing, they look better in a mustache. Their social lives are entirely masculine before marriage, and after recovering from the initial shock, I found it rather nice to see Islamic males walk hand-in-hand in the streets, kiss each other demonstratively, and otherwise demonstrate their feelings. What bothers me is that they don't observe the same gallantries with their women. Open affection between a man and a woman in public is considered scandalous.

Jackie finally went to the local drugstore to buy me some Valium so I could sleep. I've been having dreadful dreams and I still see the poor Mazhari girl's face. He said, "Your yelling wakes me, all the neighbors, the martial guards, and that goddamn Hamaze rooster. By the time you settle down, everything alive for miles is up and kicking."

"I'm sorry, Jackie." Meekly.

"It's all right, kid. Don't let this get around, but I worry about you."

Although the BHI handbook (tastefully designed in brown and blue) sternly outlines the Iranian penal code regarding possession, use, or sale of illicit drugs (opium, marijuana, hashish, heroin, morphine, or cocaine), anyone can walk into a pharmacy and order whatever his heart desires without benefit of prescription.

Iran is dead center in the infamous Golden Crescent that raises much of the world's opium poppy crop. The place could be junkie heaven, and of course I'd be the last to know. I saw

91

enough skid row derelicts in Teheran to suspect there are far more addicts than alcoholics among the natives—probably because the Koran didn't get around to covering drugs.

There are American housewives who, not having learned the restorative powers of the watermelon seed, go overboard on Valium or Elavil. And plenty of our community smoke hash and even opium. Yet among hundreds of BHI personnel, I know of only one hard core addict, a nice kid hooked on heroin. Marijuana is unobtainable here, so Americans who go to Bangkok bring back Thai sticks by the gross.

I have no idea if smuggling is widespread—or even necessary or profitable. With apologies to Guity, I have to say that Customs is a sniggering joke. There's a lane with a red light and another with a green light. A Customs official asks in bored tones, "Do you have anything to declare, Madame?" I say no and am directed to the green light, where I breeze through like a ship under full sail, and the Customs man thanks his lucky stars he doesn't have to burrow through someone's messy suitcases.

My own big drug experience in Iran happened while I was still in Teheran. One day Frank Light and I stopped in Rey, a suburb south of the city, at a photo shop, the kind where you insert your heads above the howdah on an enormous cardboard elephant by climbing a small ladder back of the stage-flat. While we were waiting our turns at this idiotic contrivance, a little, very old man on the bench offered me a pull on his water pipe. Hookahs, water pipes of all kinds, are universal in the East and, rosily polite, I accepted his kind offer.

I took about five puffs and don't remember a thing that happened for two days. Frank hauled me to our hotel in a taxi-bargh, called a hotel doctor who assured him I would live and charged him forty dollars, and I remained comatose till the following night. It scared the hell out of both of us, and to this day I haven't figured out what I had. I've never sampled another hookah.

What irritates me is that I can have all the dexedrine, morphine and phenobarbitol I wish at my corner *davakhaneh* (drugstore) but I have to argue like a debate captain to get my precious vitamins. "Uppers and downers? Certainly, Madame." "Calcium glucomate, B complex, Vitamin E, what is dese?" asks the pharmacist, glaring suspiciously. After I purchase a peck of watermelon seeds for my frayed nerves, he usually decides I'm safe, maybe just borderline and moody, and consents to sell me a small bottle of Vitamin C.

Jackie walked right in and bought a pint jug of Valium like it was Lydia Pinkham's Nervine.

Monday, 18 September 1978

We're working fewer and fewer regular hours. Word reaches us almost daily that: a/ We are not to leave for the base until 11:00 A.M., as there is a major demonstration moving down Nazar and Mir Boulevards. . . . Or b/ The U.S. Consulate, i.e., David McGaffey, informs us there will be a full-scale student demonstration moving from Esfahan University through Shiraz Circle and north on Char Bagh at two in the afternoon, and everyone should arrange to be in his appointed place well before that hour. . . . Or c/ While we are in our offices, G-2 (Iranian Army Intelligence) sends frenzied word that there will be a mass memorial for all those citizens killed by martial guards to date; or another in memory of the Abadan fire victims; or because one of the hajis was insulted by a Baluchistani and the Sunnites and Shi'ites are meeting at dawn at twenty paces for a mass duel. . . . Or d/ Oh I don't know, maybe an Iranian general picked his nose and bled to death, and the military eulogies will occupy the entire Iranian Air Force from Tuesday until Thursday afternoon.

So we are kept off the streets and behind our latchstrings for increasingly long periods of time. This is more than a minor inconvenience, as most notification arrives too late for us to make alternate plans, or to bring our work home, or to scuttle out for groceries, or even to plan something wonderful like lunch at the Shah Abbas. I'm invariably headed off at the pass just as I've worked out an *enormous* agenda of things to be done at the office that day.

Although the Mazhari attack has left me street-shy, I'm drawn to the yarn and carpet bazaars like a lemming to the sea. I love to watch the raw goat and sheep and camel yarn being brought in on burro-back; weighed, measured, and marked for quality; and in the end deftly bound and sealed and passed on to the waiting dye men who scatter to their

93

cottage factories where, from a marvelous assortment of brew pots, they mix and stir and blend vegetable and synthetic dyes.

I'm also partial to the gold bazaar. Any woman is partial to the gold bazaar unless she's a KGB spy, a congenital idiot, or in the final stages of glaucoma.

Gold here is eighteen to twenty-two carats, extremely fine, and displayed in the bazaar like glass beads in a five-and-dime store. Buying it is tricky, and Akhbar recommends establishing a loving relationship with the artisan, his family, his neighbors and his household gods. "After that," hisses Akhbar warningly, "send a boy to me and I tell you if it is a good buy or not." I gather there are as many crooks in the Esfahan gold bazaar as there are in the purlieus of Washington, D.C.

Wearing very dark sunglasses, I have viewed the Iranian crown jewels several times. They are on display in a vaulted chamber of the Bank Markazi in Teheran: an incredible array of priceless stones. Especially awe-inspiring is an orb of the world, pure gold, weighing 75 pounds and studded with 51,000 precious gems totaling 18,200 carats; emeralds represent the seas, rubies the continents, and Iran and Great Britain are tastefully done in diamonds. Not exactly your run-of-the-mill coffee table piece.

Although the bazaar has been closed ninety percent of the time since Ramazan and the start of the troubles, my biggest post-Ramazan pleasure is lolling about the Shah Abbas gardens once more. The hotel's outdoor restaurants serve the only Western-style salads in the city, and I wash mine down with *café glacé*, a kind of creamy coffee milkshake. Nothing can make a dent in this tough old caravanserai, not fire bombings or kutche gangs or politicians or galloping hordes. Zinnias riot in patchwork crazy quilts, blanketing acres of gardens; furry foliage and rich, royal purple clusters of grapes festoon four-postered and testered arbors; fountains rise and fall, their music fostering lush fantasies and embroidering the senses. Everywhere is the Persian plan for paradise: the heady attar of roses, the music of flowing water, the touch of silken carpets.

The Shah Abbas is reputedly the most sumptuous hotel in the world. Sitting in its gardens on a September afternoon I can believe it. Believe it and forget the ugly sounds of tug-of-war.

But still the vine her ancient ruby yields
And still a garden by the water blows....

Tuesday, 19 September 1978

Meanwhile, back at the base, Lieutenant Arbob, the paragon, the pure, has established his own caravanserai and teahouse. Maybe "watering hole" is the term I want.

Though he has maintained a respectful distance since our public confrontation (when we accidentally pass in the hallways, his nostrils quiver alarmingly, like a horse smelling fire), he has, in his inimitable style, irritated me again by his selection of location for the officers' new chie room.

As a burgeoning military installation, we frequently bulge at the seams. Havan-e-Ruz is the circus Fat Lady adding ten pounds a week and desperately making new alterations. One of these alterations was using peripheral space around the main hangar for desperately needed offices, including mine. Nor did I complain when a vital Ladies' Ordinary was installed next door. Some of our girls must walk a mile for their ablutions, and I felt fortunate.

With its usual lack of tact, however, the Iranian Army also filled the hallway around the ladies' room with lockers and changing rooms for their men. But I didn't take umbrage at this, either; I see them in their pajamas three times a day as it is.

It was only when Lieutenant Arbob, pride of Mashad, established the officers' chie lounge immediately outside the door to our ladies' loo—samovars, tea kettles, hot plates, lounge chairs, the whole schmeer—that I hollered Foul! I hollered foul to Jim Holland, Jack Massey, and finally Colonel Mohammed Shahnaz. Shahnaz gave me his most aloof look and said, "Missus Robin, we have a base to run, heelos to run, a country to run." I nearly yelled, "And toilets to flush!"

Always remember that we women have our ways and our means. Putting our heads together, we girls controlled our bladders and plotted Arbob's comeuppance. We were very aware that, the minute one of us entered the bathroom, an unearthly silence fell over the chie lounge. There was no slurping of tea or chattering Farsi or lively banter, just silence while those perverts waited.

For a time we went to the bathroom in twos, threes, or fours so that our gay, hysterical laughter drowned out all other sound. We accompanied ourselves with a symphony of sink water, cooler water, and more or less continual toilet flushing. We became masters of every subterfuge.

Then Margo Watkins, Karen Owens, Pat Powell and I decided the time had come to give Arbob the Water Cure. Yesterday, Sunday, was uneventful, and the four of us arrived at the base early to put plan into action. With the help of two hajis who worshipfully consider me beset by both saints and devils, we carried buckets and basins and tubs to the ladies' room and filled them with water. We filled so many containers that our humble water closet looked like a solar collector. We could scarcely worm our way from toilet to wash basin.

At the eleven o'clock tea break, the one with biscuits, nuts, seeds, and pastries, Margo whispered, "Are you sure you can manage it on your crutches?"

"If my leg drops off," I said grimly.

"Maybe two of us could squeeze in there so I could help."

"Nosiree, it's my turn with that schmuck." And, smiling fatuously, I passed into the officers' midst. I even managed a slight sashay and several suggestive glances. As I closed the water closet door behind me, I could hear the heavy breathing around the samovar.

After a suitable interval, I began. I poured water from the first handy pitcher in a steady stream down the toilet. Without a pause, I continued pouring from the next can. I emptied water into that toilet, nonstop, from every barrel, bucket and basin in the room. Eventually water seeped slowly across the floor, under the door, and into the chie room. So far as I know, it was the single longest, nonstop simulated urination in history, although I haven't checked with Guinness.

By the time I emerged, rosy and beaming, there wasn't a chie drinker in the house. They had, to a man, fled home to their wives and children.

Margo, Pat and Karen were doubled over the sopping wet floor, between howls of laughter. The Iranians had been first entranced, then perplexed, had surrounded the door in eventual horror, and finally fled in terror.

Jim Holland appeared to ask why in the devil there was

water all over the hangar when we ha̶...
months. We were too convulsed to explain ...
This morning every last bit of chie pa...
disappeared from the ladies' room and locker a...

Wednesday, 20 September 1978

This afternoon at four o'clock I ran out of time and
options. Shahnaz's little toy army, his officer elite, and a
number of highly irritated BHI men in wool and polyester
leisure suits gathered to watch weird Robin get her medal. It
was hotter than a fiddler's bitch, and I felt like an iguana on a
spit. Shahnaz wore khaki and a bushel basket of gold braid
and ersatz hardware. I wore gray wool, powder-blue polyester, and a navy-blue blazer bearing the proud crest of BHI.

All I recall of the ceremony is that it was a great big
embarrassment for everyone but Shahnaz, and my good bud-
dies stood there looking like they'd sell their souls for a drink.

Come to think of it, I don't believe Shahnaz was happy
either. He'd never decorated a woman before, and it not only
stuck in his craw, but he also got the pin stuck in my left
boob. Looking as if he was staring into the jaws of hell, he
fixed one beady eye on the small minted medal from His
Imperial Majesty and tried to get it to stay put without
maiming me. Finally he pulled himself together, pinned the
thing on upside down, and dismissed the crowd just this side
of mutiny.

The medal is an ugly little tintype a lot like the lead
soldiers we used to pour in molds when we were children.

Even Skip said out of the corner of his mouth, "How's
tricks at the Arc, Joan?"

Friday, 22 September 1978

Skip, Roddey, Ben Roche and the Libertys arrived at my
gate this morning and announced a picnic was packed and we
were going to The Dunes. Since I'd resigned myself to a life
in solitary confinement I could have hugged them all.

"Just remember you're the last woman on earth I'll ever get

p for," said Liberty. "Any more of that awards
seshit and I'll turn out in my jockey shorts, the ones with
the hearts and flowers."

Judy Liberty said, "They'll feel a lot better if we let them
shoot their mouths off till lunch-time. After that it's 'more-
talkee, no eatee.' "

We invited Jackie, who yelled, "The nightingales are singing, the crows are on the wing, and Robin's loose in the
streets. Let's get the hell out of town before she lands us in
the newsreels."

The reason these countryside expeditions are so special is
that curfew applies only to the cities; out of town we're free
to breathe open air and bask in moonshine and blink back at
all the stars we wish.

The Dunes are reached by going north on Bozorg Mehr
and turning east toward Afghanistan by way of Barsian.

Barsian is a remote pueblo which has only recently been
electrified and where outsiders are still a rarity. We gassed up
there, then crossed what passed for a bridge and followed a
tortuous goat track to the nomad village of Bar.

Bar is a long-abandoned Bakhtiari oasis with ancient village walls worn thin by time and wind, and lovely surrounding greenery, and trees watered by the Zyand-e-Rud.

There'd been heavy rains the night before, and we followed
a goat path as pocked as old cheese, which meant the natives
were unable to pursue us on bicycles and Mopeds and had to
content themselves with spying on us from an outpost across
the river.

We camped beside dunes far higher and whiter than the
Great Sand Dunes in Colorado's national monument of the
same name. Everyone regretted not having skis or sleds for
sliding but settled instead for hiking to the top of one dune
and then, breathlessly, to the top of the next. Meanwhile, I
read Dickens with my feet in the surprisingly icy river.

The Iranians across the water are presently tiered up like
an audience in a Greek amphitheatre waiting for the next act
of Euripides. Still, they are so distant that we feel nearly
alone and almost uninhibited. I'm writing beside the campfire
like a Conestoga wagon wife. We've finished the beer and
sung the last verse of "There's a Long, Long Trail Awinding."
With our collection of voices, the Iranians undoubtedly believe someone has died. Think about it: These simple people
have every reason to puzzle over why in the devil a large

group of patently affluent Americans with autos would choose voluntarily to take to the desert, bump along washed-out roads, sleep on the hard ground, abjure the comforts of barq and TV, and all the while howl strange, barbaric chants. Jim Liberty shone his spotlight, and they're still across the river, rows upon rows of them, wide-eyed and waiting. You can tell they expect another funny ritual before the night is through. I just hate to have them lose all that sleep for nothing. But when I suggested to Skip we go skinny dipping to give them their money's worth, he threatened to truss and gag me.

Judy Liberty, Minnie the Marvel, brought enough food for a pack of wolves, and she found marshmallows, which we dutifully burned to a black crisp, making it a darned fine, near-perfect, thoroughly pickled American picnic.

Saturday, 23 September 1978

Rape is extremely rare in Iran. Freud and Jung would undoubtedly have attributed this to infantilism or the substitution of the crotch-grab for other manifestations of sexual aggression. But then crotch-grabbing, like rape, is only a *symptom*.

In line with these thought trends Larry Spencer, one of our three chiefs of maintenance, told me about that strange statue out on the Shiraz Highway, a monument I've wondered about every time I drive to Havan-e-Ruz. It's a plain, ungarnished, smashed-flat, very rusted Jyanne automobile raised high on an imposing pedestal.

It seems a young Iranian married couple on their way from Esfahan to Shiraz stopped beyond the city to assist two young men signaling that their car had broken down. When the couple pulled over, the young men abducted them at knife point, took them into the desert, killed the husband, raped the wife, and left her for dead. Though badly hurt, she managed to drag herself back to the highway where she was spotted by the driver of an eighteen-wheel semi. The driver picked her up and turned back to Esfahan to take her to a hospital. On the edge of the city the girl looked up and cried, "It's them! The ones who killed my husband!" "Are you certain?" asked the driver. "I swear it on Allah's name!" sobbed the young woman, and the driver swung around toward the men, who were again standing by the road having car trouble, real or feigned. He ran them down, flattened their troubled car, and ended their mortal days.

Fred awarded the truck driver the equivalent of the Congressional Medal of Honor, gave the widow a lifetime pension, and hoisted the sorry remains of the Jyanne as a national monument to truth and honor.

I'll admit this sort of justice appeals to me. Swift, sure, and it doesn't cost the taxpayer a dime. I've inherited a pinch of red-neck from my father, and I don't give a damn who knows it.

Monday, 25 September 1978

My regular BHI physician, Afghani, who undoubtedly received his training in the fleshpots of Macao, has gone on leave to Communist China, and the new company doctor examined my knee and exclaimed, "Good Lord, child, you need immediate surgery."

"Not on your life and not in Iran!" I snapped defensively.

His name is Kemmerer, and he's patently a genius. "Of course not," he said. "We'll have you sent straight home to your own orthopedist in the States. You'll need a man who knows his patient and his business."

We'd just met, but I was prepared to name the man sole beneficiary in my will. I settled for a spate of tearful gratitude.

Although I haven't committed my concerns to paper, I've been worried sick that—if things grew much worse—I'd be wearing a plastic prosthesis and selling pencils on Chicago street corners.

I'd been conducting an endless, unprofitable, and very churlish debate with our departed Afghani physician, who contended I had "joint mice" and must have immediate surgery in Teheran—while I argued that even with pack rats camped in every ligament I would never trust a limb of mine to Persian surgeons.

The American Hospital in Teheran is American in name only: In truth it is a chamber of Iranian indignities. Oh, I know there are Iranian physicians who've received their training in the finest European and American medical schools. But there's also a plethora of local M.D.'s who've gotten their diplomas from the Afghani and Kampala Colleges of Septicemia and Advanced Miasmas. Medicine here is as full of professional fakers as the government and the armed forces.

There are four hospitals in Esfahan. I've been a visitor to three of them, and they're roughly comparable to American medical facilities during the War of 1812. It's routine in Iran for the patient to supply his/her own bedding, nursing care, disinfectants (optional), medications, bandages, syringes, biting bullets, bedpans, physicians, and T.L.C. So far as I've been able to ascertain, the single amenity provided by the hospital is the roof over the patient's head.

Nor have I been at ease with my BHI doctor pre-Kemmerer. The one who'd been clucking over my joint mice was the same sweetheart who finally diagnosed my brucellosis after six futile months trying to convince me I had advanced diabetes. After conferring long distance with Uncle Whit, who roared that there was no damned way I could be diabetic, I stoutly refused the insulin shots the man pressed on me. Word spread that our medical wizard diagnoses everything from cirrhosis to jaundice as diabetes. By now he does no one any harm. But then he doesn't do much good, either.

Jim Liberty, at the advanced age of thirty, has gone to the BHI Clinic three times about chest pains. The first time he was told they were "growing pains" and not to worry, they would pass (undoubtedly when he reached sixty-five and social security). The next time, our inspired diagnostician advised him he was developing arthritis. "In my *chest*?" asked Liberty, incredulous. At length he added doubtfully, "I guess if you say so. But old Bill Dougherty told me last year you said his chest pains were arthritis. And then he had that heart attack and up and died."

I must add in fairness that the BHI Clinic people give a lot of sound advice and sensible health care in a faraway land crawling with exotic diseases. And they do it at a very nominal fee.

The two Iranian gynecologists who honor us with their presence twice weekly are another matter altogether. Ob-Gyn is a lousy specialty for a Moslem in the first place. Just issuing birth control pills causes them low-grade agony; and the simplest vaginal infection leads to the instant assumption

101

that the patient has been conducting a thriving business at the Nobel Hotel brothel. Nor will they issue pain medication at birth, insisting that it interferes with nature's intent. Deliver me from *those* guys, Allah!

Meanwhile, thousands of Iranians attend medical school in the United States—apparently without cheating or bribery—and immediately set up practice in Beverly Hills or on Park Avenue. Instead of returning home where they're needed, the good guys go west.

When I sustained my broken hand and ravaged knee in that little motorcycle donnybrook last May, I was sent to Dr. Jamshidi of the BHI Clinic staff. After airily inspecting my X-rays, he said, "Your hand is broken in three places, Madame. Here, here, and here. Go home. It will heal. *Hodafez*—goodbye." Dr. Jamshidi is also Afghani which, on a medical scale of one to ten, brings him in at about a minus three.

Actually Jamshidi was probably right. My secretary, Pat Powell, types 110 words a minute and signs my name better than I do. With her help and a little caution, I healed up just fine. Which only proves once again that the best medicine is often no medicine.

Between the hand and "Ramon," I've endured enough trauma for one year. Ramon is an enormous, protuberant, gray-black cap that occupies most of the lower right quadrant of my jaw. He neither fits my molar nor my mouth, and in fact leads an independent life all his own. He was installed by one of the two dentists recommended for Americans after I bit into a rock in a platter of rice at the Park Pol Restaurant. I barely missed swallowing the rock, but not the half-tooth which broke off in the accident.

"So too bad," sighed Dr. Adineh, "we might have grafted." *"Grafted?"* I squawked. My reading experience had led me to understand you grafted fruit trees and an occasional severed limb. I'd never heard of tooth grafting and immediately lost all faith in Iranian dentistry.

Since the installation of Ramon, my other teeth have scrambled around in a constant, frenetic search for living space, while the new lord of the manor lurks in the back of my mouth—large, lumpy, black, and *mean*. He makes wonderful cocktail party conversation, and I can scarcely wait to show him to Rob Chatmas, my dentist-friend in Aspen.

The Mazhari family sent me, via Mercedes and royal

messenger, an Esfahani silk carpet in palest blue, muted gold, and most delicate shell-pinks. It is so lovely that I buried my face in it and damn near wept. I asked Akhbar about its history and value, and he told me the history but when it came to value just rolled his eyes skyward till nothing showed but the whites.

Tuesday, 26 September 1978

Iranian bus drivers drive to drummers all their own. And Iranian bus routes are as loosely observed as the summer solstice. Therefore I called Larry McCormick ahead of time and explained I was on crutches and would need to take a bus to work the following morning. Larry is an Iranian Peace Corps survivor, speaks fluent Farsi, and is in nominal charge of BHI's bus driver corps, the most verminous, sullen, pig-headed, and perverse bunch of psychos in latter-day Persia. Larry's job would make a graduate psychologist self-destruct.

It's been speculated that BHI bus drivers pick up their buses in the morning, drive back to their home kutches, rent the buses out to beet vendors or pomegranate sellers for an eight-hour tour, spend the day in bed, and return to the base garage at closing time.

I asked Larry, as a favor, to somehow make certain the number five's driver arrived at my corner by nine o'clock sharp. "If such a thing is possible?" I added in my most beseeching tones.

Not only did Larry make certain; he personally accompanied the driver on the bus. After I gimped aboard, we became embroiled in a discussion of Iranian Army procedures and, fifteen minutes later, looked up to find ourselves en route to some strange land. We were neither on our way to the base nor to any part of the city either of us had seen before.

"Hey!" yelled Larry. "Where the hell do you think you're going?" he hollered in Farsi, Urdu, and Arabic (to cover all fronts).

The driver pretended Mongoloidism—the single language Larry hasn't mastered—and proceeded to park in foreign parts. He said with a sneer, "Stay where you are, agha. We must cash our paychecks. It will require only a little time."

"Cash your paychecks? What do you mean, cash your pay-

103

checks and 'only a little time'?" roared the apoplectic Larry. Meanwhile, a number of janitors who had been huddled on the floor at the rear of the bus arose and filed out behind the driver.

"And just what do they think *they're* doing?" roared Larry.

"Excuse me, agha. They also must cash their paychecks," said the driver, who apparently was a bank agent on the side.

Larry followed this Persian symphonette into the bank, making an effort to control himself. He tried to reason with the bus driver, who first ignored him and then, losing his temper, ordered the Agha McCormick, his superior and supervisor, back to the bus.

About this time I hobbled into the bank and accosted the driver myself. I told him he was making me late for work. He was so livid that I, a woman, should question his judgment in a public banking establishment, causing him to lose precious face, that I thought for a minute he'd knock me off my crutches.

The hubbub finally grew to such proportions that the bank manager emerged from his inner sanctum to see if he was being held up or bombed.

I knew then, with due apologies to *MS.*, that there was nothing for it but to play Bernhardt. I informed the bank manager very softly, in Farsi, that if he did not insist our bus driver return to his job and drive us to our office as was his appointed task, I would start screaming at the top of my lungs. The bank manager looked searchingly into the bus driver's eyes; the bus driver shrugged, said he had no job, and that he was a lowly day laborer en route to his home.

Larry and I led the bank manager outside and pointed to the large Mercedes-Benz forty-passenger bus painted blue and white and informatively marked BHI Bus #5. We then reentered the bank and the bank manager sternly requested the driver's identification. If he, the driver, was denying stewardship of anything so important as a Mercedes-Benz, the Savak must be informed on the instant that a wayward bus was in his bank yard.

At this, the driver admitted boyishly that the bus was his after all, and that he would consider driving it as soon as he and his co-workers had cashed their checks.

The bank manager looked at me questioningly, I got a

good grip on a pink marble pillar, and I opened my mouth wide. It would have been a real bloodcurdler, but the banker was an intelligent man. He and his clerks ushered driver and janitors unceremoniously into the parking lot, bowed me and Larry hurriedly from the building, and locked and bolted the place till we had hurtled out of sight.

Our driver drove us in a fury at ninety-five miles an hour and blew two tires just as we roared up to the main hangar at Havan-e-Ruz. I was sixty-five minutes late for work.

I thought it was pretty funny and wrote up my "Incident Report" with tongue firmly in cheek. One copy went to G-2, and then some wag made a Xerox of additional copies which were distributed around the base with the latest Rasht jokes. It was a little bit of Jean Kerr in old Esfahan.

I received a rather kindly reply from Floyd C. Haskell, who controlled his bile, and a real literary jewel from Shahnaz. They both had talks with Achmid about his surly attitude and then the poor devil spent a week in jail for attempted kidnapping and had his head shaved. (Standard treatment, it controls lice and causes great loss of face, to say nothing of hair.) I almost felt guilty, but after hearing that Achmid is the meanest s.o.b. in the driver corps, I decided it might get him religion. Either that or me a fire bombing.

I have a good friend, Hamid, who drives a bus route on the far side of the city. He and I have been fast friends since I lived near Hakim Nezami in Jolfa last year. While I rode his bus, Hamid taught me much of my first Farsi, and we're bound together by bonds of language, *tarof,* and contempt for the other drivers. He assures me I will have no trouble with the hateful Achmid, while Donna assures one and all that this house is as safe as a cathedral. Last night, to demonstrate the exact degree of our safety, Skip strapped his ribs tight, started far down the kutche, ran full-tilt at the twenty-five-foot wall, dug his climbing boots into the adobe, and let his momentum carry him right to the top and *over.*

Donna was shaken to the soles of her Otafucu's. She is presently in the utility yard smashing up old liquor bottles and preparing to cover the top of the wall with shards of glass.

I told her not to bother. If Achmid leads a gang of revolutionary revisionists, they won't notice a few scratches, and they won't take prisoners. Anyhow, there's no way this casa can be transformed into a fortress. It's only an old

105

Iranian hacienda, crumbling at the seams, meant for geraniums and sunshine, not harquebuses and crossbows.

Jackie's room is on the far side of the kitchen, close by the handy back door to the kutche. My room is next to Donna's, but on hot nights I like to sleep in the empty room between the kitchen and the bath. It's directly over the well, which is deep and cold and wonderfully soothing to think upon. I throw down my pallet and sleep right on the floor over the well water, Persian style. This is a grand idea which I shall transplant to my vacation house in Bora Bora, along with the marvelous Persian roof planes and wall angles which protect one from blazing sun in summer and invite warmth into the house on chilly winter days.

Our personal and paltry crises have palled beside the earthquake which, in a matter of ninety seconds, killed 25,000 people in the Tabas region. Jim Holland says this particular area has recorded thousands of quakes over the past twenty years, and that it makes the San Andreas Fault look like the Rock of Gibraltar. *25,000!*

I wobbled out to the base to see if there was anything I could do to help. Shahnaz actually agreed to use his precious heelos for errands of mercy. Tabas is about 350 miles from Esfahan, and our helicopters are ferrying medical supplies, foodstuffs, and emergency equipment to the area. The biggest concern is an outbreak of typhus and how to conduct mass burials fast enough to halt epidemics.

Moqanis have been imported from all over the country to get the qanats flowing again.

Everyone at the base has volunteered blood. No one would take mine, on the grounds I may be needing it myself. I gave fifty dollars and felt a little better, but not much.

The Tabas people are hard-working country folks, the kind I care about. This afternoon's papers showed them kissing Fred and the empress, then prostrating themselves at their feet. There was one front-page picture of Fred holding an old man in his arms as the fellow fainted.

Can this be the same country? Simultaneously beset by cataclysm and revolt, by affection for and rejection of its leader? Am I losing perspective? Vision? Reason and balance?

Friday, 29 September 1978

Home, home! I'm going home!

So what if it's the scalpel that calls? Oh the bliss: postoperative depression with Mom, Dad, Whit, Dan, Gwen, Sarah, Mike, and old friends gathered round. I'll be able to savor every minute, as I won't have to scrub hospital floors, change my sheets, cook meals on the floor, or dress my own wounds.

I called to ask Mother to make all the surgical arrangements, and she is pretty excited. She'd rather have me flat on my back in Aspen than dodging cross fire in Iran.

Because of increasing strikes, travel is erratic. The girls at ER are working hand over fist to get me out on the first possible plane. My knee has ballooned to cantaloupe size, and Dr. Kemmerer ordered, "No more work for you, young lady."

Though I'm allowed three months of extended sick leave and have accrued weeks of vacation time as well, I don't plan to lollygag around the States. A month should be about right. After the time and attention I've given Persia, if she's intent on falling apart, I'd like to be here to pick up some of the pieces.

Meanwhile, it's nice to be master of your fate and your life and your limbs.

Saturday, 30 September 1978

I don't know if the high, clear, health-giving air of the Rocky Mountains affected me genetically, but I can't seem to drink or smoke dope, together or separately. I tried both at Rose Fazio's last night, and today I feel like the bottom of the Ruhi abgusht kettle. I am definitely done in and at death's door.

Suzanne Parrish of ER has ticketed me out of here early Wednesday morning, and instead of being deliriously happy, I'm too far gone to care. Skip and Jackie carried my bloated body into the courtyard and deposited me by a geranium bed. If the crows attack, they can have me.

107

Rose served a knockout farewell banquet that should have made the *Kayhan*. I do hope my speech turned out OK. I believe I made an impassioned, drunken plea for Esfahan's French orphanage, Rose's favorite charity. I told the inattentive audience that those children needed all the clothes we could give and, if I recall correctly, demanded that everyone strip on the spot.

I haven't been myself lately.

Well, I've done *my* share for the orphans. My clothes are conveniently child-size, and knowing that I can replenish my wardrobe, I've packed boxes and cartons for the sisters. There's something fine and finite about giving away the shirt off your back.

Sunday, 1 October 1978

Yesterday Roddey, Skip, and Ben Roche toted eighteen cartons and parcels to the orphanage, muttering imprecations and snarling all the way. They came home pleased as punch at having done their Christian duty. The sisters treated them like Knights of Malta, fussed and fluttered over them, and plied them with shirini and lemonade. The two-faced wretches smirked as though they'd conceived the idea, carded the cotton, woven the cloth, stitched up the clothes, adopted the orphans, and been beatified for life.

Men!

I don't need the clothes; I'll be traveling with two crutches, a single suitcase, and an immense roll of Persian carpets. The divine Pat Powell not only cautioned Lufthansa that I'll be presurgical and postprandial, but also implied that I've had a death in my family and a leak in my aorta. If she'd spread it on any thicker, clear-thinking Lufthansa would have refused to carry such a wholesale risk on their flight. As things stand, I'll probably get so much attention I won't have a minute's peace.

I'm to receive first-class wheelchair service from Esfahan to Teheran to Frankfort to London to Chicago to Denver. For the last lap to Aspen, I expect to crawl aboard on my hands and knees. Our local airlines are not noted for congenial service. Just getting you there seems to take everything they've got. (They have also become embittered by the heavy rounds of passenger applause upon landing.)

Monday, 2 October 1978

Rose's party certainly cured me, and I hereby renew my pledge to stay planted on the wagon although I do not look forward to twenty-seven hours of intercontinental flying without so much as a vodka martini.

I also solemnly swear to mind my P's and Q's. Iran is as sensitive as a girl in her first brassiere, and it's time for me to drop idle jesting and humorous "asides." Persians do not have our penchant for light comedy.

Jackie, Donna, Skip, John, Ben, and Roddey are going to escort me to the plane in a body, undoubtedly to make sure I leave town. I can hear the collective sigh of relief as they wave me off across the world.

I bade an emotional farewell to the Ruhis, and Akhbar presented me with a gift of *tizbahs*—Persian worry beads that are carried in the hands, counted, prayed over, and fingered. Iranians don't bite their nails. They massage their tizbahs. I like the idea.

Wednesday, 4 October 1978

I am comfortably draped across three seats of a Lufthansa 747 and being plied with bonbons and sherry (well, Cokes) by attentive German stewards. What service, what a show. First they unfurled the red carpet; then a rosy-cheeked young Bavarian bustled up with a plush-lined wheelchair; I was tenderly placed in a recumbent position and escorted on board with a guard of honor. I could hear Wagner in the distance.

Maybe I'll scratch surgery and spend my days traveling the world in a wheelchair.

The less said about the departure from Esfahan, the better. I was dispatched by the bawdiest bunch of "bon voyagers" ever to molest an airport—and right after my solemn oath to promote better-balanced behavior! Following a loud and very off-key rendition of "She's a Jolly Good Fellow," the martial guards, soldiery, Savak, and Customs officials began nervously fingering tizbahs and triggers and were bewildered when some of us began bawling like babies. The all-American farewell. Jackie hugged me a lot and hiccuped. I lost my voice. Skip kissed me hard. Even Donna choked up. The Iranians watched our pagan antics wide-eyed and dumbstruck.

Wafting my way across Europe in the motherly lap of Lufthansa, I am a jigsaw puzzle of jumbled emotions. Dreamily I picture the tintype of my family lined up at the airport, those beloved faces I have not seen for seventeen months. Then, unbidden, my thoughts return to those good, true friends in Esfahan; I feel nearly traitorous, leaving them now.

I examine my feelings for Iran, which are as jumbled as those of a mother toward a backward child—tenderness alternating with impatience, despair with hope. Please don't fall and skin your knees while I'm gone, kid.

Me, I promise to hurry back.

BOOK III

Monday, 30 October 1978

I just spent six ridiculous days in a dreary New York hotel, standing by without daring a visit to the Museum of Modern Art or even to the nearest Nedick's. We were waiting for Pan Am's striking (by which I don't mean stunning or even adorable) stewardesses to settle their grievances.

Eventually BHI's Chuck LaMance, a number of Grumman people, and I succumbed and booked out on Iran Air, which is possibly one cut above the Grace L. Ferguson Airline & Storm Door Company. We expected purgatory, and it was hell. When the plane took off, so did shirts, ties, shoes, and socks. The aisles were immediately filled with snoring Iranis, shrieking children, flying seeds and nut shells, and that familiar barnyard smell. Everyone talks about his cattle car experience. Iran Air is the cattle car incarnate.

I staggered off the plane and into my first experience with Iran's brave new world. The once-casual approach to Customs inspections is now a matter for the history books. I was instantly surrounded by grim men with hooded eyes who dismantled my luggage like a shipment of time bombs. The job was so thorough it required nearly an hour. I simply sat on a bench, too travel-worn and shell-shocked to protest.

When they had finished, I summoned my iciest tones and said, "This is the first time, in my many months as a guest of your country, that I have been subjected to such an outrage."

A young inspector beamed at me. *"I kar-e-xub, missus?"* (I did a good job?), he asked eagerly.

"You sure as hell did," said I, surveying the compost heap that had been my neat job of packing.

"It is the new regulations," he announced proudly in Farsi. "We must inspect bags like big bunch of locusts."

I had reactified my crutches for travel only. (Having discovered the divine service that goes with being crutch- or wheelchair-bound, a girl would be a fool not to ride that gravy train one more time.) I leaned on them like a war veteran and said to the pleased and proud young Customs man, "And now, my friend, you may have the privilege of putting it all back together."

He did, too (his instructions obviously not having covered this eventuality), folding my satin and lace "teddies" and camisoles with particularly loving care.

Tuesday, 31 October 1978

On the trip back to the U.S., I had been jet-propelled from 100 degree desert heat into a crisp, cool, Colorado autumn.

Our Aspen orthopedists had, at last count, treated a family total of forty-nine fractures and some fairly grim ski injuries. They were aghast at the state of my knee. "Joint mice?" asked Dr. Rod Kirk quizzically and, after a diagnostic arthrotomy, tidily repaired one shattered cartilage and two shredded ligaments. Because of the long delay, I endured a painful rehabilitation marked by wracking muscle spasms and a lot of unaccustomed cursing.

After wallowing in pain and self-pity for a week, I peered feverishly at the shopping list I'd brought home and somehow tottered to my feet. It is every home-bound American's solemn and sacred duty to those less fortunate souls trapped overseas to bring back the booty. If it takes weeks, his sanity, and his last cent, he must return with the whole *Megillah*. A brief sampling of my list is as follows: one Plexiglas windshield for '73 Ford pickup; Caress Travel Curler kit; *Web-*

ster's Collegiate Dictionary, newest edition, unabridged; all possible back copies of *Architectural Forum;* owner's manual for Porsche; electric toasters, sizes and models specified; case of Turtle Wax; blue jeans, sizes six through fourteen; Elizabeth Arden bubble bath; every Louis L'Amour and Luke Short paperback on the racks; Monopoly, cribbage boards, any new games; Head Competition tennis racket, grip size four-and-a-half.... The list was far-reaching, heterogeneous, endless. I wondered wearily if I'd see my family any time outside of shopping hours.

I had become accustomed to visiting the Esfahan specialty shops for every individual item—the greengrocer, the pastry shop, the butcher, the fabric shop, the appliance store, the apothecary, the magazine shop, newspaper stand and book store. I'd forgotten the convenience of the American department store, of vast superemporiums and discount empires selling everything from ant farms to zebra rugs, and this helped. Mother loathes shopping, but she shouldered half the load like a man with a mission and ferreted out the elusive machine tools, auto parts and mechanical mysteries ordered by my heelo boys.

I basked in the breathtaking beauty of local supermarkets, with everything in stock, in order, and sparklingly clean. I was as covetous of rib roasts and monastery eggs as Lee Radziwill over the latest thing in chinchilla.

It was a dreadful grind on my war-torn knee, but gritting my teeth and ungraciously ruing my generosity to the orphans, I even replaced my wardrobe top to bottom. "I'll take that and that and that," I barked at flabbergasted saleswomen. My Bedouin period was long past, and I knew what I wanted. If it was in vogue, had a belted waist and no resemblance to a chador, and the décolletage was circumspect enough for Islam, I grabbed it.

Aside from the Olympian rigors of shopping, the trip home was as restorative as a spring in Samoa. The lush greens and brilliant bronzes of the mountains were a feast for my sore eyes. Favorite French, Italian, and Swiss restaurants were a feast for my tired palate. And the comforting sound of American voices was a relief from the harsh, nerve-jangling street sounds of shouted Farsi.

We sang old sweet songs, talked far into the night, and friends called me from everywhere in the country and the wide world. I raced through back issues of the *New York*

Times, The Nation, National Geographic, Vogue, Town & Country, anything Western and eclectic. I was eager for any clues to what's happening in Iran. When the action is too close, it's tricky for us farsighted folk to see what goes on right up front.

It was delicious to talk to intelligent, composed, and well-informed adults about monarchies, absolute and otherwise; about the Americas and the Mideast in our emerging OPEC world; about manners and mores, cabbages and kings. And so very lovely to criticize our President, his predecessors, all media meddlers, our rotten postal system, the electoral college, CIA, and vast judicial muddle—all without lowering the voice and with no fear of rebuke or a barbering.

Ah, such a family reunion, community town hall, running house party, junior sneak trip, vacation with pay, and incidental surgical encounter!

After weeks that would have killed a presidential hopeful, I checked off the last item on the shopping list, again reassured Mother that yes, indeed, Iran was safe as a church, bade everyone a tearful farewell, and collapsed into the nearest plane. I looked forward to the blessed peace and quiet of old Esfahan.

I celebrated Halloween and my return to Iran at Teheran's President Hotel, donning a Steve Martin nose mask for dinner with two beguiled Grumman executives. (I know I promised to do better, but these awful urges overcome me.) A solicitous waiter inquired whether I had "nose trouble," probably thinking my sinuses inflamed.

Wednesday, 1 November 1978

I would have preferred making the trip from Teheran to Esfahan on one of Akhbar's magic carpets, but this is the lone rug service the good man does not provide.

Since all airport ground crews went on strike to mark my reentry into the country, Chuck, a Grumman man, and I, with mountains of baggage, embarked for Esfahan in a dyspeptic taxi piloted by a misanthropic driver who ordered me under the baggage every time we passed a settlement. I emerged at The Flats looking like the Wicked Witch of the North.

Skip's first words were, "Why in the *devil* did you come back?"

Roddey added brightly, "We're packed to leave. The Rags are running wild, and we're heading out."

"What do you mean, 'leave'?" I demanded incredulously.

"Actually we can't," Roddey reassured me. "All ground crews are out indefinitely, and no one can fly without them. But we would if we could, though we can't."

I felt deflated, like I'd galloped up with reinforcements only to find everyone in full retreat.

My marathon shopping saved the day. Like pulling rabbits out of a hat, I unveiled windshields and books and blue jeans and tennis rackets—trunkloads of overweight comprised of luxuries and necessities everyone had missed. Eyes lighted up, spirits rose, Christmas was in town.

We're having unseasonably wet, cold, November weather that makes old injuries hurt and new enthusiasms die. A damp chill has crept into houses and hearts. Even my singing fails to cheer. I learned some new dirty songs which I immediately rendered in a loud, clear, off-key voice.

"Oh God," was Skip's only response.

Thursday, 2 November 1978

An inspired PR man on Fred's team struck a strategic blow for the monarchy. This is Hajj Week, when thousands of pilgrims go to Mecca, making the holiest of holy journeys. With Iran Air grounded, the junior genius, whoever he may be, assigned the Iranian Air Force to transport hajis to and fro and free. That should earn Fred five hundred points and a new silver scimitar.

Recovering from the denouement of my unenthusiastic reception, I cooked tonight for a worshipful group of my own circle of men and several ravenous pilots. The sneering about Donna in my absence was ill tempered and rude. "Yoghurt," they grumbled, "that's all she lives on; yoghurt and *düg* and *saebsi* and seeds—like a Farsi."

Donna's version was: "They've been like bears since you left, sniffling and snuffing, trying to get *me* to cook. They've suffered acid indigestion, drunk gallons of Pepto-Bismol, and interrupted my writing with their complaints."

117

I made Austrian meat loaf with cheese, herbed carrots and Waldorf salad, and baked sour cream–raisin pies for dessert. I could have had any man in the place on a silver platter.

Dinner was preceded by a shopping expedition that mortified Skip. I insisted on paying for our grocery order with my surplus of limp Band-Aids and stale Chiclets.

Persian merchants do not condone, nor profess to understand, and absolutely never have on hand, small change. *"Xord nadaraem"* (I don't have change), they tell you from city to city and counter to counter, and in lieu of Farsi pennies, nickels, or dimes, they throw loose Band-Aids, matches or Chiclets into your shopping bag. The value is usually correct, so none of us has ever been able to understand why they consider it easier to count up, and deal in, Band-Aids, matches, and Chiclets than in the equivalent pennies, nickels and dimes.

On arriving back in town, I took an unjaundiced look at my accumulation of change—enough Band-Aids to stock a jungle infirmary for a year—and decided to unload the works. The incensed Super Pol clerks eventually came to the conclusion there was nothing they could do. They had been dumping the things on me as currency of the realm, and they had no choice but to take them back.

"What I don't understand," I said irritably to Skip, "is why more people don't pull the switch on them." Poor Skip quickly and quietly loaded the groceries, looking as if he'd welcome a drink of hemlock.

Jackie has found a fine-fettled friend with whom he is sharing quarters. He brought his new friend for dinner, and the friend was so shy he scarcely spoke a word.

Although everyone came prepared with sleeping bags in case we were curfewed at eight, we were rewarded for something or other with a fashionably late eleven o'clock shutoff. Curfew still changes at the whim or wish of the Majlis, martial guards, GOI, Iranian Army, Air Force, Navy, and only Allah knows who-all.

Clint Redosovitch came; his wife has gone back to the States. And Chuck Dutton was here. They're both pilots and regaled us with stories of the pilot and his experiences in modern Persia. "It's the damned *fahlawis* who do us in," muttered Chuck. *Fahlawi* is a Farsi word meaning a sharp-witted, clever person who is adept at masking his feelings, fooling most of the people a lot of the time, doing a minimal

118

amount of work and, at little expense to himself, maintaining great face. The fahlawi student pilot cheats, bribes his teachers, flatters and connives his way through his courses. He is usually admired and often envied for his cleverness in avoiding work while at the same time giving the appearance of being highly skilled. Fahlawis are the biggest menace in Islam. Here in Iran we live and work with them daily. My Farsi instructor and friend, Manucher, first told me about the fahlawi personality. "They develop feelings of inferiority," he said, "which they disguise with strutting self-importance and undisguised contempt for those of us who work hard to get ahead."

The effect of fahlawis when they fake their way through pilots' school or into high positions in government or the armed forces is disastrous. Witness, friends, Mohammed Shahnaz, who, in my absence, finally phonied his way to the generalship he so ardently desired. General Shahnaz, he of the ill temper, quick intelligence, short attention span, and very brown nose!

It was Chuck Dutton, air ace and test pilot, who, back in '74, was awarded the supreme accolade of teaching Shahnaz to fly. "See these gray hairs?" inquired Chuckles gloomily. "Shahnaz put them there, one by one."

"Oh come off it, you've been gray since you were seventeen," said Skip. He likes Chuck and Clint. They're good pilots, good pals, and they take care of their ships.

Like other Moslems, Iranians have an overweening sense of kismet, or *bakhtiar*. One's fate is one's fate. *"Inshallah,"* they say, meaning not only "God willing," but "it's in God's hands"—and they believe it. Dayle Courts, another pilot, told Skip one day, "I don't mind their leaving things in God's hands, but I wish to hell they wouldn't overwork the Poor Guy the way they do."

They also overwork their long-suffering instructors. Witness Chuck teaching the general to fly. Although Shahnaz had not yet achieved his generalship, he was practicing for it daily. What's more, he did not like helicopters, detested flying, and only forged ahead in true fahlawi fashion because he knew both were necessary adjuncts to his advancement. Reluctantly he placed himself in the hands of Allah and Agha Dutton.

"Every day for six months, ten new gray hairs," sighed Chuck in unfond memory.

Harry Reasoner writes, "Helicopter pilots are different. ... The thing is, helicopters are different from planes. An airplane by its nature wants to fly, and if not interfered with too strongly by unusual events or by a deliberately incompetent pilot, it will fly. A helicopter does not want to fly. It is maintained in the air by a variety of forces and controls working in opposition to each other, and if there is any disturbance in this delicate balance the helicopter stops flying, immediately and disastrously.

"There is no such thing as a gliding helicopter.

"This is why being a helicopter pilot is so different from being an airplane pilot and why, in general, airplane pilots are open, clear-eyed, buoyant extroverts, and helicopter pilots are brooders, introspective anticipators of trouble. They know if something bad has not happened, it is about to."

Chuckles Dutton is the living embodiment of the Reasoner helicopter pilot—gloomy, doom-ridden, and brilliant.

Managing a hovering, backing, lowering helicopter is like playing a Bach fugue on a *very* touchy clavichord. Since few Iranians are musical, and all are addicted to placing everything on automatic pilot (and into the reluctant arms of Allah), it is difficult to impress upon them the very vital details which must be handled personally by the pilot, never mind Old Allah.

As I understand it, there is a moment during run-up when everything has to be in perfect synchronization, when instrument checks and systems checks are crucial. Chuck had stressed the importance of this many times to Shahnaz. Mohammed Shahnaz is nobody's fool. But he is also, to the soles of his army boots, a Persian fahlawi. One afternoon as he and Chuck sat tensed at the 205 controls, at that exact moment when inattention could have caused a "hot start"— exceeding the temperature limitations and causing, if not an engine fire, at least the fusion of some vital engine parts— Shahnaz, without so much as a by-your-leave, leapt from his seat, tore across the airfield, and, in the words of his ashen-faced instructor, "beat the shit out of an enlisted man he spied lolling on the tarmac without a hat and tie." Then he sauntered jauntily back to the heelo, where Chuck, sweating peach seeds from every pore, had managed to abort the start.

"It gives me chronic colitis," Chuck sighed, "thinking of

120

how many kinds of aircraft that non-aero-minded nitwit is licensed to fly."

Clint is less colorful than Chuck, but he is another of Skip's and Roddey's favorites. He's the rare pilot who goes into the hangars to learn what makes his aircraft click. At night or in his spare time he does general maintenance and questions the mechanics endlessly. He's reached a point where he could at least make emergency repairs, which is more than ninety percent of the pilots would even attempt. He's also one of the most highly rated fliers on base, with some of the best credentials. "Redoso-bitch," we call him, as he belongs to the mighty ranks of chronic complainers.

Over dessert Clint told us about Ted Kopeck's experiences as a Cobra instructor. Ted is a big, tough, ex-state cop with whom casual Iranian attitudes don't "set well." He has a simple system for teaching them to fly Cobras. "Hell," he says, "I never let 'em touch the controls. They get to shoot the guns once in a while, that keeps 'em happy, and then after a few weeks I just pass 'em."

Clint says Ted is not wholly to blame for this cavalier attitude. He had a harrowing experience with one of his early Cobra students, and it marked him.

Cobra pilots wear a motorcyclelike helmet with a swing-down eyepiece that also acts as a gun sight. Wherever the pilot looks with the eyepiece is where the TOW missile will go. Upon firing, the missile remains attached for about 2000 yards and up to ten seconds—by a very thin, very tough umbilical cord of copper wire. This allows last-minute corrections in sighting on the target.

The Cobra student fired his TOW missile and, talking to Ted, kept swinging his head winsomely around to gaze at his leader. "No, *no*, you dumb s.o.b.!" screamed Ted as the missile, following the direction of turning head, helmet, and eyepiece, described 180 degree arcs in the air, scattered surrounding heelos in all directions, and wreaked awesome havoc on flight patterns and the other instructors' life spans.

"The missile!" bellowed Ted. "Keep your eye on the target, for God's sake, don't look at me!"

"What was that you say, agha?" inquired the student, craning his neck further in Ted's direction.

What astounds me is the outstanding safety record of BHI in Iran.

121

Friday, 3 November 1978

My friends, it is the Ayatollah Khomeini who has emerged from the mosques as the bona fide leader and definitive soul brother of this revolution.

And let's have no more silly euphemisms such as "unrest" or "demonstration" or "disquiet." This is r-e-v-o-l-u-t-i-o-n, and it is here to stay.

Mother has another brother as bright and balmy as Uncle Whit. Roger is also a doctor, a Ph.D. Though he's a darling, with all the social reactions of Winnie the Pooh, Dr. Whitcomb writes his treatises like every other college professor: If there's a choice between a fifty-cent and a twelve-dollar word, he'll go for the big money every time.

"Robin," he told me somberly when I was home, "you are witnessing a revolution that's comprised of some of the craziest conditions in history. I want you to be fully aware of everything that's happening." Then he mailed me a heartless, hefty tome on grade A corrasable bond entitled "Why Revolution?: Toward a New Conceptual Synthesis."

After the initial shock of lifting the thing and translating the title, I found it full of fascinating insights into the Iranian upheaval.

Roger's covering letter said: "Whether you know it or not, you're right in the middle of the biggest thing since Rasputin and the Russians."

"If it gets too hot, get out of the fire," he added. "But for Lord's sake, take notes on who's shooting at whom. You'll have to keep an eye on dozens of emerging factions: intellectuals, the Tudeh, underground/underworld, merchant class, rabid religionists, to mention a few. The coyotes will be waiting for an easy kill of a disaffected and demoralized nation. Syria or Libya may pounce. Or Iraq. It'll be confusing as hell. In a less fanatically partisan Shi'ite country, I'd have bet on the Tudeh to win. But even those cunning little Commies are no match for really rabid religionists."

He was so full of fire and fervor I was tempted to reply, "You're the expert, *you* take it from here."

With Roger's advisories and Mother's "Do not leave the

clearing" echoing in my ears, I feel for the first time that I am in an all-out, full-fledged, honest-to-God war.

"And I can prove it," says Skip. "Those old sweet sounds— bazooka fire and tracer bullets—tune up louder every day."

Or as Roddey hums, "Trouble spelled with a capital T, and that rhymes with E, and that stands for Es-fa-han!"

Saturday, 4 November 1978

Yesterday and the day before marked "The Great Protest," the fifteenth anniversary of the exile of Khomeini after his leadership of the 1963 revolt against the Shah. Five million people marched in Iran. I would have guessed, by the look and feel of it, they were trampling Esfahan underfoot. Generally, at least to date, the tone has been moderate. Slogans have run along the lines of "Long Live the Unity of Working People, Students, and the Revolutionary Movement of Iran," "We Belong to Hezbollah" (the Party of God), etcetera; although there were a few yesterday that read "Protect the Country from Usurpers," and "Britain, the Russians, China, and the U.S. Are the Enemies of the People." *China?* (Some fahlawi goofed on his geo-politics.) There were also placards praising France for giving sanctuary to Khomeini.

We did hear that two theatres were fired in Kerman and the Fluor Company offices burned in Ahwaz.

BHI and the Iranian Army are understandably nervous about our schoolchildren, and they have initiated a warning system and placed armed guards on every BHI bus. The current state of affairs is:

1. BBC announces that massive student demonstrations in Teheran lost all sense of proportion and resulted in sixty-five deaths.

2. Either the gas stations are on strike or there's a benzine (gasoline) shortage. Lines are beginning to stretch for blocks.

3. The English newspaper, *Kayhan International*, announced it is going to strike indefinitely because of government censorship. There goes our news. Up surfaces Liberty's scuttlebutt.

4. The supply of gas and naft, our only sources of heat and hot water, is seriously curtailed.

123

5. The post office is at least nominally on strike, though mail drifts wantonly in and out.

My own morale is in fine fettle, but I've had to do some fast talking to get Skip and Roddey and John Gannon to stay on. "I need bodyguards," I pleaded, appealing shamelessly to their macho instincts. The truth is, if it came to a fight, Roddey would wave his Allen wrench like a baton, Skip would try to talk the attackers into submission, John would hide his wallet, and I'd be the one who'd have to protect everybody's rear—my crotch-grabbing defenses having given me worlds of experience.

I read aloud to tonight's dinner assemblage from Roger's thesis: "Revolution is often a product of prosperity. . . . Revolution as the product of improving economic conditions and rising classes is quite as common as the product of want and misery." (Which explains why, when the average wage under Fred has risen in a decade from $150 per capita to $2500, people are still rising up in wrath and demanding a better world.) Well, "man cannot live by bread alone." The Iranians, it appears, want the stuff of dreams and democracy too.

Sunday, 5 November 1978

There's been an unpleasant "to-do" at the local youth hostel. This is a singles camping facility for travelers and some few locals run by Koreans in that overzealous section of ancient mosques and minarets and mullahs where Pat and Mel Johnson live.

Five BHI men have been bunking there in very rustic rooms—for the cheap accommodations, the ready restaurant, and in the eternal hope of meeting single girls. One of them is Mike Hamrah, who works in Medevac and whom I dated briefly.

The youth hostelers had warning notices tossed over their walls four days ago. Then, on Friday at three o'clock on a busy Sabbath afternoon, an estimated three hundred howling Mongols stormed over the wall. All of the tenants, mostly young and athletic, beat a hasty retreat through the rear—except for one stout American, an out-of-shape boob too blubbery to make it. The Korean cooks, who understood neither Farsi nor English, were trapped to a man in the kitchen. One cook was killed, the others hurt, and the fat American hid in their pantry, where he armed himself with a firebox axe. When an Iranian stumbled across him, Fatso killed him dead.

"The ass-hole," as he's been universally branded by BHI men, got out of there unscathed while the mob was delightedly torching the place. But instead of carrying his ugly secret to the grave, he bragged about it all over the base the next day. By afternoon he was en route to Paris, and every BHI executive in town looked slightly bilious. What kind of maniac boasts about killing another human being?

One awkward part of *l'Affaire Hostel* was that the martial guards found a large arsenal of incendiary devices; meaning someone in the hostel crowd, like many foreigners in the city, has been busily manufacturing Molotovs and other makeshift armaments (such as butane capsules converted to flamethrowers) in case things *do* reach a point of fighting in the dugouts. The uncovered cocktails have caused a big brouhaha, as the pervading government paranoia is that such stuff will be sold to "troublesome" civilians. Their paranoia is my paranoia; I grow wild-eyed at the thought.

Jackie tells me that illegal guns are finding their way into the bazaar, PLO-smuggled and very expensive. I not only shudder over guns in the hands of Iranian Army boys, but also the thought of kutche gangs with guns makes my hair stand straight up like Little Orphan Annie's.

The hostel dwellers, including the innocent Mike Hamrah, are now being questioned in Teheran. Aiding and abetting a revolution is a murderous charge, and BHI has sent a platoon of honchos and some top bilingual lawyers up there to bail them out.

Meanwhile, everyone is grim-faced and mum about the slob who's off wallowing in the fleshpots of Paris. I think the brass would have liked to hand him over to gloating, gleeful Savakers, but supposedly we're all civilized here.

Monday, 6 November 1978

The weather is tuning up for forty days and forty nights of rain, sleet, slubber, and sludge. Though Esfahan is nearly a mile high, it is roughly parallel to Damascus and Phoenix and not exactly in subarctic or high precip zones. Just the same, everyone has been, or is now, in the process of hauling the *alladins* (*ah-lah-deens*) and *boxaris* out of storage and into place for an early, inclement winter. Either of these heating mechanisms is a lethal weapon quite capable of killing off more noncombatants than a rock concert.

The *boxari* is a metal box about four by four by two feet, heavy as a molasses barrel, which is dragged forth and installed for the usually brief winter season. The upper half contains vents and a removable lid, and inside there is space for the naft (kerosene) tank. This vicious instrument is connected to a ceiling vent, one in every room of the Iranian house. A boxari is very inefficiently designed and blows its lid at the slightest provocation. One of Skip's exploded right through an adjoining wall and hurtled into the outer adobe, where it buried itself like a cannonball; it missed John Gannon's fair Celtic head by inches. People showed up for days to marvel over the impact and John's narrow escape.

The *alladin* is simply the familiar Alladin heater used by Americans for camping—a tubular tank that cracks in half, with kerosene in the bottom half, a wick in the center, and open space in the upper half that radiates heat through vents. On top there's a small grate, and Iranians use alladins both to heat their rooms and to keep their chie kettles bubbling hot.

Persian alladins are particularly dangerous, fume-wise, and the only time and place Donna and I will use one is to heat the bathroom before taking a bath. By spring the tile and marble bath walls are thick with black soot that must be scraped off with putty knives.

Another messy and deadly household weapon is the hot water heater, which I have as little to do with as possible. When these explode (which they invariably do), they spray greasy carbon like a Gatling gun—through every room from floor to ceiling, into beds, clothing, drawers, cupboards, and crevices. I know plenty of people who have wallpapered right over the mess rather than try to clean it up.

It's the butane bottles used in stoves and water heaters that ever-ingenious Americans are converting to deadly little flamethrowers.

Every autumn the *Whirly Bird* is filled with dire warnings about the native heaters of Iran, with Do's, Don'ts, and

Beware's listed for weeks before the first killing frost. Because heaters and houses alike are incorrectly vented, noxious fumes abound. The *Whirly Bird* insists that no matter how cold it is, or how far down one turns the heat, windows must always be kept open. This is so self-defeating that we begin to understand the Iranian custom of wearing flannel pajamas at home and abroad.

I am a proponent of the old-fashioned Persian system of bedding down—the *kursi*. The kursi is a giant communal bed, very rough, constructed like a low stage platform-in-the-round. Underneath are pails of hot charcoal. Tossed on the platform are piles of old quilts or sixth-best carpets, and everyone lies down like the spokes in a wheel, feet toward the center, over the charcoal pails, covered with piles of blankets and tribal quiltings. It's very chummy and practical, and since I love to chat in bed I'm crazy about the idea.

Lacking a kursi, our most practical solution is the electric blanket. I have kicked myself around the kutche for not bringing dozens from home; they're unavailable here. How was I to guess this autumn would not prove like last year's, as balmy as a day in May? Electric blankets require a transformer, which can be counted on to overheat and short-circuit, but what are a few shorts compared to decapitation or, lacking a bird, creeping death from carbon monoxide?

It's only November, and already my *takht-e-xab* (throne of sleep) is a sodden pile of dampish, clammy linens. Houses constructed with marble floors and adobe walls, once chilled, seem never to warm again. I use Grammy Sterling's summer-house trick and fill the bed with gin bottles full of piping hot water before I climb in; this helps but not much.

Another household nuisance is our sewer. Since the manse is at the bottom of a slight incline, the steady rains have caused sewage to back into our courtyard. We use old towels and discarded clothes in a frenetic effort to keep the drains plugged up. Sometimes this works and sometimes it doesn't. A bout of typhus would go down nicely with the next round of explosives.

Meanwhile, back at Havan-e-Ruz, General Mohammed Shahnaz is fighting a winning battle with American personnel over the hangar heat, which has been hovering around 40 degrees. "When it reaches a low of 32 degrees Fahrenheit, we will cease work," says Shahnaz from the sanctuary of his 78-degree office. We are instructed to keep temperature charts for

127

his inspection, the kind of thing that drives sane men mad. Our mechanics are half-frozen and wholly desperate; they must work with cold, lifeless fingers on all kinds of delicate mechanisms. With the wind chill factor on the line adding to their misery, and their Iranian counterparts driving our heated trucks through endless days and nights to stay warm, somehow the men keep carrying on. In more ways than one. The bitching and griping and threats of insurrection have reached epic proportions. Liberty can be heard bellowing "that *meathead*!" in the chill, damp air, meaning either Shahnaz, the Shah, or both.

The cold and the freezing rains have driven most revolutionaries inside, beside their braziers. Still, the minute there's a break in the cloud cover they manage to run amok. One current gambit is to stop up the boxari chimneys. *Tootis* (parrots) are dropping dead all over town. In the case of Americans, there are so many of us jammed into every house that someone invariably wakes up, finds the place full of smoke or naft fumes, and drives everyone up on the rooftops in freezing downpours to unstop the chimneys and air things out.

Tuesday, 7 November 1978

Pat Powell, red hair, four feet eleven, secretary for defense and attack, is the spearhead for women's rights in this office and on this base. It is Pat who insists, "Just because we're low-salaried slavies around here doesn't mean we're going to row these galleys in arctic conditions!" She inspires me daily to do better.

Pat, by dint of sheer moxie, has obtained permission for us women to have, to wear, and to cherish through the winter weather—bunnysuits. Bunnysuits are a Sears Roebuck special roughly related to the Snowmobile suits used in the States, though not as warm, and they are worn by our mechanics on the line and in the hangars. They are zippered from ankle to shoulder, easy to climb into, and are padded with some abstruse material that's probably part kapok and part goat hair. (When damp, they give off a quaint odor.)

In my heavy-duty Garmisch hiking boots, striped and tasseled Aspen Lid, and bunnysuit, I stand ready to holler

"Mush!" and drive my dog sled through howling blizzards. I'm a scream, but everyone's too chilled to chuckle.

I never thought I'd see an entire office force resembling the cast of *Nanook of the North*, but we come close. Bundled to the eyes, we grin owlishly at Shahnaz and his disapproving senior officers as we pass them in the hallways. Since they spend most of their time in steam-heated offices and only sally into the cold, outdoor world in extra flannel pajamas and massive greatcoats, they naturally feel we women should remain chic and chilblained for their aesthetic satisfaction. It was firebrand Pat Powell who won the skirmish again.

Wednesday, 8 November 1978

Shah Mohammed Reza Pahlavi has appointed yet another government—this one entirely military.

For the first time we feel really isolated. We can no longer get *Time*, *Newsweek*, the *Kayhan*, the *Herald Tribune*, or, in this rotten weather, short wave reception. We are entirely dependent on Liberty's trotlines, and on telephone calls from the States. Since most of the mechanics take these on the phone in my office, I at least get their news before it's been recirculated and totally garbled in Liberty transmission.

We've heard that the Shah's family, except for his wife, younger children, and one reclusive, very religious Shi'ite uncle, has left the country. Also that there are hundreds of new political prisoners in the jails, though simultaneously it's promised that Savak is relieved of all prison duties and there will be no more tortures, thus tacitly admitting that indeed there *were* tortures.

There is talk about investigations of corruption that appear to be little more than meaningless sops to Persian public opinion. An unwilling seventeen-man tribunal is on the job now—comprised of disgruntled lawyers who are supposed to be on strike—and they sound about one half as efficient and one-tenth as enthusiastic as the Warren Commission.

Note: When I speak of particular groups going out on strike, they are always government workers. Since eighty percent of all businesses and professions in Iran are nationalized, almost all city people work for the government in one role or another. Nationalized are: most lawyers, insurance

129

men, many hotels, all Iranian banks, utilities, schools, the oil
fields and oil and gas-related businesses, postal and Customs
systems, teachers, airfield and transportation workers, etcetera, etcetera.

We are beginning to live like foraging alley cats. Between
strikes and the inclement weather, there is erratic crippling of
everything from transportation, to police work, to bank
hours, to food availability.

Friday, 10 November 1978

I have installed Kitty Kat and her brood in the basement
over Jackie's roars of protest. It is much too vile for that dog
to be living outside, and the last of her puppies would surely
perish. She only has two left out of ten. I know what
happened to those dogs—the soldiers and martial guards
poison as many as they find, and the crows get the rest.

Jim Holland told me that with oil production shut off and
the Shah unable to borrow the vast amounts of money he
requires to keep his house of cards from falling down, Fred is
now among the profligate rich, with everything on paper and
nothing in the bank. It'll be a fine frolic when and if our
paychecks from GOI stop coming in. On that lugubrious day
the BHI mechanics will undoubtedly storm the gates, take
back their tools, disarm bus drivers, corporals, gardeners, and
second lieutenants, and punch out three-fourths of the Iranians at the airfield. The only sounds will be Pat and I
hissing "Rah, rah, siss boom bah!" and Jim Liberty bellowing
profanities in the voice of an enraged bull.

Sunday, 12 November 1978

Ron Horan appeared for work this afternoon in a shaved
head. Ron is a senior mechanic I first met when, bored with
entering his car in the same uninspired fashion, he galloped
full speed across the airfield and dove headlong through his
Volkswagen sun roof. I strolled over to inquire if he had
perchance mistaken the directions to Shahnaz's swimming
pool. We became friends.

In direct contradiction of handbook instructions, Ron has had more Irani confrontations than anyone on the base. But he has a guileless expression and is an inspired Cobra mechanic, so he wiggles his way out of one scrape and hones right up for the next.

I am firmly on Ron's side in his latest escapade. He'd engaged a telephone taxi, the kind one hires at a prearranged rate, for an hour, and when the Iranian driver announced, after twenty-five minutes, that it was time for his dinner and demanded full payment, a heated argument ensued. Ron's girl, Lynn, has gone to school here for some time, speaks fluent Farsi, and interrupted to tell the driver she understood his predicament but unfortunately he was in the wrong. The driver shouted at Lynn to "shut up," Ron pointed his finger at the driver to suggest he retract that, the driver smacked his hand away, and Ron cold-cocked him.

The final tab, not including the time it will take Ron's hair to grow back to its former crowning glory, was 50,000 rials—the $700 it is claimed the driver will lose by not working for a month due to his extensive injuries (a black eye).

These prisons worry me. Ron says he was harried and of course demoralized though not physically harmed. But I just read *Midnight Express,* and Eastern prisons and the idiosyncrasies of their guards give me the whim-whams.

Ten thousand teachers and all newspaper reporters are still on strike and demanding political reforms. Meanwhile, twice that many hooligans roam the streets doing whatever damage their evil young minds can concoct.

On the subject of minors and schooling, Jim Norris, Skip's old roommate who teaches the fundamentals class to would-be Iranian mechanics, begins his lectures: "Here is a screwdriver. This is the handle. Grip it firmly in your hand, thus. Apply the opposite end to tighten the screw, so. . . . This is a hammer. Grasp it thusly. . . ." With American kids, the use of such tools begins so early that we think of it as natural instinct, like chewing food or gum.

Despite being solicited shamelessly by his students and invited for trysts in the men's room, Jim likes teaching Iranians. He gets their attention, too, one way or another. A favorite tactic is to remove one tinted contact lens, which the boys think is the cornea of his eye, and cause them to cower and whimper in the back of the room until he has them under his spell.

131

Skip's favorite teacher is Ed Thorpe, late of Hazard, Kentucky. Ed is a seasoned backwoods wizard who spent twenty-one years in the U.S. Air Force, can assemble any aircraft blindfolded, and taught Skip most of what he knows. Once as Skip, supposed to be watching attentively during a tedious repair, was expounding lengthily on a favorite theory about hydraulics, Ed looked up and drawled, "Who's fuckin' this cow, anyway? You just hold the goddamn tail, son, and let me get on with the job."

Tuesday, 14 November 1978

I've seen it, I'll vouch for it: The American technologist in the Mideast has a terrible cross to bear.

Ron Horan is the maintenance representative on the BHI Employee Council, a sort of grievance committee which purportedly hears and tries to solve everyone's departmental, living, and emotional problems. The council plays Ann Landers to BHI's collective neuroses.

Many of the council meetings deteriorate into rounds of cliff-hanger stories about working with camel drivers and fahlawis. In the interests of fairness I wish to report that one of the best mechanics Skip has ever taught and/or worked with is a young Iranian from Shiraz. Hossein has a natural flair for mechanics, is bright, willing, and spends a lot of time trying to learn everything he can.

My theory is that it all comes back to education. As soon as the educational system in this country is updated, and students are encouraged to think for themselves, they'll catch up to the world like brush fire.

Given our Western technological and instructional advantages, I don't feel we're nearly so far ahead of our Moslem brethren as we should be. We Americans have a few fahlawis of our own, and we are beset by no-loads, those plenteous types who avoid carrying their fair share.

Having passed out merit badges and black marks, I will now proceed to the Farsi String Trick. There is an ancient Persian belief, going back to the invention of the rope, that anything, *anything at all,* can be repaired with a length of twine, rope, thread or package string. This goes for broken water pipes, severed electrical and phone lines, washing machines, TV sets, and BHI aircraft. Jahan. Guity Ruhi's husband, first told me about the Iranian penchant for string as a fix-it device. "You watch him, Ro-been," he warned me, "everybody think he fix with piece of string." Jahan's face was doleful as he continued to shake his head over the Farsi string repair of our hot water heater.

At the most recent Employee Council meeting, Ron insisted something be done about the guilty Persian who fixed a leak in the hydraulic line of a 214 last week—with string. Naturally the string broke right off at the start of the run-up, spewing hydraulic fluid like a lawn sprinkler. Though this took place during one of the rare half-decent days in the last few weeks, there were still gusty, heavy winds. The wind caught a turning rotor and the ship went into a ground spin. The two pilots were our overtried friends, Chuckles Dutton and Ted Kopeck.

The only way to bring a ship out of a spin is with the hydraulic foot pedals, in this case "strung" out of action by the Farsi String Trick. The drivers had to muscle that ship to a stop by brute force, very narrowly avoiding several million dollars' worth of parked aircraft. It all boils down to not understanding the principle of a thing. And most Iranians just don't—not if it's mechanized. Skip goes berserk at the sight of refrigerator trucks, in the summer, roaring around the city, doors wide open, sides of beef gathering dust and bacteria like flypaper. Or at seeing a truck up on jacks so the drivers can sleep in its shade when there's an enormous, shade-giving plane tree fifty feet away. His favorite goose-bumper is the story of the Iranian pilot trainee who bought a new van in Texas and, deciding automatic cruise control must work on the same principle as automatic pilot, set it at sixty-five m.p.h. and crawled in the back for a nap. He survived unscathed; the van was totaled.

MQA, Maintenance Quality Assurance, is the department that makes final inspection checks on all aircraft work.

Once, deciding to let the Iranian ace team do a PE (periodic inspection) all by their simple selves, QA even went so far as to entrust them with the final check-out. Only at the last minute did the Americans make a precautionary double check. They found three hundred red Xs. One, *one* red X comprises a grounding condition, and the aircraft isn't considered fit to fly until the red X is remedied. There was billowing blue air and black smoke on every side. The

133

Employee Council asked Shahnaz to yank the Iranian quality inspector's stamp: His license to kill, they called it. Mohammed Shahnaz, political to the core, explained that the man would lose too much face, and that this was unfortunately not possible.

The inspector continues to work, but he works with an American expert dogging his tracks. The Americans actually do the inspecting, the Iranian inspector drinks chie with ghand, and when they are finished he signs off the work with a flourish. He has reached the pinnacle of fahlawi-ism, has achieved position without lifting a hand (except to sign his name). We feel certain the man is held in high esteem by his many ardent admirers.

Ron used my office phone today, and he was hopping mad. There have been so many cases of poor work by Iranians lately that—though the mechanics don't come right out and say it—they're worried sick about sabotage. Especially since a bomb blew out all the windows in a Chinook over at one of the FASC units last week.

We have no way of knowing how much Savak infiltration there is, how they'd screen possible saboteurs, or even if saboteurs can get around the Skinny Ties. We figure it's probably a Persian standoff.

Saturday, 18 November 1978

This week at Havan-e-Ruz Jim Liberty was officially elected Rumor King. Some joker even passed printed ballots around. Liberty, that mugwump, was pleased as punch. He doesn't care about the *quality* of attention he gets, just any kind of notoriety will do.

"He's born to the purple," grinned Roddey. "Bred for the job," added Skip. Me, I'm crazy about the guy.

Skip, Roddey and I are moving into the Liberty house shortly. We've already packed most of our boxes. Donna has a lineup of standees waiting to take my place at the manse, as everyone is doubling up, instinctively reaching for safety in numbers.

Judy and Jim and the children are set for their Bangkok–Chiengmai–Pattaya vacation, with scheduled departure November 26, my birthday. Although he hasn't come right out and said it (for a rarity), I know Liberty plans to ship Judy and the children home to Detroit from there. He'll come back; he knows this place couldn't operate without him, but in the interim they'll have had a wonderful family vacation together, and he'll be easier in his mind knowing his family's safe.

Our lives are kaleidoscopes of changing curfew times, changing office hours, changing political climate, changing weather. This, my friends, is overseas life under stressful conditions. It's not the firing squad that preys on one's mind, it's the hundreds of petty irritants. I'm gulping watermelon seeds like a Brazilian parrot.

The uncertainties do not reach our wallets. GOI continues to foot the bill for this mass confusion, and we are paid for a day's work whether performed or not.

Over all, the clouds lower, and lower, and *lower*, and we wallow in seas of mud: mud in the beds, chairs, food, cupboards, and my hair. I've managed to maintain a small, dry island in the basement for Kitty Kat and her two boys, but it's been a battle of wit and will.

Tuesday, 21 November 1978

Most strikers—Iran Air, communications, Customs, steel and oil workers—have gone back to work under the stimulus of a 22½ percent pay raise. We notice an improvement in our lives already, although the *Kayhan* stubbornly refuses to publish and our news is still spotty. I got word of the government workers' return to work from Guity Ruhi, who is pleased as punch. She's as sick of the instability as we nonpartisan foreigners. To counteract the adverse effects of moderates like Guity, Khomeini raised his voice from Neaufle-le-Château to call for a *Jihad* (Holy War). His words, played on cassettes, are trumpeted from hidden high points all over the city: "People of Iran, sacrifice your blood to protect Islam and overthrow the tyrant and his parasites. The tree of oppression will be cut down! You will be remembered for your sacrifices. Blood will triumph over the sword!" Easy for him to order everyone to shed private blood when he's safe in France right down the block from Brigitte Bardot.

Despite Khomeini's call to arms, things have seemed almost peaceful. Even the annual Armed Forces Day parade on Sunday was uneventful, although Fred was inexplicably absent from the reviewing stand—an ominous portent for the monarchy. Our nervous, nattering little BHI claque wonders if the man is ill. Certainly he is autocratic, often misguided, frequently out of step, but is he also *sick?*

On the minus side, the butane shortage is worsening, perhaps because of the abnormally inclement month; curfew has been rescheduled for nine o'clock instead of eleven, our *barq* (electricity) has been mysteriously disappearing several hours nightly, and the TV broadcasts which had barely begun to fill some of the gap left by the *Kayhan's* withdrawal have inexplicably ceased.

Addendum: As part of our mechanics' equipment, particularly for use on the line at night, BHI carries a large supply of battery-operated miners' head lamps. I've borrowed one so I can keep on working when the barq goes off. Topping my bunnysuit, this apparatus makes me look like a Venus clone, or possibly a second lead on *Star Trek.*

Three months have passed since the first September blackouts, and it has now been discovered that a total of 126 BHI wives are "on the nest," including Judy Liberty. I feel that BHI owes these women just compensation. It wasn't *their* fault the lights went out and the curfew on, all over Iran.

Wednesday, 22 November 1978

Late this afternoon I was forcibly reminded that Kitty Kat, who hadn't come home last night, was still away from the manse. The puppies set up a fearful wailing—fangs and all, they're still nursing. I fed them yoghurt and mashed rice and organized a massive search.

About five o'clock every available friend and neighbor formed into parties and fanned out across the neighborhood. When it grew too dark to see our hands in front of our faces, we drifted dejectedly back to the house.

My friends love that dog, she's so intelligent and gentle and giving, and the mechanics are crazy about her because she detests Iranian men. "A real Detroit dog," Liberty calls her. "All class."

By the time curfew fell like a last act curtain, we'd said

good night to the Libertys and the pilots and mechanics who'd helped search, and I was as wretched as a wallflower at her first dance.

It's now eleven o'clock at night, and I jump at the sound of every rifle crack; I have the puppies in bed with me, and Kitty Kat still has not scratched at the gate.

I lie here listening to her boys whimper and I have no hope. I know she is gone, poisoned or shot, and I feel contempt for those massed, armed, khaki-clad cretins roaming the streets killing dogs and frightening people at will. I have not felt this totally mournful in years.

Had she been Champion Yukon Ike of Snow Plume, her pedigree and blood the clearest blue, possessed of papers pure and white, I could not have loved her more.

Thanksgiving Day, 1978

We spent hours in a futile search for Kitty Kat and I was thankful, on such a grim day, not to have a holiday dinner on my hands. Pat and Mel Johnson played host and hostess, and the guest list was the usual mélange of pilots, mechanics, Tech Supply people, and teachers. Mel is a quiet, well-educated, charming giant of a man whom I don't know well but like very much. He is a supervisor (A-14), and Pat is crazy about him.

I worry about Rose Fazio at these rowdy affairs. Rose is in her fifties, unmarried, very pure, and a devout Catholic who attends Mass most of her spare time. She is as solid as the rock of ages, letting ribald language and unkind words go unnoticed, or at least unremarked. If she's aware that much of that smoke is from Thai sticks and not straight cigarettes, well, the quality of her mercy is not strained.

It gives me a warm, safe feeling knowing that Rose prays for me along with her worthier causes.

Tonight Liberty and Skip conducted our regularly scheduled panel discussion of OPEC politics, BHI's role at home and abroad, and the pathetic lot of the reviled American in Esfahan. Every man present vies for the position of "most abused." "Never forget," intoned Liberty with a big belch of satisfaction, "that we mechanics are the scum bags of BHI."

"Along with the pilots," insisted Redosovitch.

137

"Bend over, your company's behind you," drawled Ed Thorpe disdainfully.

Poor BHI, taking it about the head and shoulders as always. Dear Rose, letting the abuse wash over her as unnoticed as the tide. Pathetic me, I couldn't get into the spirit of being thankful for a single thing.

Friday, 24 November 1978

This morning Skip lived the nightmare we all dream and dread. He hit an Iranian child with his car.

Skip is the calmest, most careful driver imaginable in a national sea of car sharks. Once we were caught in a traffic circle for hours and nearly starved to death. Skip simply couldn't bring himself to go on the attack and break through all that screeching, hurtling, circling traffic.

The accident happened this morning during early Sabbath, mosque-bound traffic, one of the busiest times of the day. Skip was proceeding at his usual chaste pace down Bozorg Mehr when the little girl, about four years old, jumped from between two parked cars into his path.

He hit her head-on, and if he'd been going faster would certainly have killed her. When he leapt out of the car she was crying and pointing to her leg.

He managed to flag down a passing taxi, locked and left his car where it was (as demanded by Iranian law), and he and a man who appeared to be the girl's father took her to the hospital. Once there, he was shoved brusquely into a corridor with a guard on each side and wasn't allowed to make a peep or even a phone call for more than an hour. Since Skip's Farsi is nearly nonexistent, the situation was terrifying for him.

Finally a doctor allowed him to use the pay phone outside the hospital, accompanied closely by the honor guard from the corridor. He called Roddey and John and asked them to get in touch with BHI and have a company interpreter hotfoot it to the hospital on the double.

Gannon, Sherman and Liberty, not bothering to notify me, double-timed it to Sepahan, and dear Liberty even thought to scrape up all his ready cash, about five hundred dollars, and handed it through the fence to Skip. They weren't permitted any nearer.

As the BHI handbook further states, all Iranian accidents are, *must* be, negotiated to the satisfaction of the victim. There is no legal question as to why or how an accident occurs, who is at fault, or any of that rot. The victim is a victim and must therefore be compensated. But this was not Skip's concern. His concern was the child's condition. Being Skip, he never gave a thought to his own neck but was plenty worried about the little girl's.

They waited two interminable hours for the on-the-double interpreter, a ferret-faced man, who finally introduced himself and announced pompously that he had been talking to the officials and to the parents for over an hour and had, he said, been covertly watching the young American so that he might closely observe Skip and his attitudes and make a judgment as to whether or not he was the type to create scenes. Judge, jury, and hangman!

Before Liberty could be stifled, he lunged at the man and roared, "You stinking ass-hole!"

"How's the little girl?" implored Skip.

"Her leg is broken," said the interpreter, first sidling out of Liberty's reach, then picking his teeth and examining the findings with care.

Ferret Face was typical of the petty Moslem official: officious, self-important, not too bright, and very maddening. After making ceremonial rounds of doctors, guards, hospital officials, patient, secretaries, nurses, parents, and relatives, he casually obtained Skip's release and escorted him back to ER.

Although it is these interpreters' jobs to act as defendants and protectors of BHI employees, this man looked Skip up and down as if he were a prisoner in the dock, advised him sternly that he would be expected to pay the hospital bill and any damages, and that if he knew what was good for him, he had better visit the child daily, bearing gifts, and ingratiate himself with her parents.

News spreads fast in a company town, and BHI began gathering here en masse about four o'clock this afternoon. Roddey had already arrived, told me the whole story, and assured me that the principal character would be along shortly.

Skip walked in looking like a wet, tattletale-gray sheet right

139

from the wringer. He was trailed by a cursing Liberty and a subdued Gannon.

By six o'clock the house was full of pilots, wives, girl friends, mechanics, consulate people, anyone and everyone who had been in an accident, heard about one firsthand, or had any sort of solace, warnings, or trivia to proffer. The place was a madhouse. Donna locked herself in her room and turned up *The Ring of the Nibelungen,* which only added to the uproar.

Everyone told story after story, washing them down with our Scotch, wine, and beer: about the pilot who killed an Iranian in a demonstration; the woman on base who was run over by a two-and-a-half-ton army truck, lived through it, and had to pay damages for getting in the path of the truck; and so on and so on. No one said anything very reassuring.

Several vital points emerged from the welter of information and misinformation: Skip had only government insurance and this, we learned, is tricky if not treacherous; those in the know use Henry Shamoon, a private insurance agency, which gets right down to headquarters, handles everything and takes excellent care of clients; a smart Persian operator with a sense of justice and plenty of necessary influence. I am switching my car insurance to Henry Shamoon the first thing in the morning.

Next, Skip has exactly twenty days to make a settlement with the family of the victim; if a satisfactory agreement is not reached in this time he will be slapped into jail and barbered; he has perfectly beautiful hair, and this information really hit him where it hurts.

Third, he was assured that he is now in the unstable hands and at the dubious mercy of the most inept, unenlightened, and mismanaged department of BHI Esfahan—Employee Relations. I will not name names or cast aspersions, but it was the unanimous judgment of the seventy-odd souls gathered here tonight that he'd be better off in the hands of the Skinny Ties than in the grip of his own ER department. My word, aren't we mutinous? I knew ER had a reputation for harboring lame brains, but I hadn't heard they were subversive. I'm going to go to Jim Holland about this, even before I search out Henry Shamoon Agency.

Skip and the puppies and I spent the night holding hands. I alternated between assuring Skip all will be well, stroking his fevered brow, and sending up further futile prayers for Kitty

Kat. He just said over and over, "My God, I'm so glad she's all right. I couldn't have stood it if I'd killed her. Thank God she's all right!"

Saturday, 25 November 1978

What with one thing and another, we only spent about three hours at Havan-e-Ruz, and I accomplished the following on the side:

...Had a long talk with Jim Holland about Skip's accident. "We in maintenance are indeed the peasantry of BHI, my dear," he said wistfully, "but I'll use what little influence I may have. Unfortunately, my relations with those ER people are not what you could term, er, cordial."

...Accompanied Skip to Sepahan Hospital to visit the Forusmandi girl, who is a sweet child. Her mother and father were there, and I liked them too. We conversed in Farsi, and they were genuinely pleased with the gifts I'd helped Skip choose: a doll for little Faruga, flowers and sweets for her parents. I felt when we parted that we were en route to a lifelong friendship.

...I then located Henry Shamoon and their charming salesman who was delighted to take care of my immediate insurance needs and who shook his head mournfully over Skip's difficulties which, I could tell from his facial expression, he fully expected to worsen by the day if not the hour.

...Finally, I organized one last posse to search for Kitty Kat and at length went home with a hollow feeling in the pit of my stomach to console the boys, who will now have to become little men and stand on their own eight feet.

Roddey and Skip and I even managed to make a hurried, albeit shaky, move to Jim and Judy's house. (John Gannon is staying behind until he uses his last month's paid-up rent.) The Libertys fly out tomorrow.

A BHI bulletin dated today announced that: the BHI Clinic was bombed, TNT wrapped in a metal can; two BHI vehicles, Jeep and Jyanne, were burned; O Cursed Yonky notes abounded on car windshields and houses; and there were a number of "breaking and entering" attempts. The bulletin ended: "Other than the above the Esfahan area was generally quiet."

141

Even surrounded by boxes and bales and suitcases, we feel a nice, settled warmth about Liberty Hall. Jim and Judy have closed off half the house to conserve heat, and it's crowded, but it's reminiscent of my own noisy, warm, cozy, comforting childhood.

I made a hurried goodbye call on the Ruhis, and bade Donna adieu amid sprinklings of tears, though I've shed so many this week I am nearly dehydrated. Jackie came over, and we promised to commute back and forth across the city—weather, demos, curfew, gunfire, and office hours permitting. This means hardly ever. I'll see them at a distance on the base, but it won't be the same. War is hell. It breaks up families and causes griefs large and small.

Jackie persuaded his friend that in these times everyone needs a watchdog. They took one of the boys, as will Akhbar's brother, who lives in the countryside.

I snuggled down with my hot gin bottles and the last puppy, who'll leave home tomorrow, and with Skip, all of us feeling slightly less dreary about the world in general and Iran in particular.

Sunday, 26 November 1978

Today I am thirty, and I think I can safely say I've aged ten years. The past weeks have been traumatic, and today was no exception.

It was one of those times when Murphy's law set in: "If anything can go wrong, it will"—and it did. First, curfew was moved up until eleven, which gave us more working time. I was asked to stay for a meeting on the second shift, which necessitated the cancellation of my birthday dinner. Then, after many affectionate farewells, the Libertys set out bag and baggage for Forudaghe Esfahan, and when they arrived, no one was home. They waited hours, hoping life would reappear on the airport planet. I was gone when they returned, but Judy said Liberty reached an all-time high pitch with his grousing and swearing. The children were stricken, although Judy had done everything possible to prepare them for such an eventuality.

Just as our phone calls were completed and my party placed indefinitely on "hold," word arrived that curfew had

142

again been moved back, and we were all sent home at four o'clock.

At five Donna arrived to find me alone in the house and said no, curfew was definitely moved up to eleven o'clock that night. Skip was off making his duty call at the hospital, with Roddey, who speaks no Farsi either, for moral support. (As prophesied, he's getting absolutely *no* help or moral support from ER.) Donna took one look at me and said, "Come on, chile, one way or t'other, we-all are gonna celebrate." She even made me put on eye makeup which, after a few hours, always smudges and makes me look like a Babylonian whore. She also implied that if I didn't retrieve my sense of humor I'd be needing a fast face-lift.

The two of us, escortless, drove straight into the heart of the city to the Kouroush Hotel for dinner. There was a floor show with an Iranian belly dancer, and after our first bottle of wine, I cheered up considerably.

Persian music, like Arabic music, is very atonal, repetitive, and tells of endless, unrequited love. The singer wails over and over about *habibi* (sweetheart), with a catch in the throat and a figurative tear in the eye. Iranians dance and sing and recite poetry from the time they are infants—always dolefully. There are no Iranian counterparts of "Jingle Bells" or "Roll Me Over in the Clover."

Iranian belly dancing is very chaste compared to other Mideast varieties. For one thing, the dancer is swathed in yards and yards of tulle, usually bridesmaid-pink or blue, and not even her belly button is exposed. The ones I've seen, usually at 1001 Nights, a local bistro and tourist trap, were all fat and operatic (Donna was mad about them). The principal part of the dance is done with the fingers, not the toes. To the accompaniment of much dipping and swaying, the hands are clasped almost prayerfully above the head, and the fingers snapped in an exceptional manner. The index finger of the left hand is clicked against the index and middle fingers of the right. This part is rhythmic and fun, but I always feel ill at ease when they fling themselves dramatically to the floor and then have difficulty getting back up. (Boy, are they out of shape!)

I like Arabic and Persian music, which I consider myself a *very* minor student of. I've collected tapes of many of the Mideastern singing stars, all guaranteed to drive my men friends bonkers.

143

The Persians have a pretty distinguished musical history, considering they invented the oboe, the kettledrum, the trumpet, the reed pipe, and the harp. The Kurds in their mountain vastnesses came up with the flute. (So much for these primitive, uncultured peoples.)

Tonight's dancer wasn't half-bad and no more than twenty pounds overweight. Donna and I sat through two floor shows, meanwhile consuming three bottles of really dandy French wine which she sprang for. We had an elysian evening. By the time we staggered out on the roof to watch Iran falling, I was completely oblivious of my problems, my friends' problems, my advanced age, and all of Uncle Roger's explicit instructions about eyeing the revolution. While we girls stargazed and bellowed "Around Her Neck She Wore a Yellow Ribbon," two banks went up in sheets of flame, a couple of policemen were gunned down on Char Bagh, and Skip and Roddey drove the streets in a frantic search for the misplaced birthday girl.

Skip's gift to me was a monstrous, ungainly stationary bicycle for exercising my postsurgical knee.

All in all it turned out one of the better birthdays I've ever had.

Monday, 27 November 1978

General Khosradad chose today to make a surprise inspection of Havan-e-Ruz. There was a great hubble-bubble as instructors sprayed students with Pif Paf and jasmine room deodorant, and foremen neared hysteria over the usual numbers of Iranians and Americans lying down on the job, which Iranians do literally, even in cold weather. They lie right down on the hangar floor and snore and belch as cozily as though they were in their toasty kursis at home. It's very arduous getting them roused and looking alert on their feet, but somehow everyone managed it just before Khosradad strode in, listing heavily to the left.

General Khosradad is Shahnaz's superior and his bailiwicks are the paratroopers and army aviation. He looks like a cross between a Welsh corgi and a fireplug and stands a full five feet four-and-one-half inches in his Adler elevated shoes. He is gray-haired and, despite a fixation about size, quite

144

distinguished looking. The list to leeward is caused by the amount of hardware on the upper left quadrant of his torso and the usual oversized Iranian officer's hat looking bigger than *he* is.

Here in maintenance we have work to do, which we continued doing while Khosradad kibitzed.

I was tickled he didn't pick today to make a speech. The applause would have cracked my head like a melon. And I don't like him. In one of his earlier speeches he was insultingly and blatantly anti-American, accusing us of having monstrous children who were evil influences on the pure and unspoiled Persian youth. (Iranian kids are the most ill-tempered changelings I've ever watched throw a tantrum.)

Maybe Khosradad has a phobia about kids. In October, he honored BHI Esfahan with another philippic, this one a complete reversal; he explained the necessity for martial law to our assemblage, and why his soldiers needed to be so strict with the populace.

"When you are dealing with a mass of five-year-old children," Khosradad said haughtily of his fellow Persians, "you must treat them as such. They must be disciplined and may not be allowed dangerous freedoms that will permit them to hurt themselves and others." Well, the patronizing bastard is learning that a nation of "five year olds" can not only conduct a revolution, they can also paralyze an army. I just hope the old rascal is the first one fired in the new regime.*

This revolution is making me schizophrenic. I can only say for certain that I'm pro-BHI but anti-ER, pro-ERA, on the side of decency, against kutche gangs, anti-Savak, and pro-republic. At the same time, my concern is that a Khomeini-led republic may be far more despotic than Fred's monarchy—and not as well intentioned, either.

Did you all know, out there, that the Taj Mahal was designed by a Persian? If you can't be persuaded of the beauty of Persian mosques and minarets and madrasehs, picture the Taj Mahal in your mind's eye and transplant it here. To Iran.

*Khosradad was one of the first four generals shot by Khomeini's new government, and I'm sorry I said it.

145

Tuesday, 28 November 1978

It seems like only yesterday we "celebrated" Ramazan, and now *Moharram* is nearly upon us. Another month-long siege of mourning, and not a dry eye in the country.

Muhammad had one living child, a daughter, Fatima. The Shi'ites of Iran, unlike the Sunnites of other Moslem countries who have accepted the Arabian caliphs as Muhammad's successors, looked to Fatima's husband, Ali, and her sons, Hossein and Hassan, as their leaders. Moharram is a festival of grief for Hossein, who was massacred while fighting the Sunni caliphs on the Plain of Karbala. He and his companions were killed one by one, and in the interim suffered terrible thirst and privation. It is for this reason that, among tribal peoples, no animal is slaughtered or sacrificed without first being given a drink of water.

For the first nine days of Moharram all public life is suspended. Black pennants hang at every door. Although passion plays celebrating the myths and sorrows of Karbala were outlawed by Fred, they're still performed. Often the participants are extemporaneous performers from the audiences.

The tenth day, *Ashura*, is that unhappy time when men strip to the waist and flog themselves and each other with leather-thonged whips, crying, "Hossein, Hassan!" and "Allah Akhbar!"

More formal grief for Hossein's brother Hassan, also martyred, is observed forty days after Ashura. And after that, for their father the Imam Ali. It's been centuries, but the Persians still haven't gotten over any of it.

Meanwhile Skip, in addition to his daily visits to the hospital, is trying to skirt curfews, supervise his men, and hound that abominable ER to take care of their BHI boy in distress. He missed his first court hearing yesterday because Ferret Face "forgot" to notify him of it. When he stormed in to see the ER director about the gross negligence, he was promised their best interpreter, an Iranian lawyer named John Hatami. Skip and Hatami had their first meeting today.

Tomorrow I am also going to accompany Skip, over John Hatami's vehement protests, when he goes to the hospital to pay the bill and escort Faruga and her family home. (I'm

146

surprised we discovered that she's being discharged.) We've heard so much about under-the-table arrangements between lawyers and Iranian families that I want to make certain there's no hanky-panky. And Roddey and John are going along so we can present a kind of solid front.

Wednesday, 29 November 1978

This morning at ten o'clock our little entourage arrived at the hospital to serve as Faruga Farusmandi's honor guard. Skip, with a flourish, paid the hospital charges, which were about five hundred dollars. Not excessive, but then it was only for the roof over the child's head. I spoke with her doctor and was assured she had a simple green stick fracture which should knit quickly.

Faruga was as proud as a peacock of her plaster cast and crutches and the new teddy bear Skip brought her; she knows she'll be queen of her kutche, and she sailed out of the hospital like Sheba, her doting mother and father trailing behind. They are, as I said, nice people. The father is a taxi driver, and their home is clean and neat. We all sat around the chie samovar and visited for over an hour. There was some very fast talk from John Hatami, however, and it sounded to me like *he* suggested to the family they not be hasty about signing a release for Skip. I should have insisted then and there, but I just smiled and bobbed my head like a witless Punch and Judy puppet.

Thursday, 30 November 1978

When Skip went to ER to recheck his accident status, his friendly neighborhood shyster informed him that, in addition to medical expenses, the Farusmandi family had decided to ask for one million rials—about fourteen thousand dollars! For a leg fracture??

Skip's slow to anger, but he puts even Liberty in the shade when he does. He rose through the ceiling and hit the floor above. He accused Hatami of being a thief, a traitor to BHI, and an unscrupulous manipulator. They say his language was awesome. He demanded his passport and resident permit and announced he was leaving the country before he was jailed for mischief to a minor. The resident idiots of ER's community relations held him down, then put their heads together and concluded they couldn't allow it. Instead they dispatched the lawyer Hatami with Skip and Skip's blank check, signed under duress, to the Farusmandi home to negotiate.

For two hours Hatami made a show of dickering, though Skip said he had a strong sense of being toyed with. Finally, 100,000 rials—$1,400, of which that high class crook undoubtedly took half—was agreed upon. Humming all the while, Hatami filled out the check himself, as though Skip were an illiterate boob. Then the family Farusmandi, in holiday mood, went back to ER to get an advance against Skip's paycheck—and their $1,400 in cold cash then and there. After that they all journeyed in tandem back to the casa for the release-signing ceremony and some chie and *ghand*. It went so smoothly, it was as though they'd rehearsed for days.

The Farusmandis were very pleasant, obviously by now considering Skip a member of the family. I'm sure Hatami convinced them Skip was a very rich American who would not miss such a pittance. Through Hatami, they told him they had a very smart, very pretty young cousin from the university they wished him to meet. (They knew a good catch when they had one.)

The whole way back to Liberty Hall Hatami, unlike the Farusmandis, was rude, cruel, and nasty, telling Skip how stupid he was, how many mistakes he had made, and that all Americans were blithering idiots. (After Khosradad, I pray John Hatami may be the next to go.)

Finally Skip had had enough. "You're damned right I made mistakes," he roared, "and the first one was not hiring an honest man instead of a cheap, double-dealing four-flusher. What's more, Hatami, it's guys like you who are responsible for the mess this country's in! When they pass out the hangings, I hope you get yours, buddy—right in the neck!" Hatami was so apoplectic that for a minute Skip feared he might have an angina attack. Skip said it was a real pleasure, however, to watch him lose face in front of the cab driver.

Through a governmental technicality, plus no Henry Shamoon Agency, and because of Hatami's undoubted connivance, Skip was not awarded insurance money. He sold his car this afternoon, swearing off driving forever in the benighted land of Iran.

BOOK IV

Friday, 1 December 1978

There's nothing like a little sorrow to brighten an Iranian life.

Everyone will soon be as tearful as a bride's mother, and there'll be grand, grievous processions through the streets, with the faithful not only weeping piteously but also spilling blood which, in view of the revolution, they might better donate to their nearest blood bank.

It is the proudest moment in an Iranian father's life if his son bleeds to death and meets his Maker on the day of Ashura, thus assuring not only direct entry to paradise, but one of the best seats in the house. It also paves the way for all his kith and kin, who apparently get free rides on the suicide's coattails.

Azhari, the Shah's military governor, has forbidden public gatherings except on Ashura itself. Flagellation and like "provocative behavior" are frowned on. But Azhari and I know together that they'll go right ahead and do it anyway. Already you can hear the whip-wielders tuning up backstage.

I wish everyone would just put up a purloined Christmas tree, hang stockings instead of effigies, and march the streets singing "God Rest Ye Merry Gentlemen." I am having one of my ongoing attacks of culture shock. The U.S. Consulate can issue keep-a-low-profile communiqués right to the disemboweling, but they neither help my emotional shortcomings nor give me much comprehension or sympathy for this entire grief, hate, and horror syndrome.

Without the *Kayhan*, and with limited barq and few TV and radio broadcasts, our news is of the dandelion variety—pick up a piece and it goes right to seed. Akhbar is one of my best sources, as news travels through the bazaars (those sections doing illicit, under-the-counter business) with the speed of traffic. We hear that the Shah and the country's political leaders have considered every solution, from a Council of Regents with the crown prince replacing his father as figurehead ruler to an actual, honest-to-God democratic parliament.

Not only are we humble peasants in the dark; the English, the Turks, the Saudis, the Afghanis, the entire Diplomatic Corps, every foreign correspondent, and the Iranian government are thoroughly baffled. Hence we all feed at the trough of rumor, side by side.

Here on the base, Jim Liberty still reigns as executive rumor monger and secretary of state for scandal. From a distance of three hundred yards he signals me, "Pssst, Rob . . ." and like a little yellow dickey bird I go hopping across the hangar to hear what he has to impart. There's an old saw (hereinafter known as Robinson's law) that the lower the whisper in which a rumor's repeated, the higher the credibility attached to it.

Liberty is a master of the sincere whisper, delivered into the left ear, the one nearest the heart, in tones that leave no room for doubt. "Rob, you're not going to believe this, but it's the God's truth: The Tudeh is arming the Russians out at the steel mill and they're taking over Esfahan early Saturday morning." I catch myself gazing at him open-mouthed and mind-boggled. But only for one heart-stopping moment. When I've caught my breath I say fondly, "Liberty, you are so full of guano you could run the pigeons out of business." This hurts him, but only subliminally and only for a second. The next time I see him he is whispering, sincerely, into someone else's left ear.

We are now directly at the source. Full-time rumor mongering "on the house." Skip and Roddey and I are comfortably resettled in Liberty Hall for the month of Moharram, although it is crowded until the Libertys make their escape. The boys and I sleep Eskimo style in the subarctic living room, which is unheated and the size of a Pennsylvania Dutch barn. I thank my stars and the Gerry Company for my down-filled sleeping bag as I zip myself up and waddle off to our frigid quarters like a beached walrus every night.

Jim and Judy are like expectant birthday children over the Thai vacation, their first trip out of Iran in twenty-nine months. Their present departure date, barring further crippling strikes: December 8. Judy's had enough of stapling *Whirly Bird*s and flower arranging at BFS and Carole Lombard movies at the Teen Center. She's three months pregnant, and she deserves a break in the monotony.

Skip and Roddey and I will house-sit with the aid and abettance of whoever turns up lonesome or homeless. Things will hopefully run along the lines of a Sig Ep houseparty—raucous, a little drunk, and with chore shifts posted by me in a prominent location. If these male supremacists think that the lone, hapless female in their midst is going to handle all the domestic chores and keep a clean apron tied under her baby-blue base pass, they'll have a revolution of another kind on their hands.

Sunday, 3 December 1978

As we've noted, I loathe The Flats, site of Liberty Hall. It's a square mile of Texas prison farm containing supposedly first-class living quarters and not a shred of vegetation. A Burpee seed salesman could send a large brood through college just working The Flats. I'll admit it—I miss the Espadana kutche, our pomegranate tree, Guity and Mama, even the Hamaze rooster.

I have been at some pains, despite social and political instabilities, to observe the amenities of *tarof*, the intricate Iranian system of courtesy, since moving here. By making social calls on my new neighbors, I have observed one of tarof's first tenets. In these trying times, not "calling" might lead to harbored suspicions, dirty looks, and unfriendly little incidents. I have therefore, in four days' time, visited all the Libertys' neighbors—excluding Americans and British, a total

153

of nine families—and it was rather wearing. I explained that I will be caring for the home of my very good friends and also acting as hostess-landlady for a number of employees from the Havan-e-Ruz military base. We can't have them thinking I'm a high-paid call girl every time a different man walks in and out of the house. Also, to make certain our stay is considered highly respectable, I told them that I am married to Mr. Maiorana (who was appalled at the news).

I further explained that in one month, when the Liberty family returns, I shall go back to my beloved home on Espadana kutche by the old bazaar—and to the welcoming arms of the Shirazes, the Mostafas, the Abarjanis and Naderis. I also shamelessly tossed the Ruhi and Mazhari names about like bridal bouquets. The name Mazhari caused a number of mouths to drop like hot stove lids, although it occurred to me later that some of these people might be on retaliatory committees, with the Mazhari family at the top of their vengeance lists.

Oh Lord, dear Allah, I hope I don't know what I'm talking about!

Monday, 4 December 1978

For some reason which I'm at a loss to explain, probably because I keep getting caught in upheavals, I have never gone into all the intricacies of tarof. The fact is that it's a subject for the *Encyclopaedia Britannica,* and at best I can only supply some basics.

Tarof is not really translatable; it encompasses all of Iranian social behavior from public prayer to private enterprise. Start with the premise that Iranian families, taken individually, are enormously hospitable, kind, generous, and friendly. One must accept all their proffered food, drink, and gifts, or serious loss of face will occur. An Iranian host will press unbelievably expensive trifles on his guests, and it's best not to admire the shirt on his back, or it'll be *yours.*

Although women's lib has made some very small strides here, an old-fashioned and still constant offshoot of tarof is the hopefully restrained behavior of women. The feminine qualities most admired are modesty, shy demeanor, and religious faith. As a guest of the country, I therefore make every

154

possible effort to appear modest, shy, and faithful. In Iranian households I abstain from smoking cigarettes, hiking up my skirts, showing the soles of my shoes or feet (a really dreadful breach of etiquette), rolling up my sleeves, cursing, or spitting. My greatest struggle is keeping a check on my ribald sense of humor. It is too easily misunderstood.

When I am on a date in public I do not kiss, caress, brush against, or even borrow a handkerchief from the hapless man, as this would involve touching in public. A good general rule is to act married, unseductive, and as sexless as a guppy.

Although many women, both Iranian and foreign, now go unescorted in public, I am not sure this is enlightened policy. If I'm alone and on foot, I try to slither through the back kutches attracting the least possible attention. But after years in the civilized world, one simply forgets, and if caught, I'm fair game for the crotch-grabbers: They patently consider me a loose and probably sex-starved female.

Difficult for Americans to understand and accept is the fact that most Iranians consider it perfectly acceptable to inquire about your salary, your possessions, your personal hygiene, your income, your innermost thoughts, and your more intimate sex practices. Their curiosity is insatiable. Yet if *you* ask such questions of *them*, they shriek like deflowered nuns. It has been explained to me that at least part of this is because they are Moslem and pure—while we are heathen and swinish. Even my most enlightened Iranian friends have had initial difficulty accepting me, a non-Moslem, as any sort of equal.

The Persians are also surprisingly sensitive and unsure of themselves in their newly modernized world and are *very* self-critical. Since they already persecute themselves mercilessly (witness their religion), the slightest indication of disapproval from you, an infidel though still-honored guest, might send them over the brink. I am surprised hara-kiri is not a part of tarof. It would fit right in.

The matter of exchanging gifts with one's hosts and friends is an endearing and wholly inane aspect of the Persian character. Here some kind of line *must* be drawn. Otherwise one could spend one's entire existence trying to outdo the neighbors with ever more thoughtful and expensive tributes. Gift-giving, and receiving, could turn into a lifelong profession, like medicine or the law. This way, of course, lies madness.

Much of the above is only borderline tarof, a mere smattering of a body of behavior that runs rampant from table manners through East-West diplomacy. Iranian culture and customs must be *felt* rather than explained. I know it isn't easy, not with several thousand light-years and ten centuries separating us non-Moslems from all of Islam.

Tuesday, 5 December 1978

President Jimmy Carter of the United States of America keeps professing his vociferous support for the Shahinshah, Mohammed Reza Pahlavi. My heartfelt suggestion is that Carter shut his great big corn pone mouf. These people are attempting to settle their own futures. For better or worse, they'll handle it without any lip from us. What does Carter know about Iran? I've been here nearly two years, sticking my nose into every corner I could, and *I* don't know anything about Iran.

We have the uncomfortable feeling, along with several million middle-of-the-road Iranians, that Moharram is one big powder keg, very short-fused, which Jimmy Carter's inflammatory talk may set off like a veritable catherine wheel.

This month, going back to ancient Shi'ite Islam, traditionally symbolizes Persia's struggle against evil and corrupt leadership. Ohboy. The more things change, the more they stay the same. The idea's good. The time's right. But they're fighting evil with evil.

Marshall McLuhan would have to see (hear?) this revolution to believe it. Media is the marvel. Khomeini telephones his speeches from France; they're taped and copied on cassettes by the thousands, hawked on street corners and played on loudspeakers from high, secret places, thus speedily spreading Old Hawkeye's stentorian outpourings from one end of the country to the other. The communications revolution is in Iran to stay.

Khomeini's recent call for a *jihad* has resulted in a lot of unwelcome leisure for us infidel workers locked up at home. If we do get to the base, the barq workers delight in playing footsie with us. Yesterday they pulled their switches, and there was no power all morning. With the cessation of IBM

156

typewriters, adding machines, power tools, kitchen appliances and machinery, Iran shuddered to a giant electrical halt. We office carrion felt like Piltdown men running through dank cave corridors.

When the barq did not reappear, and we were finally permitted to venture home, Esfahan was having dress rehearsal for Ashura. There were rioters and flagellators and would-be martyrs attired in the shrouds of doomdom (they had donned their funeral outfits and gone into the streets to plead with someone, *anyone*, to shoot them) on every public thoroughfare. I was driving with Skip and Roddey, and we backed into a kutche corner where we watched, appalled, as men marched past in skivvy shorts or pajama bottoms, beating themselves and each other with leather thongs to bloody pulps. I felt like I was in an old chain gang movie. The passing parade lasted maybe ten minutes, and then we crept shakily out of the alley, the boys chalk-faced, me trembling.

Listen, I'm no political pundit, but I don't like the look in that man Khomeini's eyes. And it worries me that these eager, earnest young zealots are all dressed up to die, not for Hossein or themselves, but for a dyspeptic old man. The trouble with his plan is that you don't ever get to change your mind, not after the trigger's pulled.

In the midst of municipal and national torment, our evenings at Liberty Hall are a scintillating round of pumping Madame (the stationary bicycle Skip gave me for my birthday), listening to Liberty electrify the air as he tries to get BBC on my short-wave radio, hovering over the broadcasts themselves (a potpourri of Colonel Blimp and Czechoslovakian interference), and me playing Yahtzee with the Liberty children.

After weeks of oil strikes, the workers are back pumping oil like an Arkansas rig. Maybe Fred's military government is gaining ground—or at the very least, oil. We might even have enough benzine and naft and butane to keep us pneumonia-free at last. Helping Judy Liberty pack bikinis and beach balls gives me a lift; it warms the heart just thinking of sand, surf, and ocean sunsets.

GOI, the army, and BHI, together and separately, assure us that Ashura will be a bitch. Meanwhile, I am aware, in the course of my job, of the inordinate numbers of BHI people quietly departing the country. Given the instability of both

157

Iran and our jobs, this is neither surprising nor alarming. Yet. But if the pace continues, somebody better hold a recount.

Since October's bus bombings, while I was in the U.S., parents are concerned for their children, and all those women who got pregnant during the Great September Curfew are thinking about the babies not yet born. They long to go home to a nice, wholesome, hand-holding American obstetrician. Who wants to be delivered, even doing the work yourself, by a doctor who's probably posting Yonky Go Home notices in his spare time?

A few departing vacationers fully intend to return. I know for a certainty that Liberty will be back. He has his network and trap lines to run. But eighty percent of these departees will never see Esfahan again. It's getting so I can smell a man who's had it. He will not look you straight in the eye, cracks his knuckles a lot, and keeps babbling aimlessly about the folks back home who need him.

Wednesday, 6 December 1978

Due to the debilitating lack of news and the powerful effects (all bad) of rumor, BHI has just published its first edition of a homey little news sheet called the *Rotor Wash*. It is comprised of reports received over BBC by American ham radio operators, plus turgid accounts by the Bell Belles of the ladies' luncheons and the status of the BHI Butterball turkey deliveries, plus late bulletins from Cub Scout and Brownie leaders regarding the children's morale. Also daily accounts of bombings, threats, incidents, and similar social notes.

The *Rotor Wash* is unadulterated American folk art, and I am going to collect it.

Thursday, 7 December 1978

Our new status as a hardship area has just been announced. The IRS, love its cold-blooded heart, will award all Americans here a five-thousand-dollar tax exemption. This will be fine and dandy, but I haven't heard the IRS discuss bringing us back alive.

Yesterday a group of enlisted Iranian Army men burst into an officers' mess at the Lavizan barracks in the north and killed twelve of their leaders in a spray of automatic fire. This is the first open mutiny we've heard about.

Iran Air has struck again. And the oil workers returned only to walk back out. I've thought of striking myself, but I have this feeling no one would *care*.

Today's *Rotor Wash* chastised the ugly Americans of BHI who have used rude and abusive language in the offices of the Persian Gulf Travel Agency. I'll admit that here we have the most inefficient travel agency on the face of the earth, but come on, boys, just because they ticketed you to Peking instead of Peoria?

Our befuddled schoolchildren are being shuttled from school to school and bus route to bus route. No one has been hurt, but there've been sticks of dynamite thrown and gas cans lighted in school doorways, and I personally think this is hitting below the belt.

The annual BHI Christmas airlift, number five, arrived yesterday. It was one of the bigger moments of our year abroad, and we calm and collected BHI'ers rushed to the Teen Center in maddened, clawing crowds, Visigoths stampeding the settlements. We lined up (more or less), piped out our names, ranks, and serial numbers, and received: one jar of peanut butter marked "Merry Christmas from BHI," one jar of Welch's grape jelly, one can of cranberry sauce (price in Esfahan, when available in mid-July, ten dollars), one superior Texas fruitcake, and one Butterball turkey fattened to obscene dimensions. Turkey in Farsi is *boogalamoon*, and my Iranian neighbors are wide-eyed at my boogalamoon, which to them looks like a denuded ostrich.

I know this largesse doesn't sound like much to all you out there in Disneyland, but to us Moharram-sated and Christmas-starved Americans, it was payday and the Fourth of July and Christmas dinner rolled into one.

Of course, the usual anglers were hard at work. One of them made a careful note of all his departed friends, presented their names and identification numbers at the reception center, and collected a total of eleven Butterball turkeys plus "extras." It was a shame he didn't trip and break his neck carrying everything out to his car.

159

Friday, 8 December 1978

I am scratching this entry by Sabbath candlelight. We have had no barq for twelve straight hours, and Liberty assures us the blackout will continue for twenty-four.

Liberty, Judy, and the children were supposed to leave again today, but *"Aeroplanes nist,"* snarled the martial guards when we appeared at Forudaghe Esfahan, all bundled and ticketed and bagged, only to troop home once more. Liberty is muttering under his breath and trying to rearrange their plans so they can fly out of Teheran instead.

Saturday, 9 December 1978

We were shaken yesterday when we were trapped with the Libertys in a major demonstration en route home from the airport. An Iranian shouted from a window, in perfect, unaccented English, "Go home, you Yankee sons of bitches!" It made the children weep, Judy nearly aborted, and of course Liberty leapt from the car to strangle the guy. It took the combined efforts of wife, kids, Skip, me, and some friendly Iranians to hold him down.

The barq was off a total of thirty hours, so Liberty was batting .350. It took us awhile to calm ourselves, gather matches, build a fire, and remember that we're experienced campers with enough know-how to survive rural de-electrification. For a minute there we reacted like Neanderthals deprived of our flint supply.

International flights are canceled for a forty-eight-hour period and Liberty is beside himself. He'll get his family to Bangkok for their promised vacation if he has to hire a caravan and go by camel.

I am head-sore tonight, as I worked double-time all day trying to catch up on mountains of work. Muhammad definitely did *not* come to the mountain. I had to whittle it down myself, with the unstinting help of faithful Pat.

Monday, 11 December 1978

TO: All BHI Employees
SUBJECT: Security Bulletin for 6-11 December, 1978

No doubt each of you have [*sic*] heard numerous rumors concerning evacuation of Americans from Iran during the last few days. This bulletin is being distributed as early as possible to each of you so that you know BHI's official position. . . .

It has been reported that the news media in the U.S. has indicated that All Americans are being evacuated from Iran. This is not true. This probably was based on the Department of Defense dependents in Iran who wanted to leave. This was on a voluntary basis and not mandatory. Since international flights were cancelled for 48 hours the Department of Defense sent into Teheran several C-141s for pickup of these dependents. It has been reported that Grumman is also taking some of their dependents out of Iran.

BHI has no plans for evacuation of dependents. This policy of early return of dependents to the U.S., of those who desire, by commercial air is still the current BHI policy. Although there were numerous demonstrations, chantings, isolated rioting, burning of automobiles and buildings there were no Americans injured due to demonstrations or rioting. . . .

A summary of the more significant incidents that occurred during this period are listed herein:

(1) Thirteen American cars were burned or partially burned.

(2) The Grumman office building, 2 banks, and 2 theaters were burned.

(3) An explosive device was thrown into the driveway of a BHI employee house causing structural damage to the building. No injuries were sustained.

(4) One residence was fire-bombed. The two BHI occupants were relocated to a hotel.

(5) The Bonsi Pars warehouse was destroyed by fire.

(6) Curfew in Teheran and Esfahan changed to 2300 hours for the nights of 9, 10 and 11 December. Curfew reverts back to the original time Tuesday, 12 December.

(7) All international flights cancelled for 10 and 11 December.

(8) The complex on Charbagh-e-Abbasi including Bank Melli, a cinema, and the Indian Restaurant were burned.

(9) The statue of the Shah across from the 33 Arch Bridge and the statue located near the Russian Bazaar were pulled down and destroyed.

(10) The Long Branch on East Apadana was burned.

(11) The water is *not* contaminated.

> Floyd C. Haskell
> BHI/Esfahan

Tuesday, 12 December 1978

Yesterday was Ashura, the long-dreaded day of Iran's "Deep, Deep, DEEPEST mourning" (the capitals are American Consul David McGaffey's).

Although the Shi'ites were out in full, screaming force, there were plenty of others, like two of our neighbors I've discovered are Bahais, crouched at home behind drawn curtains. Islam is full of such offshoots, schisms, and antithetical factions as the Bahais (I adore the fact that the Assassins, from the word of the same name, are a Moslem sect) and has been since the day the Prophet left this mortal toil. But then Christianity hasn't been any bed of roses either.

All this deep, DEEP recalls the red-letter day that *Deep Throat* opened here last summer. And stayed open, for three interminable months, right in Esfahan's largest downtown theatre. Movies are government-sponsored, cost only pennies, and theoretically keep delinquents off the streets. The thing that confounds me is why, from a selection of thousands, some imbecile American or wily Russian or conniving Persian chose that particular picture to spread intercultural understanding and breed content. Then again maybe they thought it was a hygiene movie on streptococci infections.

Although we're told the worst is over, I am still staggered by yesterday's demonstrations of grief. Ten thousand people, all in black, marched directly past *this house,* carrying pennants covered with meaningful scripture, chanting "Allah Akhbar" and "Hossein, Hossan." I don't think their fervor was meant to be threatening, but sheer numbers and noise made it so. The sound was absolutely deafening, the grief excruciating. In their wake they left graffiti like tracks of a plague of locusts, and it was neither mournful nor was it religious. In fact it was out-and-out secular: "Karter Is a Dog," "Yonky Go Home," "Death To the Shah," and crude renderings of machine guns all over our marble walls. A waste of perfectly good tombstone material!

Every crowd I've ever been in was fun-loving, boisterous, exciting. This one seemed—ominous. A clammy chill crept through my quaking limbs, and for the first time in my life I felt I might DIE (*those* capital letters are all *mine*).

The Libertys have planned escape routes and they conduct drills with the children. Allah willing, they'll be off to Teheran tomorrow.

Younger children are particularly affected by the mobs and threats and hostility. Since the bombings the American school buses have been numbered on top so helicopters can track their courses through the city; at the school in Shahinshahr, colored flags alert students and residents to the state of security in the area; a red flag means danger, yellow advises caution, and white means all clear. The white flag has not been used since the system was initiated. This kind of thing isn't designed to make a kid feel he's safe on his mother's knee.

As for me, I am astonished to find myself still shaken by Ashura.

It's been some week. Today Esfahan had its first full-scale *pro*-Shah demonstration, the only one I've seen since the revolt began. Can the two-party system actually be at work here? Skip and Roddey and I were on our way to the

Kouroush Grocery and the crowds were so jolly and inviting that we drove lightheartedly into their midst. After yesterday I'm not exactly gung-ho about crowds, but Skip said, "Let's go!" and we beeped the horn, turned on our lights and windshield wipers, and shouted and hooted with the other zanies. Halfway through we were suddenly as immobilized as though cast in bronze, and it wasn't much fun anymore. We managed to keep smiling, but my knuckles were talcum-powder white.

My office is frantically terminating people, arranging transportation back to the States, soothing hysterical mothers and, among other extraneous duties, reinventorying all our supplies (thievery on the base has quadrupled in the last three weeks).

Curfew still begins at 8:00 P.M. and ends at six in the morning. Judy and I try to entertain by candlelight, but it's like fighting quicksand to accomplish the simplest household chores. The most irritating thing about curfew is not just that it's *there* but that some petty tyrant keeps changing the hours. Once all of us went through an entire week not knowing that it had been moved from seven o'clock to ten o'clock. I think it's a plot to keep us in the dark.

Another petty but maddening inconvenience is staggered barq. It goes off nightly at eight, in time to miss the radio and TV shows if there are any, and comes back on at ten. It's said the electrical workers are showing their muscle and their displeasure with the Shah.

Ah well, I'm becoming blithe by candlelight, scribbling away like George Sand, and growing as myopic as a carpet weaver.

When the lights go out, so do the Iranians. They climb up on their rooftops by the hundreds and howl. The sound is like all the wolf packs who ever closed in on the lone troikas of Siberia. I recorded it, the sound, on my tape recorder so people back home will believe it. I'm right under it nightly, and *I* don't believe it.

We're told this howling is a brand of Iranian voodoo, and that the chanting is led by strategically placed loudspeakers playing recordings from mysterious high places. Whatever the ethnic and musical origins, it's effective as hell. Hundreds of Bell and other families leave the country daily, hoping their children won't be scarred for life.

I can't believe the Ruhis and the Shirazes and all my old

164

neighbors are on their rooftops howling too. Guity and Mama? *Never!*

Today an American pilot, a guy I dated named Billy Huston from the Bronx, was driving up Char Bagh near Shiraz Circle, when his car broke down. Breakdowns pose a problem because no one can leave a car unguarded (another reason why none of us drives anywhere alone). But he had to have help and finally found a tow trucker who agreed to pick him up. While he was gone some lovable oaf spray-painted "Down with the Shah" on the side of his car. On the way to the garage they were spotted by martial guards who stopped them, pulled the poor Iranian driver out of his truck, pinned Billy down, and nearly beat the trucker to death. Those guards did not plan to release either one of them until the anti-Shah sign was removed, if it took until the middle of next Ramazan. Since the paint was lifetime enamel, the job would have required an electric sander. The guards began scraping and hacking at it with their bayonets, until they were diverted by a picture of Khomeini in a store window across the street. While they were shooting up the window, Billy and the Iranian escaped, and Billy took the man to the hospital.

Notes on the Iranian Army: Though officers are an elite group and are high school graduates, the common soldier is on a par with the poor devils in the Russian Army. Every young Iranian man, unless he is attending university, is conscripted. Once drafted, the boy is sent far from home, where he is lonely, abused by his officers, and beaten until he becomes a sloven with little self-esteem. This kind of army is not your thinking man's militia; I steer clear of them, thank you.

Wednesday, 13 December 1978

We all arose in the dead of night at the crack of curfew to see the Libertys out of town. They left on a BHI bus for Teheran, traveling at the pace of a sea turtle. They are scheduled for a Japan Air flight out of the country.

This time I'm certain they'll make it. Already I feel alone on The Flats, with only Skip, Roddey, the telephone and the TV to keep me warm. The telephone is not an unmitigated pride and joy. By the mere fact of possessing one, Liberty

Hall is a vital link in the pyramid communications system, an informal, sometimes convoluted, but pretty effective way to keep a tangled network of BHI'ers informed.

We in the pyramid relay news along a prearranged route via phones, walkie-talkies, ham radio, and old-fashioned hallooing.

Other phone calls are a pastiche of social chats and Iranian threats and obscenities. When one picks up a phone these days it's apt to be an unpleasant surprise.

NIRT (rhymes with "dirt") is the beloved National Iranian Radio and TV network which is currently reduced to fifteen minutes of sporadic news a day, usually at 6:30 P.M. First there's a blare of trumpets, then the national anthem plays, then the Shah's picture appears on screen, faintly smiling and very haughty; then the news, then the national anthem again, and the Shah's picture, faintly smiling and still haughty. The national anthem is a sort of medley of "Seventy-Six Trombones" and "God Save the Queen."

NIRT is the channel for all English-speaking peoples, but none of us knows what's happened to the American and British announcers, who have quietly faded from view. All we know is that Iranian announcers currently broadcast fifteen minutes of garbled news nightly, and there isn't a Cronkite in the crowd.

Thursday, 14 December 1978

There were pro-Shah rallies all day today. I'm not certain I like this kind any better than the others. Soldiers *and* civilians (who don't, however, seem to be Skinny Ties) are pulling people headlong out of their cars if they don't have prominently displayed portraits of the Shah on their windshields, their wipers pulled away from the glass and going full tilt, and their headlights on bright. Woe betide the lost soul who hasn't gotten this latest message; his car is kicked, stoned, and sprayed with lewd shades of paint. With an Iranian car, this treatment is enough to finish it off.

These must be the world's most unpredictable people. Overnight the mood changed. I'd swear on a stack of Korans I saw one of the clerks from the Kouroush Grocery in both

166

the pro-Khomeini crowd last week and the pro-Shah demonstrations today.

Last week the pro-Khomeinians pulled down the Shah's statue in the heart of the city. All they left were the poor man's shoes and the imitation rock pedestal constructed (it's the God's truth) of Styrofoam.

They propped pictures of the Ayatollah in the empty shoes, until today when the pro-Shahs erected fresh new photos of the Shah, his Shahbanu, the children, his in-laws, his sisters and his cousins and his aunts. Horns honk and lights flash and everyone is downright daring. I almost expected someone to break into a chorus of "I'm a Farsi Doodle Dandy." The soldiers and martial guards, looking a little sheepish, sported flowers in their rifle barrels.

Oh, I don't know. Only one Persian emperor in the last two hundred years has died of natural causes. Persia's dynasties have ended in a daisy chain of strangulations, gunshot wounds, garrotings, poisonings and knives-in-the-back. It would be a nice change to have one of their Shahs die peacefully in bed. At the age of ninety-three.

All the Ayatollahs look like they're already ninety-three. I'm not certain how many are in Iran at present, but collectively they appear to add up to ten thousand years. Ayatollah (Reflection of Allah) is a very high level of Shi'ite "holy-dom" reached after years of advanced study and pious example. An Ayatollah is a sort of latter-day wise man. Each major city seems to have one, comparable to a bishop and often politically powerful.

We are stricken over the burning of the Bonsi Pars–Super Pol warehouse across the street from the Shah's shoes. This was a vile blow, as there went the only American canned goods in town.

The rumor today is that we have three weeks left. This sounds terminal. Do they mean three weeks in Esfahan, in Iran, or on this earth?

The government of Iran is again reported bankrupt and unable to pay us. Can this be oil-rich Iran? They must have overdone it with the credit cards. The American Department of Defense, with whom Bell has its contract, was at least farsighted enough to get six months' cash in advance from GOI. But about half of that will have been used by now, so maybe it's three months we have left after all. Lord, but I

167

miss Liberty's reliable rumors. Anything he told you, you could count on the opposite being the truth.

Because of continuing oil field strikes, we're informed the Iranian government is importing two thousand barrels a day for its own use, and three guesses from whom? Yessir, America is carrying coals to Newcastle and I love it!

Two timekeepers from headquarters were beaten senseless this morning in Jolfa, and by senseless I don't mean lightly barked on the shins and socked in the nose. I don't know either of the men, but Ruth Weems in my office does, and she says they're both ex-marines. I hope they went down in the best John Wayne tradition, taking everyone with them. The Americans had broken jaws, arms, legs, to say nothing of fractured hopes and dreams.

Mother just called! Ten thousand miles away and I heard her voice as clear as the call of the Hamaze rooster. Which is a lousy analogy, as mother in no way resembles that cock-eyed bird. She gave me a blow-by-blow account of American, international, and Iranian news. We both felt a little silly, but we in Esfahan have not seen a newspaper or magazine since the Middle Ages. She says the Shah's army rounded up supporters in rural areas for the pro-Shah demonstrations, trucked them into town, and even fed them after the show. Seems ridiculous, but maybe it's coming down to who can out-yell whom.

The butane BHI gives us is tainted. The house smells worse than the corner garbage dump. There are dumps on every vacant lot in this city. The symbiotic trash pile. When you drop off your garbage, old men and small boys enter from the wings and thrash around, heaving unwanted items high in the air while the sheep and goat herders wait their turn, then finally move in for the kill. It's the sheep and the goats that keep the dumps within manageable limits, and I always naively believed that sheep, at least, munched their way through life on green grass. Since *we* eat the sheep, I've given up lamb for Lent, possibly forever.

Yesterday's battle scars: The doorbell rang. It was the potato man. We heard, "Beeg potah-toes, Meee-sus," shouted over the wall. Just like Mexico, only in Mexico I was passionately devoted to the potato man, the chili pepper man, and the milk vendor with his little silken-eared burro and big milk cans. Our Iranian potato man is an evil stinker who whines. This time he held up a small bag of potatoes and

168

whined, "Eighty rials." Roddey gave him a thousand rials and waited, hand outstretched in the accustomed fashion, for his change. The potato man threw some loose potatoes in the courtyard and fled as if he'd come upon me cooking dinner stark naked. Not forgetting in his haste, however, his Moped and fourteen dollars of our household money. We figure those spuds cost about two dollars apiece, and that at this rate we'll be as bankrupt as GOI. We had mashed potatoes for dinner and nearly choked on every bite.

The next time I'll hose that rotter down. The Libertys own a garden hose that's almost as penetrating as the firehouse variety, and I use it freely. I spray everyone who shouts, "Yonky go home!" into the courtyard, who tries to stop up our chimney, or who stridently rings the doorbell and shrieks, *"Faroush, madame, faroush?"* (Wanting to know if we're having a garage-sale giveaway at least ninety times a day, the vultures.) I don't care if they do fire-bomb us, I'll just put out the fire with my trusty hose. After that I'll flood the kutche. Then the country.

This December is like a premature spring, nipped by the freezing rains of November only to start burgeoning afresh six weeks later. It is warm enough for sunbathing, for public masturbation by Iranian degenerates, for picnicking in the parks, and for demonstrating in the streets.

I miss the Ruhis and Akhbar and all my old neighbors, and it is almost impossible to get across the city to see them. Akhbar sometimes sends messengers. He has even sent gifts of benzine for my car. But our actions are so proscribed it's a major undertaking to move from one section of the city to another. My friends don't have access to telephones, and with the postal strikes, we can't even write postcards, for heaven's sake. They might just as well be in Seattle, and I in Syracuse.

Saturday, 16 December 1978

Consulate of the United States of America
Eṣfahan, Iran

The American embassy in Teheran has issued the following advisory notice: During the upcoming week

169

the American community should observe increased precautionary procedures, limit movement, and avoid crowds. This is a precautionary announcement and we wish to stress that there is no, repeat no, evidence that there will be immediate danger.

These habitual, wishy-washy directives give me a pain in the neck. Always repeating that there is no danger and in the same breath suggesting that if we step out of doors, take a leak in a public toilet, make use of a grocery store or pharmacy, pull into a gas station, or otherwise make our appointed rounds we may very well be shot at. Why don't they take some kind of stand, *any* kind of stand, or as Ed Thorpe put it, "Shit or get off the pot."

Also, the fool directives invariably end by repeating that we are guests in this country and to maintain the old "low profile." I don't know a soul who plans on maintaining a high profile, which we all visualize as something along the lines of Mount Rushmore. What our consulate needs is someone to write new material. I have suggested this on various occasions, but no one seems eager for my ideas or deathless prose.

Chadors used to come in prints, florals, stripes, and every color of the spectrum. Over the past months, as a demonstration of support for the revolution, all chadors have gone into the dye pot and come out a dingy black. I have identification problems with local crowds as it is, and now the whole country looks like a flock of crows. Not that Esfahanis were ever harbingers of Paris fashion, but I would not have believed an entire nation dressed in black could be so utterly depressing. I think they've even dyed their blasted pajamas black.

Many Iranian women wear European dress in their homes and, especially in smaller cities, cover up with chadors to go into the streets. Men wear Western dress. Only in Abadan, in caravans, or in Afghani tent cities have I seen men in *djellabahs* or *galabayas*. Of course tribal men wear regional costumes, but they are very far from Esfahan, in distance and in spirit. Around here the sports coat is ubiquitous—for office work, for street cleaning, for construction, for farming. Shoes are Western and crushed flat at the heels in an adaptation of the Turkish *babouche,* designed to slip easily on and off for prayers.

I have never been wildly attuned to Iranian fashion, but may I say I would welcome the return of *any* color for Christmas? Schiaparelli pink, moody blues, lavender and old lace....

After spending an entire weekend driving back and forth across this end of the city with pictures of the Shah (distributed at the base by grinning janitors) taped all over the car, Skip and Ben and Roddey and I sallied forth today to find we were the *only ones* still sporting them. I hastily ripped them off and stuffed them under the front seat, there to await the next change in political allegiances, and wished like hell I had a picture of Mahatma Gandhi handy.

We have not heard from the Libertys and presume them safely arrived at their destination. I miss them; there are days this house feels like a San Quentin cell block.

I also said goodbye to Pat and Mel Johnson. They lived in the Moslem bastion on the north side and were reduced to sleeping in their living room to keep an eye on the wall surrounding the house, when they slept at all, which wasn't often of late. Theirs was the area of heaviest after-curfew chanting, and their ears rang day and night. Even big, strong, easygoing Mel got spooked. He said, "I thought they loved us black brothers—until they started seeing the red, white, and blue of our eyes." And Pat was among the vastly pregnant September gang and wouldn't leave here without him. My batiking buddy—she's gone and I miss her.

The most important events in our lives today are:

1. Robert R. Williams, president, BHI, has arrived in this country to attend his vested interests and sent each of us a friendly notice stating that "in recognition of the current inconveniences in Iran, BHI will pay an additional two hundred dollar hardship allowance per month, retroactive to 1 October 1978." I suppose it's something, but the way the rial is shot down it would hardly pay for a casket and a shroud.

2. We are making preparations for our first *faroush* (garage sale). This is not an exigency of the times. Americans have always had garage sales when they leave, and Iranians adore them. Except we hear via the grapevine that they've gone beyond spirited fun and bargain buying. These people are so concerned about the faltering state of their currency (currently selling at half-price on the world market) that they're truly desperate for foreign goods. Mass hysteria has reigned

171

at recent sales. We plan to be prepared with bludgeons, truncheons, and my trusty hose.

Sunday, 17 December 1978

Today's *Rotor Wash* informed us that Esfahan is returning to normalcy. Hah?

A lot of shops along the main thoroughfares are indeed open, and after work I rushed across town to find Akhbar. We had a tearful reunion, but he has done scarcely any business in weeks and looked, I thought, decidedly bleak. He served me tea and shirini in the rear of his shop, explaining apologetically that it was better we not be too visible. I tried to leave; he *made* me stay.

In its next breath *Rotor Wash* went on to say that there was no reason to go all girlish and discard our security measures. To wit:

1. Do not disclose the location of your home to strangers, or the location of your job site.

2. Strangers loitering around your home or job site should be reported to security on the spot. If followed while en route to and from work, obtain license numbers, or other forms of identification on the spot.

3. Vary your schedule and route to and from work.

4. Do not be overly concerned by printed threats and notices to vacate the country. Intimidation is the intent.

Monday, 18 December 1978

As all Esfahan shops are again shuttered, everyone came to our faroush instead.

We announced the sale to two people, and at the crack of dawn this morning awakened to "Faroush, madame, faroush, madame," and a procession the size of Hannibal's army invaded the house, trampling us and our belongings under elephantine feet.

We had spent the last two days, off and on, moving

172

everything for sale into one room. We also marked prices and tagged items so the three of us wouldn't quote different amounts. We decided to stick to our guns with *fixeh*, a fixed price. Things were inexpensive, and we figured we'd let it go at that. That's what we figured.

What happened was that each customer was cheaper and more vicious than the last; with everyone hell-bent on whittling us down to seventy cents for a sixty-dollar vacuum cleaner—and they outnumbered us a hundred to one—something had to give. (It was me.)

After Skip or Roddey or I weakly agreed to the seventy cents (Barry Outcelt, Mike Montgomery, and Ben Roche next door had planned to come help but not until nine o'clock, and we were trapped behind the lines without them for more than two hours), the wretches would give us sixty, say snottily that that was plenty, and make off with their loot.

I really lost my cool when a woman came back to return a fifty-dollar pantsuit that she'd extracted from me for 250 rials, demanded I take it back, and that I promptly return her *300* rials. Talk about desperation banking!

With all the fire of the Divine Sarah, I flung open the front door and bellowed, *"Boro!"* (Out!). Though I shrieked like an inmate of a mental institution, the woman never heard me. She was busy coaxing poor Roddey to sell her a hundred-dollar wardrobe for a thousand rials. She finally intimidated him into closing the deal and said she'd be back to pick it up tomorrow. With wicked zeal I sold it right out from under her and had the customer take immediate delivery.

Listen, I can understand the growing panic. Iranian currency is falling so fast it sounds like rain. These people stand to lose their life's savings, are glomming onto everything foreign and negotiable they can, and may soon be reduced to bargaining, exchanging, and trading without benefit of currency at all. On the street corners, where most of them started.

It *is* rather fun to watch perplexed customers looking at some of our strange American thingumajigs. A perfect case-in-point is Madame, my bicycle that goes nowhere. I don't blame them a bit for peering quizzically and then turning up their noses at the old girl. I'd like to boot her right to the dump myself.

I am saving my nicest things for Guity Ruhi. The problem

173

is that the good people, the kind ones, are not the ones who go to garage sales and behave like blue-nosed gibbons. The ones who go to garage sales have greedy, beady eyes like praying mantises. Roddey has the right approach. He said to a fat, obstreperous officer's wife, "But madam, you could never use that dress. It is a size six and you are what we call a Stylish Stout, an eighteen and a half. What you are seeking, madam, is Omar the Tent Maker, he who constructs clothing for hippopotami." These smashing witticisms are uttered with an appealing smile, and the women (whose English is never as good as they pretend) smile at him fatuously. "Fat fart," mutters Roddey under his breath, and we all collapse in helpless laughter. If it wasn't for the boys, my brain cells would have short-circuited in one blinding flash.

Wednesday, 20 December 1978

Today I have numbers on the brain, and I wish to discuss some matters of numerical interest. Discounting the coming weekend and the little matter of strike-torn retail outlets, we'll be lucky to have any shopping days left till Christmas. Since none of us expects this Christmas to be particularly jolly, we're trying to tuck this particular numerical quotient away in the furthest recesses of our minds.

Has anyone noticed the significance of the number forty, biblically or arabically? For example, it rained forty days and forty nights. Moses led his people into the desert for forty years. In the case of Islam, it's Ali Baba and the Forty Thieves, and on his fortieth birthday Mohammad denounced the paganism of his country and began proselytizing Islam, etcetera, etcetera.

Why are there fifty thousand Iranian students in the United States, to say nothing of untold numbers in other foreign countries, when Iran is literally sprouting new universities and needs all the educated leaders it can get?

Jim Holland's pet peeve is the fact that the Iranians stubbornly maintain a weekend out of step with the outside world. He's figured out that only Monday, Tuesday, and Wednesday are available for international business, and with three-and-a-half hours between ours and Greenwich Mean

174

Time, coupled with the Persian siesta, this gives Iran approximately ten to sixteen-and-one-half hours *per week* in which to do business with the U.S., England, Japan, Russia, the Balearics, Germany, and Hong Kong.

In a land of one hundred and eighty thousand mullahs, there is roughly one mullah per kutche; what I want to know is why aren't they curbing those vicious kids and teaching them the brotherhood of man?

Between one-fourth and one-half of the Shah's budget has routinely been spent for arms. He controls more tanks than the British Army and more helicopters than the U.S. 1st Cavalry in Nam (I forget just where I picked up *that* statistic). He might better have used his money on penny balloons, free lunches, Bingo nights, thirty-six-piece chinaware giveaway sets, and improved agriculture. The scope of the Grand Agricultural Plan, to be achieved in five-year increments, was something to see, twenty-five years ago. Today it's a shambles; poorly administered, graft-ridden, useless. Everyone is so oil-mad that most of Iran's foodstuffs have long been imported, including their basic and very vital rice.

Since these smashing statistics are not the stuff of suspense, sex, or intrigue, I think I'll count sheep, ignore the caterwauling from the rooftops, and see if I can multiply myself to sleep.

Thursday, 21 December 1978

I've just finished working the first five-day, forty-hour week I've put in since returning to Iran at the beginning of November. I am shipping my friends and co-workers off like flotsam and jetsam, corked bottles tossed into seas of trouble. There's no way to know what's safe or certain; some are flying out via the Orient, some by way of South America, most on any carrier that will take them. Pat Powell, the finest secretary a fishwife ever had, is one of those who looked me in the eye and said, "I'm scared, Robin, I'd like to go home." I'll miss her more than I can say, but I'm grateful she's getting off. She's as raveled as an old sweater.

The long work week was a welcome relief after being paid

$150 a day to bask in the courtyard. wield the garden hose, implore someone, *anyone*, to play gin, cribbage, or backgammon, and suffer intermittent flashes of guilt.

As for Skip Maiorana, he's just had his fourth promotion and keeps catapulting up the ladder toward Vice-President in Charge of Foreign Parts. One thing about being abroad in a crisis is that talent will out.

There's no telling how long Bell will conduct its "holding action." With most of the major companies either gone or making plans to evacuate, BHI clings fast like a climber at a cornice. R. N. Mackinnon, Vice-President, General Manager, BHI, Iran, just reassessed our position in the *Rotor Wash*, and I'm struck dumb by the fact Bell has only recently completed negotiations for a *brand-new* contract with GOI! Either the Shah and his generals are in a semicomatose condition, hopelessly insane, or have the sense of aardvarks about how to quiet a mutinous country.

Uncle Roger on revolution: "The ineptness of the entrenched elite is a key. It will produce loss of their legitimacy and ultimately a series of additional factors will precipitate the loss of their power."

The Shah grows ever more inept, and "additional factors" keep gathering at the gates to storm the Peacock Throne. I've grown to love Iran in these past twenty months, and I'd be deliriously happy if their revolution were settled amicably— and in the morning. But it seems everyone must go through his appointed paces, even in this badly choreographed ballet.

There is a lull in the storm, say our bulletins and the *Rotor Wash*. It feels like precious peace to me. And good will toward men?

I'd almost welcome some of the demonstrative hullabaloo, without the howling of course. It's nearly Christmas, and so desolate somehow without street decorations and crowds of shoppers and pretty store windows and the hustle-bustle of the holidays. I'm prepared to sell my soul for a little tinsel, a tarnished angel, and some bedraggled red-and-green ribbon. Last Christmas I was in Abadan, sailing on the Tigris and Euphrates, eating crumpets and drinking Bristol Cream, elated at the direction of my life.

Skip and Roddey and I have invited fourteen people for Christmas dinner—Skip's crew and of course Donna and Jackie and Rose; the list is sure to grow. Just so our guests know plenty of carols. Around here you'd better sing—or you don't get your supper.

The maintenance Christmas party is slated for this afternoon. I suppose we'll all do our darnedest to get smashed, in the spirit of Christmas office parties everywhere, but I'd be happier doing what I'm doing this minute: reading *Freedom at Midnight* by Dominique LaPierre and Larry Collins and touching up my tan. There's no sense in rushing the season or despoiling the blessed peace.

Saturday, 23 December 1978

Whoever arrives home earliest puts fresh candles (getting scarce) in the holders and does the household chores requiring barq, such as laundry. Then, flashlights in hip pockets, we're ready for Lights Out. The guys are surprisingly dedicated about bustling back to do their share. Afterward, we play frenzied games of blackout Yahtzee, Rummy—Jenkintown or Michigan—Russian Bank, Risk, Flitch, or poker, if there's a crowd.

Although there are only three of us at the Libertys', the crew (or Merry Men, as Roddey's taken to calling them for Christmas) is right next door, and we feel like a solid front, block defenders at each other's beck and call. The crew is perfectly happy to perform slave labor so long as I cook for them.

The crew consists of Mike Montgomery, Barry Outcelt, and Ben Roche, all members of Skip's 205 team and, he says, as fine, capable, and hard-working a bunch as he's been privileged to work with.

I'm fond of them because they're ardent game players, boisterous baritones, and don't complain inordinately about what they can't change.

I'm grateful that I grew up in a whooping, competitive, game-playing, make-your-own-entertainment family. As a product of a televisionless childhood, I strongly recommend it to parents who wish to gird their children for the battle of life. So many people here have few resources, inner or outer. They're lost without TV or neighborhood bars, and I feel sorry for them.

Alcoholism is growing endemic, particularly among men

177

whose families have gone. Like skid row habitués, they work full time tracking down liquor at astronomical prices and beer at three dollars a can.

A lot of suckers like yours truly have also felt enough pressure to take up smoking again—at ten to fifteen dollars per black market carton of cigarettes. It's true that we have very little to spend our money on, but I didn't have to pick a vice that may prove fatal.

There are others as bad. Some of the men, desperate for company, entertainment, a release valve, have gambled their savings away. I wish we could declare a moratorium on poker and crap games. I hear more hard luck stories than Dear Abby, and I'm not built for that kind of strain. I break right down and cry with the losers.

At Liberty Hall we get our sweepstakes thrills by buying departees' groceries, sight unseen. Our special triumph this week was a half case of pumpkin pie filling, two quarts of molasses, a bottle of French wine (which I bestowed on Jackie and Donna as an early Christmas gift before some resident jackass could chugalug it), and three boxes of frosting mix—lemon, mocha, and chocolate. That little haul will go a long way toward stretching menus and feeding the skinny men who arrive on our doorstep vitamin-deficient and malnourished. Many BHI men, inexplicably, have lost tremendous amounts of weight—Skip, forty pounds—while we girls grow ever more chubby at the stress points.

I feed all comers what I can, and in turn they carry naft barrels, change the oil in the car, paint the courtyard walls, hang out laundry, and impart an added sense of security. (I find that role-playing doesn't work during revolutions.)

Today's rumor is that six thousand Russian guns are about to fall (or be placed) in Iranian hands. The Russian gun rumor is more or less ongoing; it crops up week in and week out.

The only Russians I *think* I've seen were two short, bulldog men wearing crumpled business suits and sporting aluminum fillings in their front teeth. They, the Russians, operate the single steel mill in Iran, about twenty miles outside Esfahan. They keep to their own ghetto—a twenty-five-story apartment house with no elevators. Skip has been there, and as Liberty would say, it's the God's truth, there are *no* elevators. The Russian steel mill is a direct trade for Iranian natural gas, which is piped north around the Caspian Sea.

178

If Iranian civilians handle guns the way they do other machinery, we'll all die in our tracks.

There must be something brewing. The martial guards are jittery as jumping beans. I drove across town to see if I could find Akhbar, Jackie, Donna, or the Ruhis, and the guards signaled me to the side of the road five times, examined me with monumental suspicion, and grudgingly sent me on my way. No more chrysanthemums in gun barrels.

> There was a Door to which I found no Key;
> There was a Veil past which I could not see. . . .

Christmas Day, 1978

My family called! Though it was ten and one-half hours earlier in Colorado, it was perfectly timed for Christmas morning in Iran.

We were all so excited I hardly remember a word we said. Whit and Dan, my brothers, are both home from ski racing and coaching; Sarah at twelve sounds twenty-three; and Gwen tried to explain how she has been investing my money. Mom and Dad see the hilarity in everything, and I love them for it.

The boys said an oil man from Denver had been killed by terrorists here. We haven't heard a word of it, and it was sad news. Otherwise our talk was all love and laughter.

I did some last-minute shopping in Jolfa's black market yesterday. A few of the stores are open, but mostly you walk the streets waiting for someone to hiss you into a corner and offer a deal. These people are born merchandisers and no paltry revolution will interrupt their sales pitches for long.

It was a balmy day with puffball clouds, and you could almost smell new hay and roses and pistachio blossoms. Things have been comparatively quiet (the world's washed out from Moharram), and old men and small babies were out basking in the sun.

I stumbled through traffic to Bonsi Pars in the vague hope of finding a corkscrew and some mushrooms, completely forgetting the place was blown up weeks ago—that and the Indian Restaurant downstairs and the Bank Melli next door. Swallowing my disappointment, I trudged over to Akhbar's and sidled in his back door to present him with his Christmas boogalamoon. He gave me such an incredible bargain on a Baluchi ("Time payments will be fine, my friend") I felt depraved, but he insisted, "Please, Robin, you are doing me a big favor to buy carpets now; American dollars will feed me and my family for many weeks. They and this fine boogalamoon!" I knew it hurt his pride to confess his poverty, so when he pressed pastries and pistachios and other delicacies into my unwilling arms I tried to accept them graciously. "An American Merry Christmas to my good friend," he said warmly with tears in his eyes. I would have kissed him if it wouldn't have made him lose so darned much foolish face.

Christmas dinner is set for four o'clock, and there'll be sixteen of us; at least, that was the count at twelve o'clock high. By this afternoon our numbers may be legion. To be safe, I cooked *four* airlifted, self-basting Butterball turkeys over the past two days. It isn't only the growing guest list, it's the ruthless tyranny of the barq that worries me, and I wanted to be prepared for any emergency. Prestuffed and prebaked, those turkeys can be heated over a can of Sterno or an open spit on a courtyard fire. I also baked, ahead of time, pecan pies made with walnuts and my precious, hoarded "Creesco," and I found cornstarch and made custard and key lime pies. One of Skip's crew men, John Alper, is married to a jolly Mexican lady who concocts mouth-watering enchiladas and burritos—she's promised quantities of both. In lieu of candied yams we'll have rice. And of course saebsi plus assorted canned vegetables which I've seasoned seductively.

Under my stern direction the boys have decorated Liberty Hall so it looks like a cross between a Tijuana strip joint and an Atlantic City souvenir stand. It isn't Christmas in Colorado, but it's gala in a garish way.

Skip's Christmas present to me was a collection of perfectly exquisite miniatures, the kind fastidiously painted with an eyelash or a lone camel's hair. I gave him the same thing I gave Mother, an exquisite Pahlavi coin on a heavy gold chain. Like all the Shah's likenesses, this one is en route to oblivion, but since it is solid gold and no longer minted, it should grow in value and interest. (I feel inordinately sad speaking of old Fred as though he were already out to pasture. But at least pasture beats the hangman's noose.)

I gave Roddey my used, partial set of Dickens, and he

180

presented me with half a case of refried beans, proudly purchased at a neighboring garage sale.

I am delighted to announce that the rooftop howling, which I ignored with the help of an iron will and double rubber ear plugs, suddenly ceased. A most thoughtful and considerate Christmas gift from our unheavenly hosts. To further enhance this newfound peace on earth, last night, Christmas Eve, the barq stayed on for the first time in thirty-seven days. Thank you, electrical workers of Iran!

Skip and Roddey, Mike, Barry, Ben, and I cozily watched the *Carpenter's Christmas Show* and Dean Martin's *Christmas in California*, both filmed, I think, in 1965. Though they were old and taped and corny, they were immensely cheerful.

The evening ended on a high note with a movie called *The Last Holiday*, which NIRT must have thought either prophetic or seasonable. It was neither. The plot featured a dying man who took all his money out of the bank to have a final fling before he croaked.

Iranian TV has been back with us since December 17, presenting enthralling programs such as natural history shorts about the duckbilled platypus. These nature pieces were initiated at Ramazan, as they are considered soothing and nonviolent. If it wasn't for our critical state, they'd be wholly soporific. In utter desperation, the guys hang on the platypus's every move, eager for whatever twist the plot may bring. We also view such ancient serials as *The Courtship of Eddie's Father* and Pink Panther cartoons. No more *Gunsmoke* or *Rawhide*. Too incendiary.

The rumor mill, ignoring Christmas, grinds on. Today's grist:

1. The Russian guns have turned up again, this time distributed to howling mobs for attack January 1.

2. David Burdick, my fine fellow-novelist who is a BHI supervisor, says DOD, will not, repeat not, let us leave because of their military and fiscal dependence on us; if they were to replace us with U.S. Air Force or other military personnel the Russians would throw a terrible fit of temper.

3. Last rumor of the day: It's said part of the reason for comparative quiet is that Khomeini's French visa expired December 16 and the French insisted if more mayhem ensued from his communiqués they would not renew it. There could

181

be some truth to this. He was asked to leave Iraq as a rare gesture of support for the Shah, and maybe the man is running out of sanctuaries.

We Americans may be in the same soup. The number of us in Iran, depending on who's counting or whom you talk to, was formerly between 41,000 and 68,000. There are now fewer than 20,000 present and accounted for. The Germans, Japanese, and Turks are leaving like bats from a clanging belfry. Most company dependents have fled Esfahan; Grumman departed in a heaving body after its offices were blown sky-high; Thor Thyssen, G.E., and B.O.C. have cleared out lock, stock, and barrel. Each company asks a few hard-core volunteers to stay behind to act as "caretakers." These last hangers-on must be the loneliest men in the world. If I could find them, I'd conscript them all for Christmas dinner.

In Esfahan, there's almost no one here but us BHI chickens.

Iranian schools are now closed for good. The university students went back to classes for one day and promptly erupted like Vesuvius. Rose Fazio says many of these students are Marxists formerly under the calloused thumbs of Savak and now popping up everywhere like berserk tiddlywinks.

The American schools are done for too. Rose will be here for Christmas dinner but soon gone from Iran. Though the students kept being shifted to safer locations, they were still moving targets, and there's been no school for weeks, with no sign they'll be able to reopen.

The sun is a blazing orb, a gift from the Magi. I am going to bask in its warmth right through the afternoon, storing up BTUs like a solar collector. The Christmas wassailers aren't due to arrive for a few hours, and if they're serious about wassailing, I hope they've procured their own glög, glüb, mulled cider, and other fixings. I'll cook and serve, but I won't brew bathtub vodka.

If someone had told me a year ago that a bottle of black-market wine would be worth its weight in twenty-four carat gold, and the Shah's coinage and future not worth a plugged nickel, I'd have accused him of raving lunacy. Sure, the marketplace is flooded with crisp new thousand-rial notes some enterprising bureaucrat has been printing in his basement, but we get the impression the government treasury has been inundated with counterfeiters and ransacked by departing bigwigs. The thousand-rial notes are virtually valueless and Akhbar warned me to unload mine fast. I did, on the spot.

After the TV expired last night, the crew and I sat there and sang every Christmas carol we ever knew. Since my family has caroled every Christmas for years, my repertoire is, if I do say so, commendable. I know all verses of more than thirty carols and am undeterred by the fact that my incurable monotone drags everyone into hideous disharmony beside me. Franny—my grandmother Whitcomb—was a concert pianist. She as slaved over my vocal cords for years, certain that no direct descendant of hers could be so tone-deaf. Dear Franny. I miss her at Christmas.

We're having eggnog. I found cream.

Christmas Night, 1978

Christmas dinner for twenty-two was jolly, tearful, sober, excessive, wonderful, warm, and enough to fill the breach for quite a time.

> We are no other than a moving row
> Of magic shadow-shapes that come and go . . .

But Christmas with gunfire, I find, lacks the proper spirit.

Tuesday, 26 December 1978

Today was quite a denouement. I spent hours trying to call Teheran and was boiling mad, once again, at our phone system, which operates beautifully between here and Aspen, Colorado, and abysmally between here and Shiraz. Naturally Americans advised on communications systems, and of course the Iranians went right ahead and did things their way, generously employing string. They cut costs, corners, and every wire in sight.

I use the phone constantly in the duties of my office, and our switchboard is unmanned and undermined by subversive Iranian operators. The trick is to give you a wrong extension or, if you should happen upon the correct one, to cut you right off. In addition, you may find yourself firmly embroiled in a toll call to someplace in Kenya. (They have crossed wires not only in Esfahan but also all over the Mideast.)

When Mother called me the first time, she was put in touch with an Iranian who chatted gaily on and on, in Farsi. After about twenty-dollars' worth, it dawned on Mother the man had no intention of connecting her with anyone else. He simply wanted to hear the sound of her warm voice.

Iranian voices are anything but warm. "Shrill" is the term I believe I seek: They think they must caterwaul to be heard. If an Iranian receives a call in my office, I immediately place both him and the phone outside the window, claiming over-crowding—not totally untrue.

Today, quite unwittingly, I reached both Yazd and Rasht. I had nothing to say to either of them. Rasht is a town on the Caspian Sea, and for reasons unknown to me, the Rashtis are the Iranian Polacks, the butt of every idiotic joke.

The only thing possibly as misunderstood or as unused as the telephone is the bath.

Though many Iranians use the imposing public baths, or have completely equipped tub-showers of their own, bathing is seldom more than the Saturday night variety. Lack of it can be so distracting in a helicopter that the American instructor pilots are expected to, and do, bump a student from a flight if he smells like a goat. Studies have shown that in close quarters—say a cockpit—highly offensive odors cut pilot efficiency by as much as thirty percent.

Over at Telemedia they keep a supply of Pif Paf (the omnipresent Iranian bug spray) and air deodorant (jasmine) on hand, and before visiting V.I.P.'s arrive, they ceremoniously spray not only the students but the air around them. The soldiers think this is an American social ritual, like the cocktail party, and cheerfully lift their arms.

Wednesday, 27 December 1978

We located the Liberty landlord, who called an electrician, who miraculously appeared in the pouring rain to repair our hall light. He arrived this afternoon soaked from head to toe, rolling a fifty-gallon barrel through our courtyard. He dumped water from the barrel all over the front hall, stood it in its own puddle, took off his shoes, and climbed aboard. The socket was defective, which was why we called him in the first place, and Roddey and I, forgetting all my Farsi, gesticulated wildly trying to direct his attention to the circuit breaker. Pointedly ignoring us, he first smashed the light bulb with his needle-nose pliers, then jammed them into the socket to remove the remains, and finally poked and prodded around repairing the fixture. Roddey kept murmuring, "My word." Skip moaned, "Good God." And I retired to the kitchen for a moment of silent prayer. I prayed either for a stroke of luck or, barring that, for the man's swift and painless demise.

After a while the bizarre electrician simply finished up, rolled the barrel outside, and ambled off.

Mr. Amiri, owner of the largest appliance store in town, was not so fortunate, he was blown to bits. He'd received many phone calls and venomous messages telling him to stop selling to xaerigi. His children came running out, cried, "Dynamite in the bedroom!" and the poor soul went to investigate. When I rushed to the Ruhis to look into the story, they told me he was murdered because he was Savak. Wouldn't you know I'd grow unreasonably fond of a bland-faced, cheerful secret policeman? Put me at a party of hundreds with just one gangster or con-man, and I'll single him right out for an evening's conversation.

I don't believe I've said how much of a constant both gunfire and explosives are in our lives, like Muzak in an elevator. We are so accustomed to them that when I say it's "quiet"—well, all things are comparative. What bothers me is that soldiers seem to fire without particular reason or plan, often without provocation. And another thing: None of us understands the Shah's erratic behavior, or that of his armed forces. He seems to use his soldiery when he should not, and to hold them in abeyance when they're needed. I'd swear the man is cracking up.

Meanwhile, the Khomeini forces have regained their old vigor, and the comparative peace ended with a resounding crash. BHI has once more evacuated its Teheran employees from their work sites. I have never heard where they go, probably straight to the nearest bar.

Bodies in the streets further attest to the fact that everyone is serious and not just playing with blanks. I will never become inured to the sight.

185

Our personal concerns still center on food. The newest scare is that there's a real shortage on the way. Robert R. Williams, still counting his losses, personally gave us his word on it. I like his style, and I'm very glad he's here. I don't *think* Bell will let us starve. Isn't that against the Geneva Convention or something?

The Liberty ménage is stockpiled for any emergency. We have 102 cans of Campbell's Chicken Noodle-O's and Tomato soup, one case of Parmesan cheese, purchased from an Italian girl who knows Rose Fazio and is married to an Iranian (and has apparently taken up saebsi in lieu of pasta), and more canned pumpkin given us by a fleeing pilot. I loathe chicken noodle soup.

Americans horde with more hell-bent determination than any Iranian, and with far less excuse. As it's no longer safe for us to hog the food or naft lines, we are forced into the bustling black market, where we pay premium prices. I don't blame people for overcharging us. They have plenty of reason to believe we're richer than Croesus after our conspicuous consuming these past years.

Uncle Rog on consumers and revolution: "According to Davies, revolution requires continued expectation of being able to satisfy basic needs, which in turn can come only after periods of economic improvement and the development of a *pattern* of expectation."

And I thought revolutions were fought for bread by hungry, howling masses!

We are back to our nightly blackout follies and I, Jane Austen, write by candlelight once more. I rather like it, as it makes me feel mysterious and romantic.

Thursday, 28 December 1978

Yesterday all demonstrators were cordoned off in individual areas—divide and conquer—and by God! . . . every marcher had a *permit*. There is an entire army of civil servants in this land, living in great labyrinths like Crete and the Pentagon, and they appear in the daylight once a year—to pick up carload supplies of fresh paper. They have been trained in the latest bureaucratic entanglements by the United States Departments of Commerce, Interior, and Agriculture. Under

186

our aegis they proudly practice the Peter Principle, perfecting the art of making one job suffice for six or seven people.

Case in point: When I bought Jack Jyanne, it was a simple transaction, for cash. I first visited a man to whom I was directed by several dozen minor lackeys. He used (it's the God's truth) a Mickey Mouse calculator. When he had finished his high-powered addition, I trotted over to the local gendarmerie station to obtain a police card (required) and after that to the government insurance offices for state accident insurance (required), then back to Hakim Nezami to the license plate bureau to pay plate taxes, and thence to the American Consulate to iron out a few minor difficulties and be quizzed as to whether or not I was buying this vehicle while in full control of my faculties.

I have omitted some details and technicalities: The entire process required more than a day's time.

I must watch myself. When uppity little clerks set me to signing batches of papers, I write "Susan B. Anthony" or "Amelia Bloomer" or "Louisa May Alcott" in the space marked "Signature"; well, it doesn't say *whose*. Given just one humorless stickler, this could lead to a prison rap on a charge of forgery. Some days, along with Iran, I simply lose control. I keep forgetting I'm a guest in their country.

There is very little benzine available. Lines are literally miles long and a full avenue wide. There was talk of gas rationing, with accompanying ration cards, but even the seasoned paper pushers of Iran balked at so vast a challenge in the current chaos.

Now how in the devil are we going to function without benzine? What will we do without gas for our cars, without taxi or bus service? It's the first time I've visualized us staggering to a complete stop, paralyzed, immobilized.

Already there's no garbage pickup in Teheran. Next the rats. Then the piper—and the plague.

And what about the millions of dollars worth of Bell helicopters? They won't exactly fall to pieces, but there's ultimate deterioration from just plain sitting around. The kind of thing I keep warning my friends about.

Because of no fuel or another blue funk, Teheran's Mehrabad Airport closed again yesterday. Everyone is trapped here three times a week, but I'm never sure on what days.

Friday, 29 December 1978

Riots break out like fresh pox, and when the guards rush to one fire or roadblock, the perpetrators have moved on to another, keeping the guards on the run and breathless as debutantes. A very effective form of guerrilla warfare, and I wonder whom they're using for instructors. (And do they wear black-and-white-checked *kefiyahs*?)

Another classy new gimmick is blowing up or deflating auto tires, causing vehicles to bog down and create enormous traffic jams. Every major city is suffering a gigantic vehicular hotfoot.

Mobs helped immobilize us over the weekend. Jack Jyanne had no gas for his gullet. So we clung to our chimney pots and watched a sea of people lap at our shores, great swells of black-clad marchers.

Esfahan is sunny and springlike, and between demonstrations we hear the *hoopoes* calling and the sound of minor scuffling only a wall's-width away. It's like having a bear snuffling around outside your tent.

When I speak of balmy weather, I refer of course to midday. One reason we sunbathe is to store body heat for the nighttime cold. We've been chilled to the marrow for two months, though I'm ashamed to complain when Teheran is frigid and snowbound.

Uncle Roger: "History has demonstrated that revolutions are not pieces of historical machinery. . . . What is needed is a mass of bitter discontent enabling the revolutionary party or group to gain a mass following. . . . Then the violent seizure of power is ripe to take place. . . ."

We can *watch* the discontent of the masses feeding on itself. Although the people are the ones who are striking, and producing the shortages, the shortages then serve in turn to breed more bitterness and discontent. And where it stops nobody knows.

Bread and flour, with their ironic revolutionary connotations, are now nearly nonexistent. The mills have no fuel to grind the flour, nor are there trucks running to transport flour *or* finished bread. Ship loads of flour are docked on the Persian Gulf with no deckhands to unload them.

188

I called ER to make certain there were no secret benzine supplies tucked away, and they didn't mince words: All the stations will soon be closed indefinitely, it's eight miles from here to Havan-e-Ruz, and we might as well be commuting to Istanbul. We're to stand by for instructions.

GOI had a novel answer to consumer education regarding benzine outages. They graciously invited the Iranian people to visit the oil reserve tanks hundreds of miles out in the country to see for themselves that there is *no oil*, and that this is not a government plot to deprive the citizenry. The problem with this divinely inspired scheme is that no one has gas or oil to drive out to the countryside to peer inside the oil tanks to make certain they are indeed empty. I wonder if they've put Shahnaz in charge of public relations?

At news of impending station closings, the boys reluctantly decided to rise at four-thirty in the morning to hit the first curfew lift and be at the head of somebody's gas line. They tried today, but automobiles are no longer allowed at the stations—only people on foot carrying gas cans (which are heavy enough, empty, to cave in a sound rib cage). This is a primitive but very effective form of gas rationing—you may have as much as you can carry.

Maybe we'll all end by eating, sleeping, giving birth, and dropping dead in a lineup. People are so adaptive it's depressing.

I am more suspicious than ever of the local Pepsi-Cola; it's the only thing that hasn't been rationed or in short supply. The Pepsi plant is downtown, across the street from that great old heartbeat of BHI—ER. Iran Pepsi turns out a syrupy-sweet product that's barely potable, but Americans adapt to that too, and we swill it down as if it were going out of style. We do not, however, drink more than half a bottle at a time. The bottle bottoms are alive with dregs, insects, and little surprises, like a Cracker Jack box. Three sips are as good as a mile, and most of us don't allow ourselves to go further.

Tonight's NIRT informed us everything is peaceful—amid a barrage of explosions and fire fighting down our kutche. I'll say this for NIRT, their Christmases go on forever. Last night it was *Christmas With Donny and Marie*. Tonight, *Christmas in Germany*. Tomorrow the world?

The night sky is as full of sound as the kutche. And I don't mean howling. Here on The Flats we're surrounded by air bases: Khatemi, the Iranian Air Force base; Forudaghe Esfahan for domestic flights; and the Crown Prince Reza Pahlavi Army Helicopter Base. There are no domestic flights due till tomorrow, haven't been for days, but tonight someone has been launching Chinooks (those immense, double-rotored troop carriers), 205s, 206s, 214s and Cobras on every side.

Helicopters, which I persist in thinking of as a force for human good, have become deadly weapons. Along with street troops, they move in on helpless people and fire away, on the premise that assemblage in groups of three or more is illegal (it is, but my God!); and we're the ones teaching the vicious brutes to fly. When I hear a helicopter these days I know it's army-fueled, and my first instinct is to run for the basement; since there isn't one, if it's daylight I sit stock-still in the courtyard in my bikini hoping to draw admiring glances instead of fire.

Tomorrow a special Pan Am charter is due to fly in and fly out, carrying good friends of mine away. Rose Fazio and Pat Powell and John Gannon are leaving. I've bid them goodbye, but only for a while.

Saturday, 30 December 1978

This morning, post-Islamic Sabbath, was a grim and terrible day. Any mobs I have described before were as decorous as a tea-pouring compared to 195,000 people on the move, a horde so vast they darkened every horizon. They moved through The Flats, their cries of "Allah Akhbar" and "Death to the Shah" drowning out all remembrance of things past; they blocked the west gate of the base so that even the army couldn't budge and finally surged north to the river. All of us waited a hushed and interminable interval, then rushed back to our homes expecting everything to be trampled flat.

There stood Fort Liberty, unscathed!

I always wonder how these mobs get under way. Does someone on a corner crook a finger and whisper, "Pssst, let's get a few people together for a little stroll," and then does it mushroom from there?

I suppose it's not impossible, as Moslems seem to have highly collective personalities. They congregate at the drop of a pin, and I have seldom seen an Iranian worship or practice

190

any sort of rite alone. Like other Moslems, Shi'ites fling themselves to the ground wherever they may be—in the street, the bazaars, the bus—to face Mecca at the call of the mechanized muezzins, but when they go to their mosques or about their business they go in groups and gaggles and great congregations. One of the worst insults in Iran is to say, "Go be by yourself."

Some poor American slob was inadvertently swallowed up in today's mob. He was attired in a lurid luau shirt and other ill-advised American mufti and was terribly mauled; a few kindly Iranians snatched him up, flung him into the back of a vehicle, and somehow spirited him away. These Persian Samaritans turn up everywhere: We hear endless stories about the man who saved a mechanic, another who rescued a pilot, always with the whispered asides that "I have a son at Penn State, agha. Run fast, and Allah be with you," or "My brother is a dentist in St. Louis, go with Allah, sir," or "We do not wish to hurt you, agha, it is only your country we dislike." So many Iranians have friendly ties abroad, and so many of them have been literal lifesavers.

It appears we are likely to be evacuated very soon. At the Security meeting this morning we were told that we'll be flown to a MAC base in Spain; a skeleton crew will remain behind to safeguard (hah!) the Bell aircraft. No women to stay, naturally. Just once before I die I'm going to be a skeleton on a crew!

I suppose I must face up to a final faroushing, for there are many items still to go. Liberty will never get back here, and we'll be responsible for selling everything he owns. Oh Liberty, the *sacrifice*!

Our evac instructions are:

1. Have two small bags packed at all times.

2. Have complete inventories and color photos of everything you must leave behind.

3. Carry your passport and residence permit with you at all times.

4. Be ready to go at a moment's notice.

Now that the time has come, it's as unnerving as a barn burning. I gather this is the feeling of refugees anywhere, anytime in history. A little hollow in the stomach. On the other hand, a shortage-ridden, trench-type existence grows exhausting and soon our whole *raison d'être* will cease. We are consumed more and more with mere survival.

All the same, I don't want my family to think we're at the mercy of ravening beasts. It's just that these people are having their revolution and they want to be left alone with it.

Our evacuation has elicited howls to put Iranians to shame. For with it has come no word that we are to be RIF-ed. BHI is operated along army lines, in part because we're (theoretically) training the Iranian Army. And, since the vernacular is the same, we thus have "RIF"—Reduction In Force—which means, in essence, that BHI asks *you* to leave and is therefore responsible for such items as separation and termination pay and prorated bonuses that are not due the employee when he voluntarily terminates himself—quits.

The difference between RIF-ing and termination means millions of dollars to both BHI and its departing serfs. It's hard to say whom to feel sorriest for.

While sweating out our financial fates, we have been instructed to fill every possible container with water and to lay hands on all possible candles. Water and electrical power stations are run by diesel fuel, and this is next on the "dry-up" list.

There's still no gas, and most of the stations are closed, and yet people line up for miles. It's my theory that it's something to do. Also a valid excuse for gathering, since it's still unlawful to "assemble." I don't believe it's yet dawned on the army that they'd better break up the gas lines. A man could stand out there and deliver the Gettysburg Address, the Preamble to the Constitution, and the United Nations charter to a ready-made and eager forum. Occasionally someone also gets five litres of benzine. But that seems incidental.

Liberty just called. They've been in Bangkok since December 13, having a glorious vacation only slightly marred by the fact he's not allowed back into Iran. He's tried every tactic. Thank heaven they shipped Kid, their dog, home in November. Positively no pets permitted on evacuation aircraft, say our instructions. Clint Redosovitch told me with tears in his eyes that he'll shoot his cats himself before leaving them to the mercy of Korean cooks. When it comes to pets, Americans are not normal.

We are now at the mercy of the bus drivers.

The first blow is that we'll have to stand, highly visible, waiting at the bus stops, which doesn't jell with the old low profile. Next, there's the matter of the buses themselves. . . .

We have forty-seven buses in the Crown Prince Reza Pahlavi fleet. Americans are not allowed to drive them because "you Americans break everything you touch"—a criticism that can only be attributable to the fahlawi transport officers. Most of these buses are brand-new or very late models. Of the forty-seven, no more than sixteen run at any given time, and not one will start with the flick of a key. All must be jumped with cables or *agha*-pushed by soldiers and drivers.

There are eight American employee bus routes and approximately the same number for soldiers living off base. Any further demands on buses and drivers, such as ferrying evacuees to Khatemi, mean that regular routes must be canceled.

The drivers are civilian employees hired by the army, poorly paid, not permitted the luxury of resignation, and uniformly craving revenge. Heaped on their many other indignities is the topper that any driver guilty of an error in judgment, like a traffic violation (oh wow!), is thrown straight into jail. There he stays while his riders wait for him to be sprung. With this kind of incentive, no wonder your average bus driver is not what you'd call addicted to duty.

I know much about bus drivers and their piteous lot through my long-standing friendship with Hamid Mahdi, who drives the Char Bagh route where I lived before I bought Jack Jyanne. Hamid and I conducted a running dialogue for months and he delightedly presented me with candy and fruit (and still does) while I in turn tendered small gifts for his family. When Hamid is not on duty he comes to my office to practice his meagre English and to assure me I will be under his careful scrutiny and close protection to the end. I am giving Hamid my Sony tape deck and radio as a going-away present.

Skip and Roddey are getting plastered on Beefeater gin, a grand and glorious Christmas gift from Rose. I keep telling them not to be precipitate, we may need it later. They act like they're going to be shot at dawn. We also have a full bottle of Grand Marnier, which I have hidden away for emergencies. We may be here longer than we think, and we may need it in the trenches.

193

Sunday, 31 December 1978

The God's truth is that we *all* got boiled last night. The resumption of rooftop howling, thunderous explosions, heavy gunfire, and a larger than usual assortment of unidentifiable noises was too much even for me.

It was our good buddy Mike Montgomery, in his luau shirt, who got swept up in Saturday's mob, beaten senseless, and blessedly rescued by unknown Iranian saviors. He's still battered, and we're providing what T.L.C. we can. I trashed the Hawaiian shirt.

I've worked like a one-armed paperhanger getting ready for the giant exodus beginning January 4. Bell has chartered two Pan American planes for the fourth and fifth, 707s holding 178 passengers each, and is dickering desperately for more. Before departure, in addition to time-consuming separation procedures, each employee's file must be copied, résumés and letters of recommendation written, weeping men and women soothed, and some sort of equanimity maintained. I spend far too much time arbitrating petty quarrels between Iranians and Americans over bills. There are days I feel like a cross between Cyrus Vance and Dr. Joyce Brothers.

Everyone is still being encouraged to leave—not the same as RIF-ed, you understand. To this end, Skip and Roddey and Jim, at BHI direction, drove all over the city today using precious gas and coping with ill-humored martial guards just to ask each employee if he/she wished to terminate and sign up for takeoff: the kind of inefficient, last-minute, poorly planned corporative bilge I abhor.

BHI, like mothers everywhere, bears the brunt of our short tempers. The beldame corporate structure is maligned, bad-mouthed, and beaten about her head and shoulders. About the politest thing I hear is that this is a company without morals, deliberately trying to aggravate everyone in the hopeful expectation they'll terminate instead of waiting to be RIF-ed. As Ed Thorpe puts it, "Play ball with Bell and they'll stick the bat up your ass." Tch, tch. Collective thought and group mentality sink lower by the day. Reminds me of the Iranians.

Few of us see our paychecks, which are now simply telexed to the States while in the background the rial sinks lower than a snake's belly. We have little to buy, but barter is running smoothly, thank you. "I'll trade you one *Captain Marvel* for two cans of Chicken Noodle-O's."

All nonessential personnel, that is, *women*, were sent home early today. I know Iran is in flames and I carp and cavil about women's rights, but I just hate being termed nonessential. It batters my ego and it burns me up. The upshot was that Karen Owens and I *did not* budge. I had piles of work to do, far more than any of the men, so I hung in there, toiled like vengeful fury until four-thirty, then stomped out with the guys, red-faced and incensed. The men, those highly essential personnel, killed the day drinking coffee.

Today's BHI bulletin closes out the year thus:

> BHI is unable to assist individuals in obtaining food and fuel.

> Until the present shortage of fuel is alleviated it is impractical to arrange departures of employees.

> By best estimates, the present shortage of naft, heating and automotive fuel will continue indefinitely.

> We must anticipate more severe food shortages.

Upon receipt of the above supportive memorandum, I, frankly, grew mildly miffed at BHI's lack of warmhearted, back-patting support. I may end by writing Robert R. Williams, president, a firmly worded letter of my own.

We canceled the New Year's party at the office, as it would only have meant singing "Auld Lang Syne" and hanging all over each other bawling like motherless calves.

Protests grow more anti-Western all the time, and American casualties become more of a possibility. Sometimes we also see anti-Russian slogans, but few of us can read the Russian or Arabic alphabets, so it's difficult to measure the quality of their vitriol. We always feel it's the Americans who bear the brunt. And that we must have done an awful lot that was wrong to have Iran so hopping mad at us.

Our most ambivalent means of home defense is the custom-made supply of personally souped-up M-80s left behind by Liberty. In a moment of madness, he painstakingly glued BB's, one by one, to these firecrackers, then dipped them in wax. I suppose it's fitting that a man named Liberty should be Ye Olde Armaments Maker. Since the things explode in a 360 degree arc, merely lighting one is an invitation to havoc. You have to leap out of the path of fire like a rodeo clown, and even then someone could lose an eye. Their greatest value is probably as scare tactics. I hid under the bed while the boys threw one into the kutche, and the noise was pretty awesome. When the martial guards arrived at our door, we told them we'd been attacked.

Our further feeble armament consists of one bow and one arrow, plus a ball bearing wrist rocket. Not exactly equipped like your First Army, Third Battalion, Boogalamoon Division. We couldn't defend our own courtyard. The boys conduct constant strategy sessions, although after covering our escape route for the thirty-seventh time, there isn't much to discuss. So they turn on me. They turn on me, and they nag and natter about how I, a puny woman, will slow their retreat and mess up their rearguard action. I of course plan to stand and fight. The guys will all flee and survive.

Even tongue-in-cheek talk of armed combat makes me feel bizarre. Deep down I have this rooted conviction that no one would ever hurt little *me*. Thus spake Joan of Arc, Mary, Queen of Scots, and Marie Antoinette.

Since the barq went off for two hours this morning, we are hoping that—as at Christmas—we may have some extra light tonight.

We are hoarding the one-third tank of benzine in Liberty's car. More accurately, *I* am the one who would kill to keep it. Skip asks caustically, "Planning to escape by car, Robinson?" Roddey adds, "I'll be happy to work out your AAA itinerary. Perhaps a leisurely three-week drive westward into the setting sun, destination Baghdad?"

They look at me as if I am addled, and of course I am. Face facts, girl. If we are not airlifted out of here under the feeble auspices and fragile good will of the teetering Iranian government, we ain't leaving.

We have barq! It is 8:45 P.M., and the world is alight, the juices still flowing. Happy New Year from the barq boys of Iran! To compound our joy and add to the festivities, there's even a rumored movie schedule for TV: *Gidget Goes Somewhere*. It's the little things that tug at our heartstrings.

I am going to abandon the journal, try to work up a block party, and see if we can't do something about escorting in the new year. Without help from us, it may disintegrate in a flash of black powder before it even gets under way.

BOOK V

Monday, 1 January 1979

Like small children who couldn't stay awake for the big
moment, we all fell asleep at eleven o'clock and missed the
dawning of 1979. Tension exacts its toll, and everyone is
ready for bed at 7:00 P.M. nightly.

We are suddenly very cautious about opening doors—
house, courtyard, or car. Locks and padlocks proliferate.
With so many street vendors and garage sale customers, it's a
tricky business. At Fort Liberty we poke a wary head and
weather eye over the wall before sliding back our bolts. And
never admit anyone after dark.

Three friends, Ken Manke, Bob Harris, and Bert Berland,
felt secure enough to answer the door to what turned out to
be *twenty* instead of the two visible Iranian front men. The
whooping invaders gathered together all their possessions and
held a communal bonfire, burned everything they owned right
down to the razor blades. The guys didn't murmur a protest.
They knew they were outsmarted and outnumbered. But it
was another warning to the rest of us.

According to BHI's solemn promise, we'll be reimbursed
for anything destroyed by fire, explosives, or "civil unrest."

Police protection is as laughably impractical as hiring a hit man. The police have their own problems. Four of them were hanged in Mashad last night—by the citizenry. Heretofore no one has defied authority to the point of stringing it up.

It seems to me it's time for a forward-thinking Savaker to get out of town. Everyone (except me, always the last to know) seems to have fingered these so-called secret police, and terrible retribution awaits them.

There *is* one Skinny Tie I'd like to get my hands on, a nasty little number with a cast in his eye and the Marquis de Sade among his progenitors. It's been more than a year, but I could still spot that baby like a brother. . . .

One exquisite September day back in '77, Frank Light and I were bicycling around town doing our Thursday morning shopping and enjoying the parks when we decided to stop off at the Iran Tour Hotel, a favorite American watering hole, for some iced chie. There were about forty Telemedia employees in the lounge and lobby, including friends talking with a British travel agent from Singapore who was selling cut-rate tickets in and out of Bangkok—where one can buy the cheapest airline tickets in the world. We were interested in a trip to Sri Lanka, so we took our places at the end of the line to see what the man was offering. An hour passed pleasantly as we chatted with everyone, and then it was our turn, and there was just one remaining couple behind us.

Suddenly, like a plague of grasshoppers, Savakers were crawling everywhere. (If anyone is interested, it's time I mentioned that Savak is a contraction of Farsi words meaning "security and information organization." If this sounds like Travelers' Aid, you're not getting the idea.)

Frank and I were shoved unceremoniously into a corner, and the Ties began frisking the last couple, Cast-in-the-Eye taking particular time and care with the girl. When it was our turn, I refused to let the pervert touch me. Frank was close to apoplexy, and I was hopping mad. When the Ties attempted to search my purse, we engaged in a ridiculously childish tug-of-war, snatching the thing back and forth. Just as it appeared I might be winning, the other couple was released, and Frank and I were placed under house (hotel?) arrest.

Through all of this the pathetic little British travel agent kept scrambling about the lobby gathering up his shabby underwear as fast as the Ties opened his suitcases and flung it out. When they began to hit him, the nasty Marquis in the lead, I set up a powerful wail. The sight of blood doesn't make me turn a hair, but I can't abide bullying. Finally the Ties pushed furniture together to make a sort of barrier and shoved the battered agent and us two harried tourists behind it. I was sure we were all going to hit the floor and engage in an Edward G. Robinson shoot-out with the hotel employees.

It never came to that. Intrepid Telemedia friends began drifting over to see what the hell was happening and then started passing me beers over the barricades to calm my nerves. One beer followed on the foam of another, and I, with my known incapacity for the grape or hops, grew increasingly disorderly and insulted all the Ties (there were at least eight of them) in loud, strident, and imperfect Farsi. I must have sounded like a cross between a Peaks Island foghorn and a Smackover hog caller. Eventually, more embattled than I, the Ties implored BHI to locate our passports so they could get the Madwoman of Chaillot off their backs.

Foreign passports are placed in the safekeeping of Persian officialdom, thus assuring that all xaerigi are trapped in the country indefinitely. As this was the weekend, BHI security officers were hastily summoned from home to the rescue. They worked like charladies, searching hours among scattered police offices and dirty files, having a dreadful time because Iranian bureaucrats use the Rosetta stone filing system. Eventually they located my passport but couldn't find Frank's. By now we had been on the Ties' hands almost ten hours, and I had scarcely shut up one minute of the entire time. I was livid that we'd been detained for no cause; Frank longed to snatch my untrammeled tongue out by the roots; and the Savak bitterly regretted the hour we had all met. At ten o'clock that night, they hastily released us on a BHI official's signature, and Frank and I staggered home on our bicycles in the dark, me roaring drunk and still complaining like a fishwife about those snakes in the double-breasted suits —particularly the slimy number with the tic in the eye.

Frank always felt the experience aged him. But it's my feeling that Savak, like most of macho Iran, will back right off when faced by an honest-to-God, spitting mad, self-righteous American female. Of course I always knew I had the American flag, Ambassador Sullivan, the Bill of Rights, the Ford Motor Company, and the Marine Corps right behind me. I wonder how ballsy I'd have been in a dank, underground tomb with Tic-in-the-Eye giving me the weekly special—say a Savak pedicure.

It's a mystery to me that, with all Jimmy Carter's talk of human rights, I've never heard him, or Andy Young either, say one word about the Shah of Iran's secret police. They've had plenty to say about those countries not supplying us with oil or gas. Why the partiality? When I go home I'm going to blab all over the place and then buy me an electric golf cart and never use gas again.

It's not only Savak who'd better begin taking it on the lam. . . . Every man on base is pressuring the few remaining wives to leave. Those who continue to hang on won't leave without their husbands, and the husbands feel the wives will be liabilities if it comes to a running gun fight. The men are Vietnam veterans, most of them, who feel fairly secure about taking care of themselves—but not a wife, certainly not small children. I play devil's advocate for both sides, a constant help and inspiration.

Fred seems to be the only one who senses his hour has come. NIRT announces that he's going abroad shortly for medical treatment. In view of these hospitals, this is among the most valid excuses a man could have for fleeing. People in the streets may pooh-pooh and snort all they wish, but I honestly believe he *is* sick. His performance has been that of a man reduced to a tottering shambles. Well, thank heaven he isn't going to hang around Niavaran Palace munching watermelon seeds and his thumbnails.

He is an enigmatic, complicated, arrogant, often kindly king, this Shah of Iran. During my time in his country, I have watched him play the harsh, disciplinary father figure—and then turn right around and figuratively ask his subjects for a big kiss and a hug. May he go in peace. He is among the last of the autocrats, and I don't believe we will see the return of the Shah or his kind again.

Fred has meanwhile appointed another prime minister, his fifth in six months. The man is named Bakhtiar and is said to be a twenty-year enemy of the Shah's who has served much time in many of his prisons; he has a kindly face.

The weather continues an enemy of the people. Determined not to be outflanked, I batiked in the chill air, and then Skip and Roddey and I washed out the fountain pool, built a fire, and scalded trash cans so we can fill them with emergency water supplies for cooking and washing. There is one fifty-five-gallon drum of naft remaining, and tonight we were finally driven to light the heater, as the house was dank as a tomb. Once the cold permeates these fortress walls, they *stay* cold. NIRT tells us our New Year's Eve was the chilliest since 1904. I'd guess it was about twenty-five below, myself.

November's torrential rains flooded the BHI Clinic. What with that, the dynamite hurled ritually at their red crosses, and having no heat, they finally threw in the sponge and moved into the Kouroush Hotel, bags and Band-Aids.

The cold definitely justifies the pajamas. I have no idea if people sleep in them, as I do not care to become that intimate with one Iranian man I've met to date. I do feel the pajamas explain why the men constantly knead their genitals, arrange and rearrange them, pat them into place and then lovingly smooth them down—it's because the pajamas keep bunching up in there and binding them. The things are patently the Farsi equivalent of American BVDs, but they sure don't give a guy the least dash or derring-do.

Tuesday, 2 January 1979

Trapped again! No buses, and no one with benzine to give us a ride.

It was cold last night and I used Madame for the sole purpose of pumping up my sluggish circulation. My color improved so markedly that everyone in the vicinity took turns pedaling and priming his blood. Skip usually lifts weights and jogs in place, while Roddey, who is turning a pale, wasted gray, huddles in five layers of clothes and reads every recycled book in the city.

I have been hitching rides to the base at any old hour I can. It doesn't matter when I get there so long as there's barq for the office machines. Picture Robin, attired in bunnysuit and miner's lamp, imbedded in a six-foot trench sandbagged with piles of paper work, only her eyeballs showing, slowly suffocating in triplicate and quadruplicate. They'll find my shriveled, cold-stiffened body one day, the small pinched face black with carbon and despair.

Though there's no formal notification of RIF-ing, the mass

resignations are doing me in. There were thirty-six yesterday from maintenance alone, along with an additional 130 dependents to be ticketed on the first ferry out. I may take my sleeping bag to the base, brave the Xerox guard, and work around the clock.

We are so desperate for gasoline that the Wright Brothers, Mike and Barry, conducted a mad experiment today—they drove Ben's car using naft (kerosene). They looked like Puff, the Magic Dragon, lumbering along in a sheet of flame. Unmechanical as I am, I understand that car engines are not designed to consume kerosene—it would be like me trying to digest hay and oats for lunch.

The boys spent the rest of the day cleaning up the engine and relining its stomach, and they are ready to try again. They think they're on the verge of an important breakthrough. If not, they've been given twenty litres of benzine by departing friends and have promised five of that (Fannie Farmer's cooking pays off again!) to me. Five litres is not even two gallons, but right now it appears a cornucopia.

Since we can use Liberty's vehicle until selling it at the last minute, Skip is trying to jerry-rig my Jyanne's muffler into enough working order to sell him.

Our present quandary is how to have anyone test-drive Jack without benzine. Interested parties will have to settle for one short swing around the kutche. And instead of selling him at a profit as I could have only last week, I'll have to take a loss and Lord only knows what kind of a home he'll have. Rather than let him fall into the hands of some thug, I'll torch him. (I regret to say that certain BHI greed-heads are doing just that, knowing they'll get more money from insurance than from an Iranian sale.)

Meanwhile, with useless automobiles cluttering our landscape, the Great Escape, or first charter, has been moved back to January 5, reducing some of our escapees to ragged wreckage. BHI, the old Earth Mother, mistress of the triplicate form and the late start, forgot to get a landing clearance from Khatemi Airfield. A mechanic who has been incarcerated in the Kouroush Hotel for three weeks tried to slash his wrists when he heard about it.

We no longer have alternatives. Teheran's Mehrabad Airport is closed ninety percent of the time. Traffic controllers, ground crews, pilots, ticket agents, Customs officials, and

204

pistachio vendors all take turns striking with atypical, near-perfect timing. We've scratched Mehrabad; we must count on the old home town.

This is a ticklish time and the Havan-e-Ruz military people are as testy as playwrights on opening night. Theoretically, we're on their side. In truth, most of our men despise or at the least barely tolerate them. I keep pleading for diplomacy. But starting from the top, a few incidents like the cartoon have made the volatile Shahnaz more short-tempered and high-handed than ever, with officers and men following right behind.

The inevitable BHI comedian snipped out a vulgar *Penthouse* cartoon showing a "brown-noser" under a board room table servicing the corporate leaders overhead. The brown-noser was labeled General Shahnaz, and those above: the Shah, his Premier, Minister of Education, etcetera. Xeroxes of this obscene work of art were made and distributed widely; and of course one found its way to the desk of our exalted leader. Let's face it, it will take the Persians another century to appreciate our irreverent brand of humor. Certainly they're in no mood for it this month.

Because of Shahnaz's fit of pique, we will get no Iranian drivers to drive the base buses to the charter takeoffs. We must furnish our own (possibly the best news of the decade). In his warped way, the general thinks he is meting out some just and terrible punishment, when instead the Americans can be counted on to: 1) operate reasonably close to schedule; 2) head in the right direction; 3) pick up all the passengers; and 4) repair equipment in case of breakdowns.

If only the Iranians were handy, or would let our mechanics repair the buses instead of worrying about saving face, we could have an entire efficient fleet of forty-seven buses on the move.

As an ex-school-bus driver from Evergreen, Colorado, I would like to volunteer my services for the charter brigade, but all those big stuffy men would only get uppity and glare at me over their cigars, and any Iranians spotting me at the wheel of their precious vehicles would have *grand mal* seizures.

We ourselves are not permitted the luxury of so much as a tantrum. Instead, I try to look on the bright side. When BHI Bus #8 wheezes past me, its driver waving antically as he wheels around the corner and heads for the base with a quarter load of passengers, I get to go back home and read or batik.

Among the first to "charter out" will be the American doctors and nurses. The BHI Clinic has abdicated in force and joins 1200 other employees who have been "signed off" for departure. Plenty of people will have to settle back and await their turns, as each Pan Am plane holds 178 people; we're due for just one a day from the fifth through the tenth, and the numbers simply don't add up.

Rioting at the gas stations grows more rife. Soldiers, martial guards, and other government personnel are the only ones with benzine, and their cavalier attitude as they drive merrily about the city makes people madder than hornets. Such conspicuous consumption is insane. All these junior military jackasses should be made to eat, sleep, and stand at attention at their respective posts for the duration; instead they are turned loose to bedevil Esfahan like swarms of bees. I wonder if Fred and Bakhtiar have heard about the low profile?

Barry and Mike and Ben hotfooted it over here with a gift of charcoal last night; a little only, but enough to cook several meals, and it was very welcome; we're almost out of butane for the stove. We celebrated by lighting the heater and then holding a campfire around its comforting, bite-size flame.

My public is undoubtedly wondering why I hang on. I'll admit there are days when the year-end bonus looms large, but mostly it's because I am needed and I am a madcap fool. There are just two of us left to handle hundreds of evacuation processings, and like every self-styled heroine, I feel all would be lost without me. Furthermore, I have a phobia, which my mother considers aberrant, about quitting. I expect to be the last one standing on the paper parapet, holding the Ties off at the gate.

Wednesday, 3 January 1979

To my everlasting delight, the Kurds came thundering down out of the hills. I was disappointed Peter O'Toole and Alec Guinness weren't along, but you can't have everything.

206

They didn't do much except thunder back home again, but they put on a hell of a show while it lasted. The Kurds are a mighty subnation covering much of western Iran, Iraq, and Turkey, and, like the Basques, have been seeking self-determination for years. They are a great warrior people, they support the Shah, and they wished to express their disapproval of this whole tawdry business.

Unless Bakhtiar, and possibly Khomeini, have extensive plans for soothing a lot of ruffled feathers, thousands of Kurds, Baluchis, Turks, Bahais, and other ethnic, tribal, and religious groups (including eighty thousand Jews, a very large Arabic contingent in the south, and hundreds of thousands of Armenians; in fact every group but the Fars or true Persians, who are very much in the minority) may just decide to stand up and fight an untidy little civil war like that between the Indian Moslems, Sikhs, and Hindus back in 1949.

The Bahais entrance me. Theirs is a comparatively new, very progressive and enlightened religion, started in Iran in 1844. At present they have a large temple in Wilmette, Illinois, and followers around the world; they espouse such tenets as the abolition of prejudice, equality of the sexes, education for all—everywhere; agreement between science and religion; and a universal faith based on the identity of the foundations of the great religions. And so on. The original Bahai animus was to make Islam more enlightened. Since Islam wasn't interested, the Bahais, despite terrible persecution, managed to survive and eventually flourish on their own. I think their faith admirable. There are many Bahais in Esfahan, and they are a freethinking, literate, kind, and very open-minded people. They are tolerated because the Shah orders it, and despised by their Shi'ite neighbors for daring to be different.

One of the younger guys in TID, Rick Brunton, has been wooing Mahine, a Bahai, for eighteen months. She speaks exquisite English, is lovely to look at, has one brother in the Philippines and one at home, and her father is an architect. Though she is still a Persian, and he has never so much as kissed her, he continues to court her in a fine, old-fashioned way. It's impossible to get either Mahine or her family out of the country, but he is trying every maneuver to move their money into the States—illegal but essential for survival. So many Iranians are trapped here, unless they have improbable escape routes across the frontiers into Turkey or Iraq.

The Bahais have no way of salvaging their savings, will be helpless without the protection of the Shah, immigration officials won't give them papers to leave the country, and they seem headed for certain doom. Our boy says he won't leave Iran without Mahine; it's like *The Last of the Mohicans* and makes me feel very tearful and tragic.

I was additionally reduced to near-tears when the barq evaporated on base, and we were all transported home.

Electricity in Iran has always mystified me. Even in the newest and best-designed houses, American appliances won't run without special transformers—big black stinkers which weigh about fifty pounds and must be hauled bodily to the bathroom to use the hair dryer, to the kitchen to use the coffeepot, and to the bedroom if one is blessed with an electric blanket. They are expensive and a royal pain in the American communal ass. Furthermore, we profligate xaerigi are accustomed to plugging everything in at once. Here, if we wish to iron a skirt we must carefully unplug every light, stereo, TV, and other connected appliances in the house. Forget, and you either blow the fuses to kingdom come or yourself across the room. Wiring is done by espionage agents, and sockets throw out showers of sparks, appliances explode, and many a house, adobe or not, burns right to the ground.

Since all of us were at home today, we decided to get on with the January White Sales. Among the fast-movers to date has been my year's supply of Ban Roll-On. After ascertaining its exact purpose, the army officers' wives snapped it up like hot cakes and I think the Ban people ought to look into immediate Mideast expansion. I actually made a profit on the stuff. That, and the guys' hair spray, and Pretty Feet.

Popular in Iran is something called *sefid,* a kind of pumice which women rub on a washcloth and use to scrub the dead skin off their faces and bodies. When the ladies reached the conclusion that Pretty Feet is a kind of liquid sefid, there were pitched battles up and down the halls with women shrieking *"maele maen!"* (mine, mine!). I only had two bottles, but I think they sold for ten dollars apiece.

I am attempting to mark things now and keep muttering firmly to myself, "fixeh, fixeh."

Perhaps because of my ill humor over the barq workers, our sale prices were, comparatively speaking, high; to my astonishment, people snapped everything up. "Crazy na-bashid, old boy," Roddey kept repeating to himself and the

208

jostling crowds. The whole scenario was a big change from Act I, Scene I of the first faroush, although some dirty dog stole the dice out of my Yahtzee game. I suspect a colonel from our base.

There were hundreds of people outside howling to be let in. This time we were ready for them. Mike and Barry and Ben and Roddey took turns manning the barricades and helping me deal with a manageable handful of customers at a time. Even so, Skip nearly called Security to come to the aid of our party when we heard a battering ram on the courtyard gate.

I was far too busy juggling money and sales slips and kleptomaniacs to bring the Liberty fire hose into play (but I got that rotten potato man good yesterday when he had the nerve to come around again, whining, "Big poh-tah-toes, missus"; the water pressure was fortunately strong and I nearly blasted his head off his shoulders).

During today's sale I felt like one of those nice Hindu gods with twelve arms, answering questions calmly, completing sales, making change, and surviving with equanimity.

Army and air force officers drive around searching out faroushes with their wives (few Iranian women drive cars; they have no aptitude for it, and it's a woman's right I'd be the last to push in this part of the world). Some of these officers are on a higher plane than your regular run-of-the-mill sale-goer, but not all. I've noted that Lieutenant Arbob never graces our door, though I hear he bought a number of things from David Burdick. The officers today kept reiterating, "But surely you are not leaving, madame," meanwhile snatching up my worldly goods and the last of the Ban. One was refreshingly direct. He said, "If you leave, missus, we will have to work too very hard. We will most certainly not let you leave." I was so tickled I sold him the sewing machine at half-price.

With tears in my eyes I also sold Jack Jyanne. To Captain Hamishey, the Iranian supply officer. He dates one of the American girls on the base and is a gentleman. He's always had a kind or polite word for *this* child, without any perverted undertones, so I happily bequeathed him Jack for 110,000 rials, about a $420 loss. Still not bad, considering I drove him for eight months, and he has a good home with a nice man who won't strip his gears.

We have a new member of our family. His name is Majid,

and he lives in the university section of the city, which is here on the south side but still not what you'd call right in the neighborhood. Majid knows Skip from one of his former homes, and now he's latched onto our little company of three plus the crew next door. He has trap lines he runs all through The Flats.

Majid and Skip became fast friends after Skip caught him stealing his Marshall Tucker tape, lectured him on honesty, and let him keep it. When the faroush chatter gets too fast and colloquial for me, Majid translates. He also brings us "bicycle news," which he pedals with fast feet and a glib mouth. As he helped me make change this afternoon he informed me cheerily that an American on Mardavich was beaten badly for setting his faroush prices too high. And this was right after I'd sold a perfectly good GE steam iron for ninety-five cents. The little scamp can't terrorize me and he knows it, but he keeps trying. We have developed a wary but mutually beneficial relationship.

Even at their best, these sales are still scary. Not that I think the shopping crowds have murder on their minds. It's just that they're so desperate for negotiable goods, so excitable and easily carried away, that you feel things might get out of hand and somebody hurt, however inadvertently. Once people gain entry, it's like pulling teeth to get them out, and the courtyard bell continues to ring nonstop, the waiting mobs to beat on the gates despite all shouts of *"farda sob"* (tomorrow morning). Faces keep appearing at the top of the walls, and there are a hundred reasons why everyone must be allowed entry this minute. "But madame, I have just driven all the way from Shahinshahr," screams the old termagant who lives at the end of our kutche. Or, "I have only just borrowed some money . . . just closed my shop . . . just picked up my aged mother . . . just received special release from my job." "And," I mutter menacingly, "are just about to talk yourselves into the hosing of your venal, lying lives."

In a small way, these people are mobs. In a very big way, they're nearly uncontrollable. And we are *very* hypersensitive about uncontrollable mobs.

The guys agreed as one that today's faroush was successful but traumatic. The din was deafening, and the behavior of the women appalled them. They had never seen that kind of eye-catching and hair-pulling outside an old Cecil B. De

Mille movie, and it marked them. I thought it was comparatively peaceful myself.

We could have sold every stick of Liberty's belongings, but he has not called us with final instructions. Though he himself is unwilling to give up, the U.S. Consulate insists no one will be allowed back in Iran, probably forever. I do hope the U.S. Marines are excluded from that directive. We may need them.

Tonight's NIRT, which we watched like shipwreck survivors, announced that unnecessary foreigners will be asked to leave Iran. Women again? Me? We were tossed fleeting glimpses of continuing riots in Esfahan and Teheran and told that the unholy stink on every side is that of burning rubber—tires. Local guerrillas must have received fresh instruction sheets from George Habbash and Yasser Arafat.

NIRT's nighttime news closed with January 1 (a few days late) shots of Chicago's snowstorms. Chicago's troubles were our delight; we felt positively warm and wonderful seeing news and views of any place at home.

Today's temperature in Esfahan: 75 degrees.

Thursday, 4 January 1979

There will be no weekend for any of us. After BHI's initial muddle over the landing permits, the first two charters will finally lift off tomorrow, and I spent hours soothing departees, juggling papers, locating passports, arranging baggage shipments, and assigning plane seats. This will continue until the tumbrels bear us off.

Candlelight, even without wine, is a welcome balm tonight. My eyes are weary and because I have long since ceased writing letters home, or anywhere, I feel as though I am reaching out to touch the world with my journal.

We may have very important mail hand-carried out in a BHI pouch and posted from the home office in Bedford, Texas. I myself think pouch mail should be reserved for life or death situations. And anyway, Mother is calling regularly, and we chat like two hens at an egg laying. (During our latest talk, Mother fiendishly announced the menu for my first meal at home. "We'll start with hot chicken noodle soup," she said. . . .)

211

I just finished several dozen calls in Esfahan, saying good-bye or sending messages to old friends who will leave tomorrow. We all tearfully promised to meet in Florida, in Arkansas, in New York, California, every corner of the old home country.

This week's *Rotor Wash* informs us that the hydroelectric plant is indeed endangered. If that goes, everything goes. We are again cautioned to store large quantities of water, to stockpile food (from whence, pray tell?), and to be prepared with ample supplies of warm clothing and blankets. Listen, the *Rotor Wash* is filling a need and I'm grateful for any kind of published news, but unless the old *Wash* can come up with a few more "how-to's" and "where-to-get's," I'll suggest where to stuff the entire next edition.

Oh well, maybe the loss of the hydroelectric plant will have an adverse effect on the rioters. It isn't easy to riot all day when a man can't go home to a hot meal and a steaming drink of chie over his nightly propaganda pamphlets.

According to Majid's bicycle news, Esfahanis are buying gas on the black market for two dollars a *quart.* I'd guess the army men at our base, like underpaid servicemen everywhere, have elected to do a little pocket-lining on the QT and are cynically siphoning military gas into every civilian tank they can find. Majid the Sly has made his own connections, as he sold us a half gallon of gas at a very pretty price. Despite danger to life and limb, I have stored it under my bed. I'd rather have it explode and take me with it than fall into the thieving hands of a kutche gang.

I am almost but not quite too tired to write the heart-warming story of three more friends who held their final faroush last week. Les Brennan, Augie Vargas, and Rick Brunton decided, after turning down the landlord's blanket offer for all their household goods at an insultingly low price, to hold a faroush. The landlord refused them permission (I never knew we had to have one), so they locked him in the hall closet and held the sale with the man's gagged and stifled cries lost in the ruckus. Then they checked into the Kouroush Hotel. They're still there awaiting evac, and the landlord stayed in the closet seventy-two hours before someone finally found him, unharmed but squawking like a barren hen. I know he's dying to prosecute but has no idea where to find them among the hundreds of people piled into every hotel in town.

Friday, 5 January 1979

Bakhtiar is forming a new, all-civilian cabinet at the direction of the Shah. Maybe I'm wrong, but I was under the impression that Fred was no longer directing so much as the menu for his next meal.

Bakhtiar himself is more of a change than anyone expected. He and his people seem to be struggling valiantly to bring order out of anarchy, but as any fool can plainly see, a revolution, once started, isn't easily stopped. Bakhtiar or no, these people appear willing to settle for nothing less than their revered Ayatollah Khomeini. Don't ask me why. I certainly can't judge by the lone picture of him, reproduced by the millions and designed to frighten babes in arms and palsied old women. He has cruel eyes like hot coals. It may be his religious fervor, but if you ask me the man's either some kind of a weirdo or has chronic conjunctivitis.

I did listen to his speech on Iran Radio Wednesday night. He sounded reasonably calm and very assured. He promised to return to Iran and his people soon. He further said that he wants no Americans or other nationals hurt—only out of his country forever—and that Iran is to be an Islamic Republic, a nation unto itself, created by and for itself, without mimicry of Western ideas. I'll admit this sounds reasonable. Everyone has a right to his own revolution, we Americans had ours. But if I had my druthers, I'd lay down the following rules:

1. Noise levels to be no higher than the allowable motorcycle decibel level, which is ear-splitting as is.

2. Let's outlaw name-calling. "Karter [sic] Is a Dog" and "Khomeini Eats Pork" do nothing for the tone and class of a really topflight revolution.

3. Only one explosion per block, and for Lord's sake don't hurt anyone.

4. One demonstration per week per side is plenty.

5. No live ammunition, all guns to use blanks.

6. Positively no firing squads. As sure as you shoot someone you're going to need him later. *Then* you'll be sorry.

I have more ideas, but they can wait.

The *Kayhan* is due to begin publishing tomorrow; it'll be the first edition after sixty-two interminable days on strike. This will mean the demise of the *Rotor Wash*, the shortest scat sheet on record. I may have maligned it, but I will miss its homey news.

Jackie and Donna got together and to a landlord's telephone, and we had a long, choked-up talk. Movement about the city is now nearly impossible. I felt like I was talking to distant relatives in a foreign land.

Saturday, 6 January 1979

I am developing a split personality. There's cleavage in my brain cells and doubt in my mind. Just as I had psyched myself up for inevitable departure, word spread that we are going to stay—that BHI's contract is so vital to the U.S. it must be fulfilled. I may have a stroke from the stress.

Or I may be shot in my tracks. Today as I was chauffeured through town in a company car, we passed a gas line seven or eight miles long. It's getting easy to buy black market gas, or to pay someone to stand in line for you. Nevertheless, if looks could kill . . .

Among those quietly evacuated yesterday was George Coles. George accidently killed an Afghani worker a week ago, hit him with his car. If the man had been Iranian, George would now be hanging by his thumbs in the local torture chambers. But he was only a poor coolie. Even so, BHI put up a million rials as bail, plus George's residence permit, and the gendarmerie shaved his head and cooled him in jail for a couple of days, then let him out until his trial next week. He would have served a long jail term and probably been trampled when they turn the lions loose on the Christians. He was smuggled out under his first name, Thomas, which he never uses. His passport was miraculously not yanked and BHI simply forfeited the fourteen thousand dollars, cheap for a man's life. They were delighted to spirit him safely home to his family.

The reason there are so many Afghanis and Pakistanis in Iran is because, with this country's new oil affluence, there are few remaining Persian poor. The Iranians used to do the

Arab world's dirty work. Now they have others do theirs for them—Afghani Baluchistanis in colorful tribal dress who live in bedraggled tent cities, make sixty cents a day, work cruelly hard, and always manage to look cheerful.

Along with George, the BHI medical fraternity finally departed, leaving behind a lone nurse plus the infamous Dr. Jamshidi, known to BHI'ers as Jam-Shitty.

Almost immediately Barry Outcelt dropped his two hundred pound toolbox on his finger, nearly amputating it. He didn't yell "Ouch!"; he yelled, "Oh, Jesus, not here, not now!" Jam-Shitty got it sewed back on, but the stitching looks like it was done with leather thongs and the finger crooks decidedly to the left.

For the third time in as many nights we had exactly one minute of news from NIRT. They did promise to return to normalcy tomorrow, which must mean a return to their regular, substandard broadcasts.

My informants, meanwhile, are either Majid on his fast cycle, or Mother, ten thousand miles away. She called again tonight, and again had no difficulty getting through. CBS News, according to Mom, showed all the oil workers going back to work a few days ago. There were also pictures of denuded grocery shelves and incredibly long gas lines. "Are you warm and fed, darling?" inquired Mother. "There doesn't seem to be much left there in the way of necessities. Have you considered roast revolutionary for dinner?"

Since there is no mail, and I'll believe the *Kayhan* when I smell the newsprint, Mother is going to keep calling with out-of-town bulletins. I promised her I would not leave the clearing.

She also said in what sounded like a wistful voice that Bakhtiar's government seems pro-Western. I didn't tell her that's the kiss of death for poor Bakhtiar. It's restless natives who'll rule the roost—not pro-Western premiers. One small purge and one new civilian cabinet are not going to satisfy these madding crowds.

Strife has become a way of life, and we wonder what will happen when everyone must settle back into his old humdrum existence, standing in the chie shop, hawking souvenirs, counting coinage at the mint, selling hot beets on the corners.

There are now to be *scheduled* demonstrations in the cities, orderly and by appointment only. Hah?

215

"By appointment only" is the way we're conducting the last of our faroushes. We got the idea from Alfonso Clark, who said his wife caught a girl shoving a toaster under her chador, and when the wife accused her point-blank, the girl punched her in the mouth. End of faroush. He will sell nothing except by private appointment.

Faces as featureless as cabbages keep shrieking over our walls to sell them Liberty's refrigerator, TV, and other appliances. We've sold almost everything of our own.

Thievery is not exclusive with garage sales. Though I've talked about an increase in thefts at the base, I must say that last weekend's losses moved into the Brink's Robbery class. Every inch of the main hangar was rifled, and hundreds of irreplaceable tools and parts were stolen. Some of this stuff is marketable, but helicopter parts are not in general demand, and mostly it's plain malicious mischief.

Liberty and his crew built a kind of cage for the toolboxes back in October, and that slowed the thefts down, but the cage is locked with mere padlocks, not elephant bolts, and it's only a matter of time before some local Houdini cracks them. Carrying tools back and forth on the buses is still not permitted. GOI professes to be terrified that our people will steal their own tools, so they refuse to sign them off the base. At the same time, they can't seem to guard them while they're here, and the upshot is: hardly a tool left in the garage.

Though there doesn't seem to be anyone watching the helicopter equipment, I've got a sure-nough guard on my Xerox mah-sheen. Actually, he's been there since the copying and distribution of the dirty cartoon featuring General Mohammed Shahnaz. At first we thought Shahnaz was making certain his Xerox was never again put to ignoble use. On second thought, we decided the guards are Savak. It's OK by me. The daytime guard is named Achmid and I find him very helpful. His job is to inspect everything that goes in and out of the mah-sheen. I'm not sure he can read, but then he only has to watch for salacious pictures and keep his ear peeled for seditious conversation. He grins a lot and is very cooperative about helping me stack and staple my copy material. I could have used him a year ago.

Sunday, 7 January 1979

We have had an all-points bulletin saying BHI will pay no insurance on goods left behind unless destroyed by civil unrest—and that we are required to have police reports and BHI Security personnel on hand as eyewitnesses.

"Hello there, Security? This is Robinson Sterling on the thirtieth block of Char Bagh, south side of Zyand-e-Rud, corner of the Mehr Kutche. I am twenty miles from ER, and my car is being dragged through the joub by a kutche gang. Will you please be here in three minutes to act as my official witness? The police are busy shooting demonstrators."

The kutche gangs grow bolder. Last week Arlene Anspach and her husband (from Mineral Wells, Texas) were walking from the bus to their house in The Flats, two blocks from Liberty Hall, when they were attacked by brutes with clubs. They were fortunate, they ran full tilt into security guards with guns. No wonder Arlene has asked to be on an early ship-out list.

Jim Holland said that following the first charter runs our volunteer bus drivers made sure all sixteen buses were returned with repaired ignitions, started at the flick of a key, and hummed along like tops; the guys had to work on some of them half the night.

Here at Liberty Hall we have a precious first edition of the *Kayhan* which we spent the evening devouring inch by inch, column by column. PARS, the Iranian UPI, is back churning out news releases, all morbid, but *they're* happy; they say they're finally free of censorship.

Curfew is now to start at 11:00 P.M. and end at 5:00 A.M. I feel like a college girl who's been given senior privileges.

The entire town of Yazd, which was under house arrest, has been freed. Yazd is about 180 miles east of Esfahan, which means dead ahead in the desert. I never heard of locking up a whole *town* before. Wonder what they did?

Furthermore, martial law is to be lifted any day. This is a dubious blessing that makes me distinctly uneasy. With all its irritants and obscene performances, I think the military is needed to preserve *some* kind of sanity; I can't see where the

217

new government is achieving any more order than prior ones. Kutche gangs and fires and pipe bombings keep rolling along like *Wagon Train*. What will happen if there are no restraints at all?

Monday, 8 January 1979

The Great Landlord Freakout has begun.

Iranian leases require either thirty days' notice of departure or thirty days' additional rent. Under our present abnormal circumstances we have been feeling fortunate to have twenty-four hours, let alone thirty days, notice of *anything*.

And, facing the grim spectre of unemployment lines and the long, expensive process of getting resettled and rehired back in the States, neither are our people eager to pour five hundred unwarranted dollars down their landlords' sewerlike gullets. I keep pumping for a compromise, while ER is adamant about payment in full.

"This is an international emergency," I say firmly.

"A rule is a rule," he maintains stubbornly.

"But we didn't start the revolution," say I.

"All rents must be paid," says he.

"Even when we're being *driven* out of their country?" And so on and so on. I am unhappily trapped between the entire bullheaded ER department and the grasping Iranian Landlord Trust.

Telephone, electrical, and water bills were supposedly submitted regularly but often the bills came in once every eight months or once a year. Now suddenly the utility bills were flocking to the BHI offices right on the heels of the landlords. Talk about Inshallah! They sure aren't leaving things in the hands of Allah now that word's spread we're going.

I know Moslems refuse to be ruled by the tyranny of time, but I wish to pete people had collected bills when they should have. I am adjudicating more and more problems between Iranian business people and American consumers, and it's not even my job.

Officially, I promise all landlords to settle matters in their favor. Unofficially, I'm not the least bit sympathetic. They've been practicing full-scale extortion on us for years. An Iranian family pays only half the rent for the same house as

218

an American, and such words as "upkeep" and "repair" aren't even translatable into Farsi.

When we are gone, I pray every landlord fills his rentals with pigeons and crows.

Coming home to the *Kayhan* is almost as comforting as going home to Mother. Sample headlines: MARTIAL LAW LIFTED IN SHIRAZ. . . . BAKHTIAR PROMISES TOTAL FREEDOM OF PRESS. . . . SHAH TO LEAVE IRAN. . . . OIL REFINERIES BACK TO WORK. . . . HEAD OF MILITARY LEAVES IRAN. (I wonder why on earth he didn't take Shahnaz with him?)

Although Khomeini's "National Day of Mourning and Projected Funeral Procession for the People" is not scheduled until tomorrow, there have been massive country-wide demonstrations last night and today, and we were dismissed early from work. I don't know what their current complaint is, but I do know mine: We are out of liquor, wine, and good spirits, and I have a raging sunburn (contracted in a sudden burst of Esfahani summer).

Two more BHI people were hurt. One had his bedroom gutted, the other his car. The one in the car was Mots Nostdahl, our American friend from Oslo, Norway; it burst his eardrum and changed his lifestyle—nothing too serious.

With typical macabre humor, BHI sporting types are now wearing T-shirts saying "Keep A Low Profile"—with a row of bullet holes printed across the chest.

Americans refuse to get down and stay down. Many of the mosques are sporting "Jesus Saves" signs. And the biggest graffiti coup of the year occurred when a psychopathic American got himself a stencil and went to work across the city. Khomeini's portrait is remarkably like that of the old man on packages of Zig Zag (joint rolling) papers. The unknown madman made a Zig Zag stencil and tiptoed about like Wee Willie Winkie imprinting it under all the Khomeini pictures. Controlling our hilarity, we are very mum and totally ignorant of the perpetrator.

Tuesday, 9 January 1979

From blazing pink to black and blue in twenty-four short hours! I look like Sonny Liston's punching bag.

Skip and I were cornered by a kutche gang this morning. There were charters going out, but we'd been promised a bus or car along our route, due about nine o'clock. Though we increasingly move out in squadron formation (me playing the fife or drums and the guys armed with bike chains), Mike, Ben, Barry, and Roddey had gotten an early ride with Dan Buck, a company honcho with enough benzine to commute; Dan makes every trip worthwhile by filling his Peykan with riders who pour out like those midgets in the circus cars.

Skip and I were late and concerned about missing our bus, so we hurried carelessly across a vacant lot to Mardavich Xyaboon, in front of the Picnic Box Restaurant. As we headed into an unused alley, a big bunch of teenage bullies, your typical wholesome kutche gang, jumped out of the sewer where they'd been lying in wait.

The leader bore an astonishing resemblance to young Al Capone and brandished his *shiv* like something out of *West Side Story*. He also made pseudo–Kung Fu noises, which in retrospect were pretty funny, but at the time were plain terrifying. Skip stood up taller than his usual six feet and kept repeating under his breath, "Don't show them you're afraid, for Christ's sake, don't let them see any fear," and somehow I kindled the old fire in my eye and kept walking right toward them. When they started throwing rocks I was hit on the shoulders and neck and once on my cheek. They howled and whirled like dervishes and acted as if they were juiced up on drugs. Maybe they were just high on Khomeini, but their behavior sure verged on the berserk.

I could sense the murder in Skip's eye, but if he'd started to fight we'd have been buried alive in minutes.

Somehow, without flinching, we kept moving and came out on the Xyaboon right at the bus stop; there wasn't a soul in sight, but that beautiful, blessed bus was moseying up the street toward us. "Oh God," I prayed, "don't let him pass us by, not today."

Then we saw the driver, and it was my friend Hamid! He threw open the door and shouted at the kutche boys, who had us surrounded and were pushing and punching and sneaking little jabs, *"Karkas-e! Sag-e!"* (Vultures, dogs!) "Go home to your mother's milk!" He slammed the door in their faces and rolled right over someone's feet: We could hear the howling behind us.

As we sailed off, Hamid looked very stern and said, *"Xub*

nist, missus Rob-een. Bad, very bad. Alone nabashid." He didn't have to tell us. My knees sounded like a woodpecker's chattering, and Skip was dead-white around the gills.

On base I was the object of a lot of sympathy and many hastily improvised ice packs; but there was so much work to be done that no one had time for idle commiseration. I wrote up a faltering "Incident Report" and a glowing recommendation for promotion for Hamid, with copies to General Mohammed Shahnaz and G-2.

Then I shakily pulled up a sky-high stack of out-processing papers and got to work.

Thursday, 10 January 1979

Because this is the weekend, and I look like a wife-beating case, we decided to celebrate something or other last night. The crew, with me a tattered rose among thorns, piled into Ben Roche's car, and we went into the city for dinner, feeling very brave indeed. As Skip sternly advised through his whopping shiner, "We either get back in the water or we may never swim again."

We arrived at the Kouroush (with only three inspection stops), and no one was home. But the Esfahan Hotel, the gourmand's choice in any case, was open; the Esfahan says "the hell with it" and even serves liquor, which the Kouroush wouldn't dare, not since they got so many letters accusing them of being Western capitalist pigs and are trying to dry out and clean up their act. I drank Lucky Beer and felt as if I were sipping Dom Perignon.

This ill-advised excursion took place only after an intensive seminar at which we came to the joint conclusion there might never be a better time, or place, to use the last precious benzine. So Iran burned and we drove. We've been under virtual house arrest for six weeks now, prisoners of the chador cabal. The last time I had dinner on the town was my birthday, November 26. And we're sick to death of scuttling in and out of our burrows like rabbits and prairie dogs.

After our brazen excursion of last evening we stopped by Dan Buck's for an even more brazen nightcap (he'd found black market hooch, and we were invited). Dan's wife, Sally, is still here, and she's a charmer. We were all very gay, not

221

only from the effects of three beers, but from the mere fact of being abroad till the decadent hour of eleven o'clock.

Also at the Bucks' was a co-worker who shall be nameless. Old Nameless is an engineer who informed me in one hot breath that he was in charge of much of the gas, naft, and butane on base and that his own gas tank, capsules, and naft barrels are full to the brim and in the next panting breath suggested with a lopsided leer that if I went to bed with him, all my tanks, capsules, barrels, and submerged desires could overflow too. Now *there's* a genuine, full-blooded, ugly-mother American from the old Slewfoot Tribe. I told him as delicately as possible where to shove his proposition, his tanks, capsules, and naft barrels. Nameless's wife has gone home, and I like her and feel sorry about this. Plenty of Americans have no more class than Iranians.

In Fort Liberty there is an area called, simply, "No Room," a sort of large, open hallway. The boys and I have moved our beds in there, and attempting to stay warm, we hold evening court like a Louis XIV *levée*. Ensconced in No Room, we at least get some heat overflow from the hot water heater. I wear my Aspen Lid to bed, Skip has an ancient set of earmuffs, and Roddey wraps himself in a plaid muffler. We look like characters from a Grimm's fairy tale.

We leapt from summer back to winter overnight. It's been raining and snowing in the mountains around the city for two days.

In addition to being multicolored about the head and shoulders, I hab a cold id my nose from living in this dank sarcophagus. However, I am prepared to brave double pneumonia without benefit of medical care before bedding down in sweet Nameless's toasty house. Ah, but it would be glorious to have our naft barrels filled to the top and be able to fire up the works—hot water, heat, everything. I've had more Saturday night armpit spongings than I care to count, and yearn incessantly for a long soak in a deep, hot tub.

Benzine's as scarce as naft and there are still enormous gas lines, although Iranians may once again queue up in cars rather than on foot. It's rumored people have been camping there, some for days at a time. We paid Majid nine dollars for ten litres of gas that I'm sure he siphoned out of someone's tank.

We were just notified that we will receive ten litres of naft per person on base. Huzzah and Happy New Year!

John Callahan, a BHI supervisor who lives beyond the crew, had a narrow escape that we missed. He happened to look outside and saw two men pouring gas on his car, set to torch it. He and his roommates sprang to their roof and bombarded the arsonists with bricks. To think of that precious, wasted benzine *outside* of a car! John said they cleaned it off with tears in their eyes.

Today was the big day of mourning, but none of us attended the funeral.

Khomeini's memorial service words were, "May every drop of martyr's blood turn into a tulip," which I thought rather lovely, until·he segued into another round of blood-chilling screams for revenge and called not only for breast-beating but for death-dealing. I know these are dolorous days, but my word, don't these people *ever* feel like a big belly laugh? Or even a quiet chuckle?

Friday, 12 January 1979

Guity and Jahan found me! They had never been to the Liberty house, but Guity had my general address and location. They drove up in their Peykan and joined the throng at the front gate. They thought, from all the dither, that we'd either died or burned down, and if I hadn't heard a familiar voice calling "Ro-been?" I would have ignored them as more would-be faroushers. I was so happy to see them! When Guity smothered me with kisses I felt like spring was here.

They didn't bring Tina, as the streets are still rocking with blasts and gunfire and dynamite and heelo door-gunning and other aftermaths of the Great Day of Mourning. I knew very well they were risking plenty to visit a Yonky friend and I told Guity to pretend she had an appointment for my faroush. I gave her armloads of gifts to bear her out when she left.

Mama is in the hospital with a bronchial infection, and I sent along some plastic orchids left from a bygone Bell Belle affair and other small gifts I knew would please her. Papa and Guity have been on strike with the Customs officials for months.

Guity said the Ayatollah is a good and wise man, but they are very worried about the street gangs, those nasty acorns

223

from which ugly mobs appear to grow, and about their jobs and their devalued money and their futures. Guity's face was drawn and she looked *thin*.

They came to make certain I was still here, still safe, because they have worried much over me. She said she is sorry about it, but there is big, very big anti-American feeling. "Not against you, my friend, it is your Agha President Carter, he keeps saying America loves the Shah, the Shah must stay." I assured Guity that immediately upon arrival back in the U.S. I am going to stuff a great big gag in Agha Carter's great big mouth. She was horrified at such blatant disrespect, but I convinced her I was only joking. I was never more serious in my life.

We drank glasses and glasses of chie, and I was grateful we had enough butane to heat the water. Jahan says they also have very little naft, and I know they used scarce and precious benzine to drive here. Guity was appalled at our beds lined up hospital style, our bare, tatterdemalion digs, and what I'm sure is my dirty as well as bruised and battered face. When she heard about our encounter with the kutche gang, she kept crying, "My friend, my dear friend!" She even offered to send cousins to guard the house for us, though I assured her the incident was trivial and entirely due to our own devil-may-care attitudes.

When I asked Guity if she'd ever been to a faroush she said, "Never," and I hugged her some more and piled extra gifts in her arms.

We said goodbye pretending it was not forever, although we knew it would be. I will never see her again. Sad nabashid, Robinson, sad nabashid.

The doorbell continues to ring morning, noon, and night, and those of us manning the barricades shout, "*Hichi, hichi*" (nothing), "*hichi dacrim*" (we have nothing), or "*faroush nist*" (there is no sale). And then our public shouts back, interminably, "Is all right, we only want to look at your things in case you might sell later." "And stick a few choice items under your chadors," I mumble hatefully under my breath.

Today's *Kayhan* informed us that upon the lifting of martial law in Shiraz there were horrendous fires, riots, and killings. So much for that noble experiment. We remain under martial law. The army, I suppose, should be given some kind of credit for keeping violence within limits. Although I'd like to state here and now that that's the *only* credit I'm giving this ridiculous, toy-soldier military establishment.

All universities are due to reopen permanently (it says here), and it is my considered opinion that the feces will then hit the fan. These students are organized and primed and ready for action. There'll be no peace in the land until they pillory every rotten, graft-ridden bureaucrat who ever stuck a hand under a table in the Shah's regime. And hang the Shah's legions of bloated relatives. And get their hands on every Skinny Tie in the country.

When they're finished here, maybe we should ship them to Washington to mop up. (Except they'd take over the country in the names of Marx, Lenin, and Habbash.)

Other news is that Japan and South Africa and Israel are freaking out because Iran won't sell them oil. (How can they, it's currently all underground.) Japan gets twenty percent of its fuel from Persia, South Africa, ninety percent, and poor little Israel, seventy percent. Israel will be supplied by the U.S. and Egypt, but Egypt as an ally makes me jumpier than a flea. I have dark suspicions that there's an Islamic uprising spreading like spilled ink, that a kind of moral revolt is brewing from Madras to Rabat. Even in southern Russia, where there are literally millions of Moslems, we hear there are signs of dissidence.

I admire everything Sadat is trying to do, and I fear for his political and personal safety. He has great charisma, but is it forceful enough to mesmerize a nation and outface the whole Arab world?

I think that suddenly, now, this year, the modern world is too much with, and against, Islam. That this sudden spate of violence is partly backlash from people who have lived for centuries in a very different world, the prey of poverty and of traditional fears about "shame," "face," and a lot of other foolishly entrenched notions.

One of my favorite stories about the Moslem's exaggerated idea of honor and face-saving is of Musa Alami, the Palestinian Arab leader, being told by the president of Syria during the '48 Israeli War of Independence (and this is the president of a people, mind you), "Not to worry. I can tell you in confidence that we even have an atomic bomb ... we fortunately found a very clever fellow, a tinsmith. . . ."

I think we've been stupidly precipitate in expecting nations whose centuries-old heritage is unequal to the demands of modern technology to do an overnight about-face. And we may pay a terrible price for it. Right now Islam strikes me as a victim of "angst," the kind of waiting and brooding and hate-harboring which afflicted those in Hitler's bunker awaiting the end of their world. Moslem hostility, once aroused, is patently an awful thing to see. Yasser Arafat and George Habbash and the Ayatollah Khomeini have totally blocked out memories of Muhammad's respect and affection for the Jews and instead harbor a blind, unreasoning hate for them. Oh Lord, let it pass, let it pass.

I can't help it. Sorrowful nabashid? No Guity, no Kitty Kat, no more Iran, no oil for the lamps of Mishmar Ha'emek.

Sunday, 14 January 1979

From January 5 through January 10, BHI and Pan Am successfully flew six charters carrying 1063 people, one baboon, and one boa constrictor from the city of Esfahan, Iran, to Dallas, Texas. I had no dealings with either the baboon or the snake (whoever said BHI isn't all heart?), but I did have considerable interaction and mountains of paper work involving the 1063 escapees. BHI and I share a nice warm feeling of satisfaction, but if it had been me, I would have shot the snake and the baboon.

BHI still manages to contribute to my creeping insecurities. Yesterday morning they announced a RIF, the first "Reduction in Force." At long last, instead of appearing to outwait people until they resigned voluntarily, Bell agreed to do the terminating and even went so far as to ask for volunteers.

When the volunteers clicked their heels and stepped forward, I was not among them. The reason I cling to my desk like a wet towel is that I have enrolled in courses next semester at Esfahan University: Revolution I, II, and IIIB.

As afternoon worked its way toward twilight, BHI announced the RIF was in error and instead was only a contingency plan. Like a fire drill? Many employees were so unnerved they quit anyway. Could this have been a calculated move on the part of Mother Bell? A little push for the old natural selection process? Maybe I'm growing as paranoid as the rest of the population, native and foreign.

226

Some of the men were so livid they actually discussed herding all BHI executives at gun point into a stockroom and holding them there till they agreed to a RIF.

BHI undoubtedly has plenty of problems we haven't heard about, but in wartime a well-informed work force is the *only* kind to have.

The insurrectionists don't much care for Norwegians either. This time Mots Nostdahl had the front half of his house blown off: two pipe bombs in perfect concert through the front window. Fortunately Mots and a friend were in the kitchen and relatively protected by thick walls. He left in Band-Aids on yesterday's charter a defeated but still cheerful young man. The bombs destroyed everything he owned, and as he said with a shrug, there wasn't a soul from Personnel or Security on hand for verification of the damage. No witnesses, no insurance. Tsk, tsk, BHI.

Everybody on the base is in a quandary about self-defense. No one goes anywhere without some kind of weapon—chains, pool cues, steering wheel locks—and yet if they used them there'd be the devil to pay.

A defense decision may be just around our own corner. Yesterday in our absence Fort Liberty received another threatening note. In well-run revolutions these notes are served, like subpoenas, on house and car owners before they are attacked. BHI insists that upon receipt of any threat we must evacuate to a hotel immediately. We have neither informed anyone of our warning notes nor evacuated. Nor have we been bombed. The boys and I discussed the current guided missile, a "Yonky Go Home," and we decided that until we can indeed go home we are staying right where we are. We've seen so many warnings, in every size, shape, idiom, and color, they scarcely even strike a chill.

Then too, Majid has not stayed away or otherwise acted suspiciously. We feel sure he'll let us know, directly or indirectly. We can read that boy like a book.

Tonight he galloped up and said he'd been able to get us two fifty-five-gallon drums of naft, but he'd have to have the use of Liberty's car! The little monster claims he's seventeen, but if he's thirteen I'll eat my Aspen Lid. Like any kid in Sioux City, Iowa, he's dying to drive. Talk about heartrending decisions! We need naft so desperately, but we can't countenance the destruction of Liberty's car. Voices croaking, we said no to heat, to hot water, to heaven—maybe forever.

227

Majid is a funny kid. He takes good care of us, but we're sure he'll steal us blind the first chance he gets. He's a smart and resourceful lad who should have a bright future with the new Iranian government. He was born for politics and dirty tricks.

We currently take turns having a very fast shower. Every third night one of the partners rises at 3:00 A.M. to light the naft heater so there'll be just enough warm water for one short morning shower. Last night it was Skip's turn, and he lighted it too late and slammed out this morning unwashed and in a vile humor.

As for me, there isn't a bloody cigarette left in the city. I was planning to stop smoking anyway, but not in this half-crazed condition.

Skip has the enviable knack of getting along with everyone. One reason we're not unduly concerned over threatening notes is that, strictly on the QT, he has promised our remaining household goods to at least fifty different people, and has all of them guarding this place like hawks around the clock.

Late this evening one of Skip's black marketeers came through, and we purchased two cases of Iranian wine, Château Rezaye and Château Sardasht, at forty-two dollars a case. The white is a bit fruity (says she, sipping with one hand and holding her lorgnette with the other), but has a pleasant aftertaste. The red is hearty and dry. We find they go down nicely against a backdrop of soft gunfire and acrid, burning rubber. Almost immediately Majid came pedaling up with a carton of Winstons for a measly 650 rials, only ten dollars.

The crew bounced in and we all huffed and puffed and drank, so happily furtive you'd have thought we were snorting coke and drinking Mountain Dew. I am in complete accord with the Moslems about the rotten influences of the West. We acted like Romans before the Fall and even lightly flicked on the TV. As we thought NIRT had faded from the air forever, imagine our astonishment when *Casablanca* appeared amid a haze of technical problems. It reminded me of the time I saw *Lawrence of Arabia* in San Miguel D'Allende, Mexico. The screening required a total of twelve hours, as a small boy shuttled back and forth on the bus between there and Queretaro, forty miles away, ferrying cans of film—there was only one copy for both towns.

Me, I was happy to see Bergman's divine face coming and going and to try to remember Bogart's lines as I *guzzled* Château Sardasht and puffed happily on Winstons. If the barq workers (the barq still flickers on and off according to conservation measures and political whim) were trying to give us a signal, I was too far gone to get their message.

Monday, 15 January 1979

Every single soul in my office except Faye Graham announced today that he/she was leaving on the February 1 charter. And that they are going to use their accumulated vacation time, effective immediately. This means holing up at home or in a hotel until they make the embarkation lists. They can no longer abide the hateful stares and ugly remarks of the Iranians on the base. The army counterparts, clerical help, and bus drivers have become so haughty, their tone so infuriating, that it's demeaning to work with them.

If an Iranian calls to plague me, I break the connection. If one wishes to use the Xerox machine, I tell him it is broken. Since their sole purpose in calling or knocking is to deliberately harass us, I have no compunctions about shutting them out. My heart is further hardened by the fact they've stolen everything not nailed or glued down.

The tumult and the shouting increase along with general destruction, hate, and attrition. Yet withal, cars on the streets grow more and more numerous. It's as though two antithetical worlds coexisted side by side.

For better or worse, this revolution has accomplished something: It's trained Iranians to stand in line. Furthermore, they *love* it. They build bonfires, read the newspapers, and chew the fat in a sort of big, wide-open house that's a perfect excuse for struck but non-rioting types to get away from squalling children at home.

Tomorrow I shall be alone with one distant Xerox guard, Faye Graham, and 1653 pressing problems.

Typical trauma: One of our youngest mechanics, a nice small-town boy from Wormleysburg, Pennsylvania, had his house blown up. His landlord insisted he, the tenant, pay for the damage. He further announced that the boy owed him three months' back rent, and though the kid had paid in full, he'd sent all his rent receipts home with his bride. I tried to help, but he was trapped like a hock in a ham. BHI won't release passports to anyone unless they're squared away with their landlords and word has spread fast—among the landlords. They have their new scam rehearsed in unison: "Pay your blackmail or rot in jail." I can smell out the phonies and I was sick when that boy forked over his year's savings, some $2500, to the biggest phony in the city. This could set one hell of a precedent: "Hey, fellas, let's all go bomb the BHI people; if we burn them out, they must pay damages to our friend Abdullah." Double indemnity.

Roddey came home tonight with a dead bird—an emaciated chicken three days past its demise which he'd proudly purchased on a street corner. I don't mind plucking a chicken, but this one was definitely barn-sour. I patted him, Roddey, on the head, thanked him gently, and said it was OK if he left the reconnoitering to Skip.

Tuesday, 16 January 1979

> Think, in this battered caravanserai
> Whose doorways are alternate night and day
> How sultan after sultan with his pomp
> Abode his hour or two, then went away.

The Shah is gone. The king deposed!

The truth is that his leaving is as pathetically anticlimactic as the retirement of a stock clerk after thirty years with the company. He has been so patently finished for weeks now, his departure so inevitable, that he was already a half-forgotten man.

Still, it is hard to believe that this proud, hawklike leader should step so quietly from the awesome Peacock Throne. He *must* be ill, emotionally or physically. He's quelled rebellions and survived coups d'etat before. What was so different this time, how else explain his dispirited acquiescence? Maybe forty-three million subjects, that's what. Vox populi. The man didn't have a lot of options.

When, where, how long past did this king forget the heritage of the great desert khans—the art of strong, just leadership combined with love and respect for one's people?

We have remained firmly barricaded in the compound where, from behind bolted courtyard doors, we ourselves hear the people's voices loud and clear. The entire city has gone mad.

When Khomeini returns, he'd better be wearing his wizard's hat to create order out of *this* chaos.

Dr. Whitcomb: "If no group is ready and able to establish effective rule following the collapse of the old regime, many cliques and social forces will struggle for power." I suppose Roger's right about Khomeini being the requisite "charismatic leader." But a new Iranian world will require much, much more. Experience, for one thing. Patience and compassion, for another.

Modern Persia is still a loose confederation of many tribal and ethnic groups. Ask a man his allegiance, and he will never tell you he is Iranian—always that he is Baluchistani, Bahai, Qoshgai, Turk, Kurd. And although national pride is being born in this struggle, a citizen's loyalties are divided in many ways. I see power passing from hand to hand, internecine government squabbling, and many changes of power. Rubbing my murky crystal ball, I see no Shi'ite peace on earth—only flame and smoke, death and destruction. And men armed to the eyeballs with those bloody Russian guns.

According to that young passe-partout Majid, who brought us a fourteen-dollar carton of cigarettes minus one pack for his trouble, Khomeini is due back in the country on Thursday. We all pray his reception will be joyous but tranquil and that the man may even smile in lieu of beetling his eyebrows.

I should now like to submit my personal request for brotherly love. Good will toward men. Kind hearts. Flowers. Oooooommmmmmmm.

In preparation for the grand entrance, I have become the official maintenance barber and hair stylist. While the guys have a haircut, they also lightsomely belt down our wine. And they call this Sassooning? Fortunately, a number of BHI men have taken the easy way out and reverted to the hippie look. With few women around, no generals giving a hoot, no water, and no heat, it's simple to drop personal hygiene from the top of one's priorities. There's no more inspection either, and that *does* make a difference.

The Liberty Jyanne is deteriorating like a beached whale. The underside has some kind of root rot, and Skip and Roddey have spent the day trying to metal-set the accelerator back together. We have to have a healthy car, for emergencies like kidney stones and flying bullets, and of course to sell for our buddy Liberty; by spring he'll have three children to support. When he called he said Judy looks like a warthog. If I didn't know he adored her, I'd have told him what to do with his faroush and his Jyanne.

Between haircuts I am rereading Lee Uris's *Mila 18*. He's a dear friend of Mom and Dad's and a fantastic writer. Going back to the Jews' last stand in the Warsaw ghetto, I realize how insignificant this seems: a passing pustule on the face of Iran and history.

Thursday, 18 January 1979

There was too much excitement to "journalize" yesterday. With the Shah's departure our world really went mad.

Although Fred's cabinet and Premier Bakhtiar are still nominally in charge, Iran seems oblivious to the fact. It's Khomeini, Khomeini, Khomeini. The night of the Shah's leave-taking (for parts unknown) there were hundreds of thousands, well *millions* of people in the streets. Nasser Sanjabi, Mahine's brother who is not even Moslem, he's Bahai, told me, "Khomeini's face, it was there in the moon!" Majid insisted, "The master's face was on the moon, I saw it myself!" Great crowds of people had a mass hallucination that Khomeini's face (undoubtedly scowling) was peering down at us from the moon. I started for our roof to see for myself, but Skip and Roddey lassoed and chained me to the cold naft heater. The rooftops were filled, and the sound was a giant sea swell of "ooh-ing" and "ah-ing." Very shiver-making, that vast tidal wave of sound; it was *enormous*.

In Hamadan, which is five hundred kilometers west of Teheran, villagers sacrificed sheep.

With time on my hands, I have a question dear to my heart: Why have the great majority of demonstrators and mob participants been *women*? What do they search for, hope to achieve—those lumpy, muffled, amorphous creatures in black chadors? It can't be more rights for women, not in an Islamic republic. *Fewer* rights for women?

The *Kayhan* is loaded with articles and pictures on women and their rights; e.g., a group of university women demonstrated in Teheran in Western dress yesterday, calling for a government that would respect equality between the sexes. Where were they when the Shah faded into the sunset? It was he who banished the chador and veil and began the education of women and gave them legal rights such as representation of their side in divorce cases. Only a few days ago there were statements from the "opposition" saying women must respect their "place." And there have been publicized threats in Tabriz, Kerman, and Hamadan that women not wearing the chador will be knifed or have acid thrown in their faces. There's nothing I admire more than big, strong men who threaten females with the cold acid treatment.

Since everyone, man and woman alike, has a mustache, it's possible the women also have the balls. I don't mean anatomically; I'm merely reverting to my instinctive feeling that these downtrodden ladies actually direct the homes, the country, and possibly the revolution. I'm dying to see how things work out when Khomeini starts issuing palace proclamations. Move over, Madame Defarge.

As for Khomeini on women's rights, he is a mass of outrageous contradictions. On a given day he declares that Islamic law shall prevail, including the traditional subjugation of women. The next, he ardently promises equality for the female.

The truth is, low profile or no profile, I'm just itching to get out there and march. I would like to state here and now that it's pure hell being in the midst of a really hot revolution and unable to participate.

Instead, we have been warned via the "communications pyramid" to take to the mattresses or else to our basements. Without a basement and with my back to the courtyard wall, I have no alternative but to await my fate, plan next month's budget, and gird myself for a hot game of Risk with Mike Montgomery, whom I cajoled into playing. One haircut for five games of Risk. We're not expecting Khomeini on this kutche, and I for one plan to remain calm.

I am incensed by a *Kayhan* article, dateline Damascus, Monday, January 15, 1979, and I paraphrase: George Hab-

233

bash, that pirate who runs the Popular Front for the Liberation of Palestine, said his Marxist group will fully cooperate with the opposition here despite ideological differences. The bloodsucker! I'd like to see *those* differences remain irreconcilable till the end of time. He'll be the first to turn on Iran the minute he decides they can't do *him* a world of good.

It's tragic that Khomeini is anti-Israel, anti-Zionist, and anti-imperialist. Well, we American imperialists can take care of ourselves, and we deserve plenty of the castigation we get. But why is poor little Israel subject to everyone's wrath? I myself find hate nonproductive and very unhealthy.

Life has narrowed down to one's roommates, immediate neighbors, and whoever works in an adjacent office, when we work. The isolation, along with the unceasing harassment, is the most difficult thing to endure.

If I were to describe Bell's people at this point I would call them generous, selfish, brave, cowardly, one-for-all, and me-for-me.

I suspect it is time for one Bell person, John Maiorana, to go home. He is so wired he can no longer discuss the literary synthesis of Sylvia Plath without reverting to Iran's toil and trouble. I mean, the guy is a literary bore. Roddey is in better fettle, but his tastes lean to Mayan and Incan civilizations, and they're just too remote for my wartime mentality.

I am busy as a beaver.

Here at Fort Liberty it's a herculean job keeping everyone fed and entertained and out from underfoot; it's like operating a kindergarten. I get the distinct impression that every grown man on this kutche follows me around waiting for my next instructions. I have even been giving occasional *haute cuisine* cooking lessons (the recipes depending on what ingredients I can beg, borrow, or swap).

To date I have taught Skip, Roddey, and the crew, plus casual infiltrators, how to: bake yeast bread from scratch—men have great hands and arm muscles for kneading dough; make tortillas, enchiladas, and tacos; bake cakes and roll pie dough; and why you tear lettuce for salads instead of cutting it. Not one of these guys had ever cooked more than an egg, and every one of them has a natural flair and will make some girl very happy one day.

Another home front diversion is playwriting. Roddey, Skip, and I have been collaborating on a musical revue starring BHI personnel. If we didn't have to spend so much time on

234

the logistics of bare existence, I think we might have a hit on our hands.

The show's big production number features the Nobel Hotel, a high class bordello that's a blight on local Islam. I'd give an eyetooth to get in there but haven't found a single man who will confess to ever entering its doors. I gather it's patronized by rich Iranians and wealthy foreigners.

Since Iranian soldiers are adaptable to either sex, I'm surprised there's a need for prostitutes. But there is. And there are. One buck, and she'll lift her chador. I was the unhappy witness to one of these transactions on a sunny afternoon in June; the end result was that I worried for weeks that she was some poor wife whose husband clapped his hands three times, said "I divorce you," and left her the sole support of four small children.

At the Nobel the going price is three hundred bucks, and I hear they're Asian and Iranian whores who are terribly talented.

Some of the Thai wives run a nice little business on the side. They import Thai girls for lonely helicopter pilots and mechanics. The girls make good wives and the men are as happy with them as Iranians are with *their* arranged marriages. Just the same, such mercenary matchmaking sticks in this freedom fighter's craw.

Saturday, 20 January 1979

Just this side of open mutiny, Ma Bell came through. After weeks of deprivation, each of us is to receive ten litres of naft. With careful rationing, that's several weeks of heat and hot water!

I am back at work on the base, and as I explained to Mother on the phone last night, there is simply no one but mini-directress Sterling to keep flight plans and paper work flowing for the clamoring maintenance masses. She in turn thinks BHI contemptible for keeping us overlong at the fair.

I explained about manning the fort for the Defense Department. Mother said, "Let the Defense Department do its own dirty work!" I repeated that Bell's contract is with the U.S. government, not Iran, and it's the American embassy that has not yet ordered us to evacuate in full. "And there's *another* department with a lurid history of overstaying its welcome," sniffed Mother. "Mark my words, those poor souls are going to sit down to lunch one of these days with manacles in lieu of napkins."

Mother has thoroughly refreshed my memory about the historic reliability of our State Department from the Boxer Rebellion right through Pearl Harbor.

She's so hopping mad she plans to call both senators, Bell Helicopter International, three friends in Washington and David Brinkley. They'll be sorry, with Mother hot on their tails.

We, the children of Bell, are the last American pawns in a teetering game of diplomacy. I don't mind being a pawn at all, so long as I can go back to being queen of the prom. We assumed an element of risk when we contracted to work here; that's one of the reasons we're well paid. Sometimes I close my eyes and hear brass bands playing, see flags waving, hear a deep voice intoning, "Robinson Sterling, you have represented your country's interests with valor. When it was not possible to send in the marines, you carried the flag." After a rending belch, the voice continues, "I therefore award you the Betty Crocker Good Conduct Medal, with Haircutting Kit."

Last night Skip and Roddey got high as hooty owls on the last of our Iranian wine and engaged in a nonstop diatribe about those bestial Iranian students, guests in *our* country, who tried to attack the Shah's aged mother in Beverly Hills. Accompanying our brave mechanics in the orchestra pit were the joub dogs.

Our personal pack at Liberty Hall is without a doubt the finest dogs I have known, nearly as noble as Kitty Kat. Monica Bloodworth, who worked at Telemedia, felt these animals such an outstanding breed that, at great expense, she shipped five of them back to the States, hoping to start a new American Kennel Club strain. The AKC was too shortsighted to see it, but the veterinarian who looked them over was astounded. They are about the size of our family Labradors, and their jaws are twice normal size, like a wolf's. Though they could snap my head off, they are friendly and loving.

I feed ours, even if it's only Campbell's soup and saebsi, and they in turn guard me like a rajah's daughter. My favorite, Luke, is an awful sight to see. His large bowel hangs out of his hindquarters and he drags it around behind him, all

236

the while churning away doing whatever it is supposed to do. He has magnificent, soulful eyes and never complains about his hard lot.

Our next charter flights are due to arrive at Khatemi on February 2, though we're having all sorts of difficulties with them. Pan Am enters Iran very erratically. Either the control tower operators are on strike. Or the ground crews. Or, again, the Pan Am stewardesses. The *Kayhan* informs us that our beloved Pan Am stewardesses refuse to fly into this benighted land, and there is some sort of international flight law which requires stewardesses to be aboard. What on earth for? We'd all be tickled pink to provide self-service.

BHI maintenance is now, field, fort, hangars, and offices, down to less than two hundred souls, eighty-three of whom can't be counted as they are "on vacation"—holed up awaiting evacuation in house or hotel.

Skeleton crews left by other companies are hanging on in the ridiculously faint hope of keeping their government contracts and their company secrets. Iran is the biggest gravy train foreign companies have ridden in years, and plenty of people aren't ready to get off until the very last stop. There are hours and days and whole weeks when I don't blame the Iranians for being anticolonialist and anti-Western.

The *Kayhan* is chock-full of news about other nationals' departures. At the request of the Imperial Japanese government, the last 3979 Japanese have been flown out. There were seven thousand here before the unrest. Gerhard Rizel, the West German ambassador, ordered the last remaining German nationals to leave Thursday on Lufthansa charters. Ambassador Sir Anthony Parsons of Great Britain has requested that the final three thousand Britons leave forthwith on waiting British Air Force Hercules. And what have we heard from Ambassador William Sullivan of the United States? "Your move," says he to the pawns.

The Kouroush is jam packed with waiting Americans. I took stacks of papers and went over there to work today, and the place looks like London during the blitz. There are no chairs in the lobby so that no one will be tempted to lounge around inviting attack, and fire hoses are strung everywhere, at the ready.

Supply and demand being what they are, the Kouroush has doubled its room rates to one hundred dollars per day.

As for the Iranians, score them five hundred points for

taking care of their own. Islamic co-ops, supported by wealthy citizens and the mosques, have been set up everywhere to provide cheap food for those who are hungry. If one has no money, the food is free. Some of the co-ops have been attacked by soldiers; but, staffed by volunteers, they continue to operate. Most have been in existence since December and are very effective in forcing prices down and preventing looting. The co-ops, as much as anything, have given me a good idea of the determination of these people to have a democratic world.

Majid, like his family, believes ardently in this new world and is a zealous Khomeini advocate. He tells us proudly of Khomeini's promises to all: free gas, free mah-sheens, free food, free schools, free everything. Majid is partaking generously of the old pie in the sky. I haven't sought to disenchant him, nor to shake his simple faith. He is so pleased at the prospect of his magnificent future I wouldn't have the heart.

And who's to foot the bill for this national Nirvana? Oil money, properly applied, could do it. Nevertheless, revolution exacts its tolls. Look at the disintegrated heelos. As for oil refineries, if they remain idle overlong they require extensive rebuilding and refitting. And Iranian foundry workers let the fires in their coke ovens die, which in turn cracked the furnaces, and Lord only knows how long it'll take to repair *that* destruction.

Iranian Army and Air Force morale is at an all-time low. With the Shah gone, officers and men alike are at sixes and sevens. I expect the enlistees at Havan-e-Ruz to mutiny any morning now. If the army collapses, Liberty's M-80s are at the ready. If not for self-defense, at least for the best road show in town.

We have given careful thought to the goldfish. He belongs to Dawn Liberty. I do not wish him to fall into unfriendly hands. Roddey and Skip suggested we poach and eat him or sacrifice him to Khomeini. I myself will not condone torture at the hands of Iranian infants. I'll save him from that fate by slipping him down a qanat to live to a sightless but advanced old age.

Sunday, 21 January 1979

There has been heavy gunfire outside our courtyard all day. Since we were on Down Time, we were right here to serve as handy targets. We crept into the kutche during a lull and found tic-tac-toes of bullet holes in our walls. Finally we darted across the city to wallow piteously in Akhbar's carpets. We decided if we left home, whoever was trying to scare us—and succeeding—might quit. It could have been anyone from *qomani* snipers to rebellious army units to kutche kids who've finally gotten their hands on those Russian guns.

Akhbar and his bazaar friends were glad to see us, and we them. They seem to be suffering as much deterioration as we; everyone is starting to shrivel before our eyes. It's a funny thing about these rug merchants: Born traders all, they tell us with hollow cheeks yet stars in their eyes that under the coming socialism profit will no longer be important—everyone will be content with a modest living only!

Monday, 22 January 1979

Skip and Roddey insist on getting up hours before time to go to work, and we're confined to such close quarters I can't sleep a wink when they crash around. I was so weary yesterday, and then our next-door neighbors to the north, the Amejiris, partied all night; their son had come home from the wars. He's been a conscriptee in Najafabad, which must have been a strain. According to Majid and the *Kayhan*, the army burned down half of Najafabad and murdered a number of people there. Majid told me this with a suggestive shrug toward the Amejiri house. I was a little hesitant about going over there to drink chie and welcome home the conquering hero, especially if Majid's crowd has marked the place for swift and violent vengeance.

Schizoid feelings about whose side one is on continue. Mostly I try to smile at everyone and stay the heck out of their quarrels.

Even with help from Bell, we are on very short rations.

239

The single supply running merrily along, rhythm and function unaltered, is the sewer below Liberty Hall. The smell has been so vile that I wondered briefly if the underground was trying to gas the populace.

I think we finally have sources for most of our needs. Mr. Amejiri's oldest son, Hamid, whom we'd never met until last night, is going to buy Liberty's household effects in one fine fell swoop. He offered a very fair price, and he owns The Flats gas station, or rather operates it, as all gas stations are owned by the government. To conclude our deal, he appeared with extra food, naft, and benzine, everything we needed, though our needs, after so much privation, are not exorbitant. Our lives have thus taken a strong turn for the better.

Skip was so delirious at the sight of an honest-to-God roast of beef that, to Mr. Amejiri's delight, he threw his arms bodily about him. As for me, I will go happily to my grave if I never see another chicken or noodle again.

All this was nothing compared to today's uproar! The three Esfahan departmental heads were fired. "Off with their heads!" roared the merry Queen of Hearts, BHI. They are all very bright and decent men who made a stand and insisted Bell was being profligate with its employees' lives, that someone was going to be killed. Pyramid communications immediately scorched the airwaves with the news. Apparently the Big Three were told that the Department of Defense really *does* need us as a last toehold for the U.S. in Iran. So the Big Three announced, "Screw the U.S., let's get our people out of here." And were fired for their trouble. I wonder if we should commission an oratorio on this?

With the execs gone, we junior helots will keep what's left of the store going. Skip and Roddey insist the mechanics and pilots who remain are the cream of the crop. Me, I see only the ones who are barely making it and am aghast at the big strong men falling apart. It's my observation that men are less adaptable to stress than women.

Listen, no matter how many severance checks, tax breaks, and hardship bonuses overseas people are given, they're completely justifiable. Leave unforeseen hardship and hectoring out of it; simply moving wives and families around the world from culture to culture, investing in new homes and automobiles, getting one's life reorganized and refunctioning in a strange corner of the globe, takes a tremendous toll physically and psychologically.

240

As for your average American abroad, some adjust gracefully to change and alien environments. Plenty should never leave their home towns. There ought to be a test, some kind of psychological screening, which would determine who's a good candidate for foreign service and who's not. Every company abroad should then conduct obligatory indoctrination courses so new employees learn *in depth* the history, habits, manners, mores, and culture of the people they've been sent to live with. Here in Iran we might just have made ourselves and the U.S. a lot of new friends instead of so many bitter enemies.

Right now we're *all* mad at each other. The Iranians in the avionics and armament shops went on strike today, saying we are not sympathetic with their cause. As they are a generally shiftless lot who seldom worked but devoted their time to petty thievery, our avionics and armament men were thrilled to pieces. The Iranians had also taken to being overbearing and baiting our men to fight. The situation was becoming untenable, as there are American mechanics in those shops with fuses shorter than my little finger. With tempers so taut, it's a relief to have the Iranians out of there and chattering in the naft lines.

It's impossible for me to show unmitigated support for their revolution until I've heard Khomeini's final stand on ERA.

With the sound of the axe falling on the Big Three came the chop-chop that everyone, no exceptions, must move to Shahinshahr immediately. Details to follow.

It's easy for the company to enforce such a move by taking away housing allowances and providing free housing only at Shahinshahr. The ranks of soon-to-be-unemployed will fall right into line. I think even *I* can tolerate Shahinshahr, which is unadulterated American suburbia, though I'd never join the restless hordes at the Kouroush, even at gun point. I'd go stark, staring mad locked in a hotel for weeks on end.

Meanwhile, I've got the office shipshape and running like a destroyer at twenty-eight knots. All the decisions I always wanted to make, and didn't dare, come rolling out of me like a seasoned first mate's orders.

Tuesday, 23 January 1979

Concertina wire, barbed, suddenly appeared around the hangars and outbuildings, and I feel as though I'm up here directing a prison camp. It's very unpleasant.

Over at Telemedia, Donna's life is indescribably bad. Their teachers and personnel have always endured a minor purgatory, what with heckling and catcalling and lewd commentary. Now it's plain hell. The officers are as unnerved as chickens with a skunk in the yard, and discipline has gone the way of naft supplies. The soldier-students are rude and unruly, and only a few of the women teachers have been able to tough it out.

Khomeini the messiah is due home this weekend, and this seems to be giving everyone moral carte blanche to wax more wild and wooly. Our message, natch, is to keep a low profile. Bakhtiar has his back to the wall and can no longer fudge with airport closings and other delaying tactics. He will be forced to open Mehrabad, Khomeini will land with a thud, and the military will split right down the middle and undoubtedly kill each other off.

Jim Holland says that without his Shahinshah, even Shahnaz is running around like a chicken with its head cut off; that he and the other officers can't believe their beneficent leader has fled, leaving them holding a Pandora's box of disagreeable surprises. The land will be rent asunder, and we Americans will drop into the cracks and pfttt!—drown in the qanats.

Yesterday John Moffit tried to rebel, do what many of us have longed to. His landlord offered to buy the Moffits' furniture at rockbottom prices and then refused him permission to hold a sale, so John piled everything out front and began touching matches to it. He was immediately surrounded by an enraged mob of would-be shoppers. They opened his head like a coconut, and he had to flee in a bath of blood. Botched the job, but his heart was right where everyone else's mouth is.

To top the litany of heart- and headaches, a Bell wife was raped. And I was so smug in thinking that a certain reverence for women, not extending to the crotch-lift, would keep us safe. The woman answered the door thinking it was her husband home from the base, and instead confronted a grinning kutche gang. Ma Bell has issued stern directives about no woman living alone or stepping into a street unguarded.

It's been a very long, very, very hard day, like so many of late, trying to keep abreast of terminations, threats, demoralizing information (to be transmitted as gently as possible), moves to Shahinshahr, inventorying stolen equipment, and so on. I am too exhausted even to locate my sense of humor.

I find myself wishing it were over and done with, that we could fly through time, and that magical spring would be here. Spring and *No Ruz*. No Ruz is the single happy-go-lucky, jolly event on the Iranian calendar, the Persian New Year at the spring equinox. In parts of the country people dress in Mardi Gras splendor or their best tribal costumes and dance in the streets; the equinox is hailed by the firing of cannon (into the sky), and the traditional No Ruz feast contains seven traditional dishes beginning with the letter "s": e.g., *sib* (apple), *serkeh* (vinegar), *senjed* (olive), *sir* (garlic), *siah daneh* (fennel), *saebsi* (herbs), etcetera. On the *haft sin* table are the traditional settings of as many candles as there are children, the Koran, rosewater, a fish, and colored hard-boiled eggs—startlingly like Easter! On the thirteenth day everyone in the country, *everyone*, leaves his house empty so the spirits may frolic and then won't disturb the household for the remainder of the year—reason enough for all of Iran to go into the beautiful, flowering spring countryside, picnic, play, and socialize.

Seeing No Ruz, one sees the best of Iran.

Wednesday, 24 January 1979

Early this morning it became hyperofficial: All housing allowances are cut off, and everyone had better hie himself on the double to Shahinshahr. It's no fun assigning families living space, as they angrily proclaim that among a thousand petty tyrannies this is another company plot to tear them away from their happy hearths, get them to terminate instead of waiting for their RIF-ing, give up, leave town, go home. We plead that it's dangerous as hell out there. But this is a last stand being made by people who are unbelievably stubborn about their own lives.

Chuck Dutton told me yesterday, swearing it's the God's truth (voice low, tone sincere; he's inherited Liberty's mantle) that the reduction in force will proceed shortly, and when the numbers or equations are exactly right, the rest of us will leave en masse for Red China. The Chinese premier *did* visit the Shah last September, but I'd swear it was only a little chie klatch, probably to swap oriental carpets and insult the mutual enemy Russia. Just in case, however, I am offering up a prayer that Ma Bell might use an able administrator in Nanking.

Since the departure of the Big Three (huddled now in the Kouroush Hotel), we unfortunately have some of our less desirable leaders in charge. I have work to do, and when they issue me idiotic directives, I ignore them, as they seldom get around to asking if I've followed through anyway. The charters are as slow as molasses in January. One plane sneaked in and out on the tenth, another on the fifteenth, and a third on the twentieth. Our emigrés, we hear, are standing in line to use the hotel bathrooms. One enterprising entrepreneur has found a quiet corner and is printing up carloads of freshly inspired T-shirts. Many of the fellows already sport his latest: "Stay and Die with BHI," which is a little macabre even for my tastes.

Friday, 26 January 1979

Khomeini was due in the country again today, but Bakhtiar, in conjunction with the Shah-loyal air force, closed all the airports so there could be no ingress or egress (I'm really pleased at this opportunity to use the words ingress and egress).

Newspaper articles and NIRT radio indicate Khomeini is promising all things to all people, and good gracious me, he does sound like "them crooks in Washington," as Ma Kettle used to declaim. It's said that the Moslem leaders of Iran mix in politics like no Islamic leader in any other country, and I believe it; this man sounds practiced. In one speech he promises all material goods will be shared equally. In another, that the mullahs are to regain their traditional wealth—in trust for the people. And so on.

Meanwhile, I do hope he has some plans for law and order. After the lesson of Shiraz, when Bakhtiar lifted martial law and there was unholy pillaging, looting, and murder, we learned in a hurry that no matter the leadership, however chaotic the country, some kind of a police force better be on hand or the reign of terror starts. I am even, I suppose, glad to have Shahnaz immediately on hand.

Joke of the week (repeated by me in feeble tones): What is the difference between a holy and an unholy war? Answer: blessed bullets.

Eerily, the Iranian world has not heard a word of the Shah since his departure. It's as if his people had literally willed him out of existence. We heard rumors he was in Switzerland, in Mexico, in France. Then Mother called and informed us castaways that he is in Egypt! No one here even made a near-guess.

With Khomeini closing in, I'm not certain why the fighting grows heavier; the only thing we conjecture is that people are afraid the army will attempt a coup. There are constant armed clashes, and we don't know if the public has been stealing or buying contraband weapons, or if it's different factions of the military fighting it out joub to joub. An armed fire fight is not exactly the place to poke one's nose inquiring as to methods and motivations—not unless you want leaded tongue for lunch.

According to Khomeini, capitalists and Marxists will be allowed to exist side by side while being guided gently "to the right." I'll just bet they'll be guided gently—with .38 caliber guns indelicately nudging their backs. It'll be firing squads for breakfast, and a nice thick noose over dinner.

Dr. Whitcomb: ". . . terror occurs in the latter phases of any revolution and is employed by the radicals after they come to power. . . ."

It is the face of terror that we recognize already. And already my moderate friends like Akhbar and Hamid Amejiri are beginning to think this wasn't *all* such a grand idea. They wished for democracy and inherited anarchy. Bless and keep them, Allah, every one.

I still go along if the revolution really means more freedom, better government, and real power to the people. That's why my great-great-great-great-grandfather died at Lexington. But I remain skeptical about Khomeini, who's no Washington, and touchy about the Tudeh, whose rough Red hands grow ever more apparent. Yesterday there were cassettes of Red army songs playing from our corner minaret!

I now have in my files a stack of written threats and "Incident Reports" that would gag a goat. One of my favorites was submitted by Ernie Pfeiffer, he of the Arkansas Ozarks, long beard, no socks, and Old Testament profile. Poor Ernie. He has lived and boarded with an Iranian family for five years and is a decent, God-fearing, Iranian-liking man who still can't comprehend why his Persian friends have suddenly disowned him. *Everyone* likes Ernie, he is so happy and willing to help, and as Liberty says, is such a goddamn jewel.

(Note: Your usual run of helicopter mechanics is not noted for literary fluency.)

INCIDENT (WHAT HAPPENED) *Myself and 4 other Americans were waiting in the mess hall line and 1 or 2 Iranians said loud enough Yankies go home and us Americans just ignored that, and while me and another American was sitting at our table eating our lunch we kind of looked around us, and the other Iranians waiting in the mess line looked at us real weird like with hate in there faces toward us. As we are not welcome to much anymore in these mess hall, so I said to the other American, I get that feeling we are not welcome much no more, and he agreed with me. That's all.*

POLICE INVOLVED _____ YES ___ X ___ NO
BHI ACTION _____ none _____

Ernie has been packing a lunch and eating in the hangar, and it has taken a lot out of him.

Our communications pyramid informs us the last Grumman people guarding U.S. radar equipment at Khatemi Air Base were forced to pull out two days ago when their soldiers went bananas. The handful of Grumman men just had time to snatch the computer keys so the radar would no longer be operational. And so it appears that at least one air force detachment is moving away from the Shah and Bakhtiar and toward Khomeini.

This division of forces between Khomeini and Bakhtiar is ridiculous and unhappily bears out Uncle Roger: Two old revolutionaries, long-time enemies of the Shah and proponents of the people, one banished and the other imprisoned, both with the same goals for Iran, are not only reaching for each other's throats but are also leading their country step-by-step toward civil war. It's power they want, and not for their people.

This is the Sabbath, and Skip and I ventured into the streets to try to find a kutche store open so I could buy some desperately needed groceries. Stores and co-ops are operating at fuller and fuller capacity, the co-ops still very nicely keeping retail prices from soaring sky-high. Again we thank you, inspired creator of the co-op scheme. We were waited on at a kutche store with a minimum of scowling, undoubtedly because private enterprise is taking a terrible licking.

For the first time in months we walked streets *not* filled with troops, and we felt ectoplasmic, like the world had become a gelatinous blob. Then we peeked into a back kutche to see if it looked safe, and there, camouflaged and keeping a low profile in vacant lots and side streets, were hundreds upon hundreds of troop trucks and tanks. It was positively terrifying.

We had ventured past the Kouroush and Suite hotels earlier, and were able to wave to old friends like Nancy Reason and Dan Allen. Everyone had the look of caged animals.

It's true that people there are surrounded by armed guards, which is an impossibility in private homes, but I have ambivalent feelings about this fishbowl existence. One irritable Irani sergeant could easily turn a tank gun or bazooka right on the nearest mezzanine and annihilate a whole big bunch of people.

It's really a dreadful existence. The Kouroush shows non-stop movies in an effort to prevent open rebellion, but everyone there is crotchety and trapped and beginning to think it a huge plot to make them eat in the hotel's crummy, high-priced restaurants, reopened for the seige.

Skip and Roddey informed me this morning that I look like warmed-over death. Even if I felt like primping, which I don't, I own not a hair curler or a jar of face cream: Everything's been sold at faroush.

Saturday, 27 January 1979

Today I proceeded downtown to ER to assist in the process of moving all BHI personnel to Shahinshahr. Also, RIF-ing finally began for real, on Wednesday last. I didn't mention it because I didn't quite believe it. Reduction in force is actually happening, if only, thus far, on paper. This quieted the crepe-hangers but did not wholly shut them up, a blessing too monumental to hope for.

The *Kayhan* tonight reports that Carter's White House snubbed the Khomeini envoy. Furthermore, he, Karter the Dog, has publicly rebuked Khomeini for not supporting Bakhtiar's government. Will the nincompoop never pipe down? I can't believe my ears or his mouth. Khomeini is a proud old man, jealous of his prerogatives and his righteousness. He won't forget such a slight nor the insult to his face, and he is the one who will direct this corporation.

Perhaps it's overeasy for us here at hand to feel Iran's pulse. Nevertheless, I can't believe, with the many Iran experts in our foreign service, that the U.S. is so insensitive to what is happening here.

If Washington had an ounce of sense, it would hold chie parties for everyone who drops by, court them all, and support whoever comes out on top.

I just hope it's true there are contingency plans to evacuate us via a military corridor. I can see myself now, fighting hand to hand, retreating toward Saudi Arabia, cursing Carter every hard-fought inch of the way.

Sunday, 28 January 1979

There's been a war! Word spread like wildfire up and down the communications pyramid that Shahnaz's army finally took sides and battled it out at the Crown Prince Reza Pahlavi Base. No one is sure of details except that there was bitter in-fighting between the pro-Shah and the pro-Khomeini forces. It lasted two days, and they apparently used everything that came to hand, including the heelo guns, and the

248

whole base is reported to look like Berlin after the bombings. We don't know who won, only that a lot of soldiers were killed or hurt.

The telephone and wireless trotlines say many officers are dead. I'll bet my socks Arbob wasn't among them. Probably hid in the ladies' toilet through the whole thing. Someone in top Iranian military circles has informed us officially that our safety can no longer be guaranteed. My word, I never suspected it was—guaranteed, I mean.

Thus, with a muffled bang, endeth BHI's official existence in Esfahan.

The news caught everyone totally off-guard. I don't know why, when we've talked of this possibility for weeks. Most military mutinies have been in the army, and why shouldn't we at Havan-e-Ruz have expected some of the same? Nevertheless, the moaners and wailers are mad as wet hens that they can't go back on base to pick up tools, personal effects, etcetera. They are indignant and affronted, when they should be thankful they didn't get their heads blown off.

When the news came, Gary and Terry Peyson, brothers who are both 205 pilots, were here at the house talking to Skip about the condition of the helicopters. Millions of dollars worth of ships have been sitting on the line for almost a month. First there was no fuel to fly them, then parts and tools were stolen in wholesale lots. Our boys cranked them up and started them idling as often as possible, but eventually there was no fuel even for this. So, untended and unused, they're deteriorating at an alarming rate. If they're to be serviced and flown by the typical Iranians we've worked with here, the crack-up rate should run about eighty percent.

Our men are sickened at the waste. They've tried to keep the parts oiled and greased, and Mike Montgomery, in a frenzy of misguided intention, even took to Turtle-waxing and shining the bodies so they wouldn't look so bedraggled.

These ships belong to Iran, but everyone wishes we could have flown them somewhere to safety for the duration. Their slow disintegration is like watching the end of the age of the dinosaurs. Awesome and shattering.

Later: I did exactly what mother warned me not to, and nearly paid with my scalp. Roddey, chewing his Allen wrench, was engrossed in *Mila 18,* so Skip and I decided to step over to Mike and Barry and Ben's for breakfast before my ride to downtown ER arrived. Right beyond our courtyard we came on an Iranian man being beaten by soldiers, and when he managed to break through a courtyard gate and run into a nearby house, shouting "I am your brother," neighbors appeared, children shrieked, and soldiers ran up and down our kutche screaming "Get him!" Then they began firing at everyone in sight. By this time they were between us and our gate, so with a fat Iranian woman, her little girl, and a quizzical young man who appeared to be a retarded son, we climbed over a kind of hedgerow into what we thought was a vacant lot and dead end. Skip and the young man had to stop and hoist the woman across, which attracted the soldiers' closer attention and then they were shouting "Get them!" at *us*. The woman said harshly, "Follow me," and led us through a small gate behind an abandoned grape arbor, around a garbage dump, and out into another kutche. She unlocked a courtyard gate and steered us into a very poor, shacklike house where she made us sit down and keep quiet while she boiled up some chie. She was very close-mouthed and disapproving and calm through the whole affair. When the little girl started to whimper, and the young man looked like he might, she gave them a brutal tongue-lashing and went back to her chie-making. She made us stay for almost an hour and finally, via some inner alarm system, indicated it would be safe for us to leave. She never said thank you, but in her strange way she sure repaid any favors.

We returned to find Roddey pacing the yard and my ride to ER come and gone. He had ventured into the kutche to search for our bodies and was so distraught he was clammy from head to foot. As for me, it was my first experience being shot at, and the more I think about it the madder I am I couldn't shoot back. It gives one a vivid conception of how these people have felt at the mercy of their own armies.

Skip analyzed the whole fire fight step-by-step and declared all of our attackers lousy shots.

Gary and Terry told us earlier that the increased street fighting is because there's a firearms pipeline operating in the bazaar, and all the latest weapons, smuggled in by Libya or the PLO, are on sale in back rooms and under the counters. University students are buying them as fast as they can take up collections.

I think the men who shot at us were *homophars* (NCOs). Skip says so, he recognized their insignias. Lord, but he's calm. I examined him for grazes and scrapes and he didn't even have a goose bump.

As for me, I glanced in Liberty's remaining mirror and was not surprised to find a vision as unlovely as Redd Foxx's "seventy-year-old white woman."

Tuesday, 30 January 1979

There has been a serious lapse in this journal and in my life (to which I feel I have added another ten years). After months of writing up "incidents" about others, I now find most of them happening to me.

Late on the afternoon of the 28th, known as one more Bloody Sunday, an escort appeared to take me to the Kouroush, the current ER headquarters. (We've been moving around like Yugoslavian guerrillas, snatching up papers as we run.) It was about five o'clock, but I thought, "Oh, well, maybe I can help for a few hours."

I was greeted by a scene of such utter insanity that I decided I'd be needed till the middle of next month. I typed and shuffled paper and filled out embarkation orders until my eyes rattled in their sockets. By the time I'd finished, it was too late to call the boys, and anyway I'd found Donna so I spent what was left of the night in her temporary hotel bunk room. At six in the morning, after borrowing a toothbrush and wallowing gloriously in a hot tub, I went back to work and worked nonstop until seven o'clock in the evening, when the feces hit the fan.

It was then that an American shot an Iranian taxi driver—over a lousy two-hundred-rial cab fare. The shooter was a Puerto Rican guy from New York City, and he got the shootee in the jaw. The New Yorker had been goaded and baited to the point that the cabdriver's snide remarks added the last straw to his camelback. The American had smuggled the gun into Iran, and oh my Lord, there was trouble in River City.

Within minutes the Kouroush was besieged by twenty thousand howling Iranians clawing at the doors, screaming imprecations and insults. Eventually most of us xaerigi were layered like sardines on the second floor, with every mechanic, pilot, and executive trying vainly to shut off the elevators,

251

which I thought was a damn-fool idea. If the place had been torched, we'd have been trapped.

McGaffey, the U.S. Consul I considered no leader of men, arrived to speak to the crowd. He had a great deal of difficulty getting their attention. We never did hear him over the din, and we made continuous surly remarks about his total vocabulary of "now, now, everyone, let's keep a nice low profile."

Finally the army arrived. Not to cordon off the place, but to stand across the avenue tugging at their pajama bottoms and speculatively picking their noses.

The mobs attacked the rooms on the lower floor, while several hundred of us stayed tightly jammed in the upper stories in helpless misery. Then McGaffey earned his pay and his Distinguished Service Cross. He gathered us up like a flock of fluttering chickens and led us, single file, through that ranting, screaming mob. My personal exit was made with eyes and head so lowered I could count the stitches in my stockings. I was spat on and shoved and preparing to die, but the crowd wasn't quite hopped up enough for mass murder.

David McGaffey was so cool I could not believe it. He bore the brunt of the crowd's wrath and emerged bloody and bowed. But he got every one of us safely through in the finest exhibition of pure guts I've ever witnessed. His poor head is full of Dr. Jam-Shitty stitches, and I certainly hope when we get out of here that the State Department will treat him to the best plastic surgeon in the business.

Old and defeated, all of us, over a two-hundred-rial cab fare.

Since I had called the boys that morning and told them not to worry, I shakily hopped a ride to Donna's familiar manse and collapsed into the nearest bed. She poured us both a drink, and I threw mine right up. So much for the bold, brave bandita in her first and last full-scale battle.

The Kouroush and Suite hotels have swallowed their profit motives and banned Americans forever. BHI's final stand is taking place at the Esfahan, which has fair food and inferior rooms. I believe this is our last resort, short of the Nobel Hotel. We are in no shape to cavil and will take anything we can get, thank you.

Wednesday, 31 January 1979

Our days are hectic and our nights sleepless. After Mr. Hamid Amejiri bought all the Liberty's possessions—we found to our horror that we still had scores of things to dispose of. So I took a rest from the rigors of hotel life, girded my loins, and we called over the courtyard wall, "*Faroushinja.*" We were immediately inundated. There were even soldiers and martial law guards, bristling with weapons and hot to shop.

Since the economy is nearly paralyzed, the rich industrialists and businessmen have left the country, and most of the banks are closed again, I can only come to the conclusion that there's been one heck of a lot of under-the-mattress (or under-the-carpet) hoarding going on all these years. Everyone had money to spend.

What they didn't buy, the shoppers stole, right down to the toilet paper from the holders. I was embarrassed for them.

I salvaged a few things to bestow on my favorite garbage man. He's been wheeling his barrow around our neighborhood picking up trash for seventy cents a month, and is one of the politest, gentlest men I've met here. He was so excited with my meagre gifts that his sad rheumy eyes nearly popped. I cursed myself roundly for not giving him more of my worldly goods instead of selling out at five cents on the dollar. Then I gave him a twenty-dollar tip which I could ill afford because none of us has much cash to escape on, explaining that the tip is an old American custom for services well rendered. He thanked me with tears in his eyes.

I gave the last BHI turkey to the joub dogs, who relished every bite of it.

Then Skip and Roddey and I caught a ride with Ben Roche, and we walked into the Esfahan Hotel and picked up our RIF papers, a step I never thought I'd take. It's fine to have the satisfaction of knowing I didn't quit, and that the end came only when my job was extinct. Everyone else's job is also extinct—along with Havan-e-Ruz, the helicopter fleet, the Shah, most politicians, all of Savak, and women's liberation.

After having BHI telex Liberty's faroush money to Detroit,

we were free to move bag and baggage right next door. We'll share the Crew's quarters until we can all troop out to Shahinshahr. Definitely a barracks-type bunkhouse, but the rent's cheap, and, having contributed our Campbell's soup supply to the larder, we feel we've done our wicked duty.

The boys here are, oh my Lord, holding a final farewell faroush. Despite my best-laid plans, I am in the midst of another stampede of maddened cattle. It's terrible to see the growing hate that envelops us. There's no attempt to hide it. And Ms. Robinson Sterling, lover of mankind, cheerleader for the women's world, queen of the prom, can barely endure it.

A bright spot is seeing BHI operate, for the first time, like a top-grade, ripsnorting, rootin'-tootin' copter company should—razor sharp, smooth, and efficient in the teeth of adversity. RIF-ing and evacuating proceed like a day in the General Motors executive suite, and I'm proud of my company.

Literally overnight BHI transferred its operations into the Esfahan Hotel. We're just a roving, hip-pocket corporation without any fancy equipment or superfluity of brass. A few ballpoint pens, and a gross or two of paper, and we could set up shop in a bazaar basement. I repeat that I am proud to be a part of it.

Khatemi Air Base has been reopened as a special dispensation to get us all the hell out of here. There hasn't been a charter since January 20, and someone must be nervous about an American bloodbath or maybe an Allied invasion. We're a thorn in the Iranian side, and it would be fine to have us out of sight and mind. Everyone is entirely too busy sorting out the country and taking up sides to bother keeping track of xaerigi.

BOOK VI

Monday, 4 February 1979

Khomeini is with us at last!

From the moment he arrived I've played hide-and-go-seek all around the town.

I don't know how I hung onto my journal—I certainly couldn't write in it. Not after Khomeini announced in his inaugural speech that he wanted all foreigners' hands cut off. He was speaking symbolically of Islamic law, implying that we are thieves deserving of the traditional Moslem punishment for thievery. Since I need my hands for any number of things, I've kept them in hiding.

After his arrival at Mehrabad Airport, Khomeini was chauffeured across the city in a blue Chevy Blazer and, following a number of inflammatory remarks, prepared to be lifted above the crowd like the angel Gabriel. A 214 helicopter, piloted by several of Iran's ace fly boys, kept trying to put down, gee'd and haw'd, aborted and reaborted, and finally staggered off without him. To Skip's and Roddey's undying delight, he made a disordered retreat in the back of a flower truck.

The guys think the whole affair a preposterous but fitting climax to the Age of Bell Helicopter International in Iran.

Khomeini is sure no Mahatma Gandhi or Martin Luther King. He is purported to be devout, honest, willful, and cruelly uncompromising. I can vouch for the fact that he makes intolerable statements that feel and sound like the pent-up hatred of years in exile pouring out; his continued shouts of "shutting the mouths" of Islam's enemies and "redeeming the rape of Iran" were enough to send the lot of us into seclusion for a day and a night. We literally hit the floor at Montgomery's place and stayed there, afraid the sight of our faces at the windows might incite someone to shoot.

When the tumult and shouting quieted to a dull roar, we made a run for Shahinshahr and arrived without incident.

We can't comprehend why Bakhtiar continues to cling to his nonexistent support. To date, he and Khomeini have done nothing but spar verbally, but last week Bakhtiar made the mistake of supporting the military when they fired into crowds and killed innocent people: I think that'll be enough to hang him. This country is ninety-nine-and-one-hundredth's percent behind the Ayatollah Khomeini, and more and more civilians are armed and eager to shoot. Please, Allah, don't let it be us BHI pigeons.

The first sickening sight to greet us at Shahinshahr was one million pounds of American trunks piled in the offices, parking lots, and courtyards. There's an additional million stacked up at BFS, the Teen Center, and in our warehouses. BHI swears they will eventually be shipped to the States—right after the men, women, and children. This seems improbable.* Those trunks hold people's baby pictures and memories and family treasures and irreplaceable mementoes. It's tough to feel totally impersonal about them.

Shahinshahr, like all our bivouacs, is full of makeshift offices, so I rolled up my sleeves and pitched in with more realignment processing.

The first priority is still evacuation. Pan Am's stewardesses, we hear, have once again refused to fly to Iran (I believe I will have a good, satisfying fist fight with the first one of those dolls I run across in the States), and after that the air traffic controllers went on strike once more. I won't defend the merits of flying without traffic control, as it would be appalling to load a plane with people and have it go down in a mid-air

---

*Score another five hundred points for the revolution. Most of them got home, although rifled, water-soaked, and damaged.

collision. Although there's so little air traffic even this seems unlikely. As for those stewardesses . . .

It was confirmed late this afternoon that we're to be salvaged by MAC, the U.S. military-cargo plane fleet.

There are, we think, some two to three thousand Americans left in Iran. One MAC plane carries 125 passengers, so this will hopefully be a high-intensity operation. MAC flights also mean being bused to Teheran, a 290-mile trip which is against everyone's better judgment, better instincts, and better ideas. Nevertheless two buses made the trip this afternoon in the face of positive information that Khomeini is en route to Qom (directly in their path), and that civil war is imminent.

BHI, faced with more pressing problems, is dismissing housing assignments as third-priority business and sometimes carelessly places three families in a one-bedroom Shahinshahr apartment. It was sheer luck that, as the Crew and I roared into the place, I came upon Ray West, one of the men from my department, just departing. He bequeathed me his house, leftover food, dishes, blankets, and hot water. Otherwise our Cub Scout troop would be roughing it with one blanket, and no heat or hot water. My coterie of Merry Men admitted that it isn't so bad after all, having a lady lookout. We are now comfortably settled with the necessities for the good life— lacking only a favorable climate and country.

The lone inconvenience is a faulty thermostat, which astonishingly provides scalding hot water and scarcely any cold at all. At least it's a change. We borrow cold water from our neighbors and they carry hot water away from here in buckets and barrows.

Though I feel like Jean Lafitte, everyone assures me that we have the departees' blessings to go into empty houses and apartments and help ourselves to whatever we need: canned goods, extra bedding, a mattress. I'm assured this is legitimate scrounging and what we don't use the Iranians will pilfer, but I still feel like a sneak thief.

We have the real variety aplenty. Even in this well-guarded compound—and it *is* a compound, complete with guards, gates, and walls, where Iranians are not permitted entry—the old faroush crowd seems to crawl through cracks, infiltrate the sewers, bribe the guards, and otherwise invade our sacrosanct premises. These final, persistent shoppers are as loathsome as jackals. When one of them looks at me, his mouth

259

fixed in a death's-head grin, his eyes brimming with malice, and says, "I am your friend, please help me"—which translates into "Sell me the fillings from your teeth for two cents apiece"—I look him straight in the eye and say calmly, *"Boro dige cungeshat"*: the sum total of my Farsi curse words. I will never feel trusting again; in my heart I know this is the man who knifed Warren Hollis or fire-bombed Elaine Busbey's car or threw rocks at Martie Balderson's little boy, David.

Skip Maiorana, the Italian wunderkind, is among fifteen men asked to volunteer to stay behind as a BHI rear guard which is quite an accolade if one is of a mind to "Stay and Die for BHI." He refused with what decorum he could muster. The FASC units have also asked for volunteers. Bell is desperately hoping to maintain any kind of toehold, to salvage something from their multi-million dollar operation and that incomparable fleet of aircraft.

Thieves Khomeini may brand us, but everyone down to the file clerks took pride in those ships.

The only statistic we've heard about the fight on base is that 103 men were killed. I keep thinking of the soldiers I knew, of my Xerox guard and Hamid the driver, and Captain Hamishey, wondering where their allegiances lie, wondering if they are wounded or dead.

Tuesday, 5 February 1979

I don't believe I mentioned that one week ago, like a good girl, I collected my year-end, several-thousand-dollar bonus. On promissory paper.

This morning, ever the unhappy riser, I shambled wanly into our new kitchen and looked straight into the repugnant eyes of an Iranian shopper. For all I knew, he had watched me through the night. He signaled like an eight-armed octopus, indicating he wanted my gas capsules and, when I turned my back on him, began pounding the door with a sledgehammer fist. This woke all the guys who, in their assorted boxer and jockey shorts, escorted him through the streets to the guards at the gates of the compound. There was no rough stuff, let's just say that the man will bear the imprint of muscular hands for the rest of his natural life.

I wonder if these crazy shoppers are PLO or Russian spies?

Safe as we seem, it's still not pleasant. While I walked around the streets taking families final forms to be filled out, a carload of Persian charmers followed on my heels haranguing me. I finally turned and spat right on the one dangling from the nearest car window. He came out of the car like a madman. I felt cool as ice. (There was a guard down the street.) I stepped right into him, as casual as a belch, sneered, and spat again. He backed off, squeezed into the car, and away they all drove into the noonday sun. But they grow more emboldened every day. I just hope to heaven my mother never hears about this spitting and snarling and animalistic behavior. Both of us will be mortified.

I have also been asked to notify every mechanic I can locate that General Khosradad has purchased all the tool-boxes and personal equipment on the base (he must have gotten his hands on the crown jewels) and that personnel who had to leave equipment behind will be justly compensated. It was simply lovely to deliver news which, for a marvel, was greeted with cheers, hugs, kisses, and universal joy. A helicopter mechanic's tools, in a box the size of a large cosmetic case, cost him around two thousand dollars.

As Ed Thorpe would say, the remaining men are as useless as tits on a boar hog. They spend entire days playing Hearts or Twenty-One and repeating the conversations of yesterday, last week, and the month before. They continue, like broken records, to gripe at poor BHI, all of Iran, the U.S. government, the United Nations, UNESCO, Rosalynn Carter, Zbigniew Brzezinski, and Cyrus Vance. The single thing they seem able to discuss with joy in their hearts is their bank balance. I am, frankly, a mite sick of them all.

When I've done what I can to be useful, I sit in the sun and read voraciously, this time from the splendid supply of books left behind by Shahinshahr residents.

I, who abhor communal living, am amazed at how delightful I find Shahinshahr. Having a real Western house with real wall-to-wall carpeting (in a virulent turquoise) is downright comforting in times like these. The landscaping is magnificent, reputed to have cost ten million to import seed by seed and blade by blade from the U.S. There are beautiful trees, the grass is as thick and green as a golf course (and the only real grass we've seen in Iran), and the pansies are abloom in January. A ridiculous waste of money, though, when Persian flora would have been exquisite.

There is so much love here, even among the crepe-hangers; everyone is as kind and thoughtful as though dealing with bereaved relatives. If one needs anything at all, one knocks on the door of a perfect stranger, is welcomed with open arms, and one's smallest or largest wish is fulfilled. Everyone acts a little like it may be his last day on earth.

Just down the street is the oil refinery built by Fluor Thyssen, worth billions and it never refined a drop of oil; the company fled in January just as it was completed. There's a half-finished BOC helicopter manufacturing plant nearby; their contract wasn't canceled until they'd invested an initial billion or two; and Boeing, which maintained all aircraft for Iran Air as well as training their pilots and mechanics, left in December. There's also Grumman and NAWASI housing; they were the F-14 people. The F-14 is the highly classified Tomcat, and though the remaining skeleton force is pretty secretive, we gather some of their ships have been flown out of the country to Egypt.

As for the Russians and their toeholds, we haven't heard whether they've departed their ruined steel mill or not; we suspect that they, like BHI, will linger for the company flag and the glory of the motherland. In their case, however, they're probably under strict orders.

Opposite our Shahinshahr bivouac is the pool table, transported from the downtown Teen Center and ensconced in someone's living room. Across the way, in a private home, the ASI Club has again taken root—with booze and food à la Korea. The Koreans from the base, who have unmercifully not been evacuated, are selling mediocre drinks and very bad food at piratical prices. I could never eat their food at Havan-e-Ruz and doubt I'll start here. Koreans are great survivors, natural-born crooks, and poisonous cooks.

Last night we took a gift bottle of wine, Boone's Farm Apple, walked down the street to a neighbor's, and saw *The Choirboys* screened in a private living room. The language was on a par with that of the men in this compound.

Everyone talked about the bus trip to Teheran; we've come to terms with the necessity. If only we could bypass Qom. I've suggested detours through the desert and the mountains, but apparently none are feasible because of 1) quicksand, 2) thousand-foot cliffs, 3) wolf packs, and 4) crazed camel herds. Also, there's only one road.

The Iranian military is escorting Americans from their Teheran hotels to the airport, and certainly we should move out while the army is functioning, however haphazardly. I know the trip is comparatively safe, or was as late as last week, and the sooner we go the better. But still I hesitate.

A drive to Teheran suddenly holds the same terrors as a trip to Mars. Here in Esfahan we are acquainted with our terrain, have established escape hatches. Teheran is an enormous city in an alien land. And we are not even in communication with anyone there, don't know if our people are arriving safely. They could be swallowed up in prison encampments along the way, betrayed for a dollar a [   ] so wayward bus drivers.

I am writing again by candlelight; barq problems [   ] as consistent, if of a different variety, as those of the city barq flickers on and off like twinkle lights on a Christ tree—which is undoubtedly the origin of the term "alter ing current." The heat also goes off at least a little during night, so that our steaming water cools to a bearable temperature; I am perfectly happy to stay up until 2:00 A.M. to have a shower.

Wednesday, 6 February 1979

We sallied forth in throngs to see another bus off for Teheran. There is no pushing, shoving, or panic. If we don't depart this trip, we say goodbye to everyone and return to our packing. BHI is doing a good job making sense of priorities, people, even luggage.

There is now an occasional phone connection to Teheran, and we've ascertained that every bus load to date has arrived safely. We are also told that the street fighting between counterinsurgents grows heavier daily. Since Uncle Roger's thesis on revolution went up in flames at the base, I am unable to make a pithy comparison, but I'd say it's about what he predicted.

All of my office on base, with its administrative files,

equipment, IBM machinery, Xerox, and classified material, was destroyed in the fighting. Damn! There was a picture of an old boyfriend in there I really wanted.

Since I too am as useless as mammaries on a stud horse, I am ready to go. Worse, I can no longer even abide the Iranian women I've championed for so long. They also invade Shahinshahr, and though they don't resort to the bawdy and vile-mouthed harassment of the men and boys, I see them watching with evil glee. How too bad, oh too, too bad I can't say goodbye to Guity or Mama, have a last look at their good faces. Nor Akhbar's. We are running too scared to set foot in the city.

Three Americans, Jack Charles and Billy Huston and Augie Vargas, decided to chance some errands in town and got shot at for their pains. Jack was waiting outside a store, and the others had just joined him in their car when a motorcycle roared up, screeched to a halt, and an Iranian opened fire with a rifle. Whether it was Allah's will or rotten marksmanship, he missed them all at point-blank range.

Another pilot, Jake Pomeroy, came over for morning coffee (yes, coffee!) looking like he'd lost a ten-round fight. He too slipped out of here, and when his Jyanne was wrested from him by a crowd, made the mistake of fighting for its life. The odds must have been a hundred to one, and he not only lost the car, he got forty stitches in his head, administered grudgingly by Jam-Shitty, who further refused him the courtesy of Novocaine.

Jake would never have escaped with his skin if another friendly Iranian hadn't literally heaved him into the back of a truck and driven off; told him he owed Americans a lot of favors and was happy to repay at least one.

In the fight for his car, Jake remembers breaking a baseball bat, literally, over one man's head. It not only didn't knock the man out, it didn't even slow him down. Jake kept babbling, over and over, "I couldn't believe it, Jesus Christ, I couldn't *believe* it!"

If it's about hard heads, *I* sure believe it. I just called Security because more indefatigable Iranians were wiping out the house next door. They are still, theoretically, not allowed in Shahinshahr, but there they were, blissfully trashing a house which Americans left early this morning.

When the Security Police arrived, four of the men fled and

the two who remained tried to cover up their mess, loudly insisting they had bought everything in the place, calling me a devil liar and other sweet nothings. They had emptied the refrigerator contents over the carpeting, defecated on the floors, stomped food into the furniture, and absolutely destroyed the place. Good heavens, don't they know all of this belongs to them, that they should be preserving it for their children and grandchildren?

I kept my voice low-key and made a good impression on the guards, who handcuffed the monsters and then pounded them with their gun butts. I must be getting brutalized; I didn't even flinch.

Tonight we have an additional four people bedded down in our house: Elaine Busbey and Ruth Weems and John Pitts and Kevin Frost. We moved them in here when we found they had neither heat nor hot water in their quarters.

Most exciting of all, Donna and Jackie arrived group across the way. I have been trying to trace the the Havan-e-Ruz War, and we were so relieved at b fellow-survivors we darned near did a dance around American flag.

We have planned a glorious dinner with candlelight and, in lieu of wine, beakers of loving-kindness and a canned ham.

Jackie has given me a terrifying account of his misadventures, most of which nearly caused me heart and kidney failure. He also ran his "attack" vocabulary past me two or three times. He's found that "son of a vulture, rotten bastard, and filthy fucker" scarcely evoke a change of expression, but "dirty whoreson of a sow," rendered in faultless Farsi, gets an Iranian where it really hurts—right in his "face."

Khomeini, ignoring Bakhtiar as if he were a gnat on a screen door, has now begun announcing his own government. Yesterday he named Bazargan, a former university professor and a moderate with wide experience in politics, as his prime minister. Then he, Khomeini, asked for demonstrations of support in every town and city today. I should think he would have had enough parades to last him into his grave, but maybe he feels demonstrations are a force for solidarity. Whatever his purpose, I am grateful not to be out on the highways and byways. We felt certain BHI would cancel the bus trips, but they think it more pressing than ever to move us out, so we keep rolling to Teheran.

Thursday, 7 February 1979

It's me again, Allah, and I'm ready. Our names have been called on the roll up yonder. And our group, Skip and the Crew and I, are awaiting the next bus for Teheran. It's our turn to move out.

Sad *nabashid*. Here I sit like a baffled mud hen, two scarred suitcases at my side, about to leave Iran under a black cloud through forests of unfriendly faces. I have never felt so abjectly miserable in my life.

All the love I had for this fascinating Persian land, for this history-rich city, is it now so shriveled and sere it will never [flo]wer again?

> Come, fill the cup, and in the Fire of Spring
> The winter garment of Repentance fling:
> The bird of time has but a little way
> To fly—and lo, the Bird is on the Wing.

Iran was my adoptive country, and I was happy here, if only for a while.

As I wait in this crowd of anticipatory Americans aquiver like greyhounds, I try to rise above wretchedness, to think of the stuff of good memories: a striking Bakhtiari girl in a goatskin tent; a wonderfully loving Iranian family, Moslems who befriended a Christian and made her a Christmas; a gentle garbage man who cried gentle tears; a fair, fine rug merchant who treated me with scrupulous honesty and great dignity; a grateful family who repaid me handsomely for a favor done one of their own; a humble bus driver who brought me gifts of fruit and candy bought from his meagre salary.

Perhaps if I fix these faces of Iran firm in my mind, I will one day, when its people have found their destiny, be able to return with love. Perhaps we can even begin again, our people and our countries. Maybe, Inshallah, even forge a friendship.

GLOSSARY OF FARSI WORDS
(*except where noted*)

ab: water
abgusht: a "slimy" soup resembling boiled seaweed
agha: mister
alladin: space heater
Allah Akhbar: religious chant; literally, Allah—God, Akhbar—
    proper name of a Moslem martyr
apadana: audience hall
Ayatollah: "Reflection of Allah." Shi'ite religious leader comparable
    to a bishop, position reached only after years of reflection and
    study.
babouche: flat, heelless shoes with pointed toes
barq: electricity
baksheesh: gift
benzine: gasoline
boogalamoon: turkey
caravanserai: wayside inn; originally built to accommodate camel
    caravans
chador: a bulky, sheetlike dress
Char Bagh: THE street in Esfahan
chie: a beverage comparable to tea
dasht: dessert
davakhaneh: drugstore
djellaba: (Arabic) voluminous robes worn by men
dug: Persian drink of yoghurt, salt, and soda. Ghastly.
dust: friend
fahlawi: "practiced" faker or fraud
faroush: a garage sale
fedayeen: (Arabic) native
fixah: fixed price
forudaghe: airport

267

galabaya: (Arabic) voluminous robes worn by men

ghand: sugar

habibi: sweetheart

haji: a Moslem who has made the pilgrimage to the holy city of Mecca

Havan-e-Ruz: Crown Prince Reza Pahlavi Base

homophar: high school graduate (it's a big deal)

hookah: (Arabic) water pipe

hoopoe: thrush-like bird native to the Mideast; has cinnamon and buff plumage with bold black and white bands on wings and back. Large head crest is often touched with red. Call is reiteration of "hoop."

Inshallah: "God willing; it's in God's hands"

jihad: Moslem holy war

joub: irrigation ditch

kebab/kabob: literally "roast." Refers to small squares of meat skewered with vegetables and broiled over fire.

kefiyah: (Arabic) headdress

khan: tribal chieftain

kuku saebsi: omelette with herbs

kursi: a large, round communal bed

kutche: an alleyway

lütfan: "Please"

madare: a school

Maidan: a square, royal Maidan is located in the center of Esfahan

Majlis: parliament

Moharram: Iranian festival of grief for Imam Ali and his sons Hassan and Hossein

moqani: a digger and tender of wells

mosamma bedenjan: eggplant and chicken stew

motshakeram: "Thank you"

mullah: a Muhammadan priest

nabashid: an idiom used with an adjective and having the force of the English "don't be"; e.g., "angry nabashid" means "don't be angry"

naft: kerosene

Otafucus: brand name for Iranian plastic sandal

pesteh: pastry

Peykan: the Cadillac of Iranian cars

qanats: ancient system of underground canals and wells in the desert

Ramazan: month-long religious observance that commemorates the revealing of the Koran to Muhammad

rial: monetary unit of Iran. Approximately 70 rials in one dollar at time of book.

saebsi: dried herbs; often used in open compound words that refer to particular dishes, e.g., gormeh saebsi, kuku saebsi

Bantam Book Catalog

Here's your up-to-the-minute listing of over 1,400 titles by your favorite authors.

This illustrated, large format catalog gives a description of each title. For your convenience, it is divided into categories in fiction and non-fiction—gothics, science fiction, westerns, mysteries, cookbooks, mysticism and occult, biographies, history, family living, health, psychology, art.

So don't delay—take advantage of this special opportunity to increase your reading pleasure.

Just send us your name and address and 50¢ (to help defray postage and handling costs).

Savak: the Shah's secret police; a Savaker is a secret policeman. Actual Farsi words for which these initials stand are "Security and Information Organization."

sefid: cosmetic pumice

Shahbanu: Queen, Empress (*banu* means woman)

Shahinshah: King of Kings

Shahinshahr: American housing complex outside Esfahan; "shahr" means town, thus "The Shah's town"

shirini: sweet pastries eaten as dessert

takht-e-sab: "throne of sleep," bed

tarof: loosely, hospitality: a system of courtesy

taxi-bargh: a three-wheel, motor driven "wheelbarrow"

tizbahs: worry beads

tooti/tuti: parrot

Tudeh: the Iranian Communist Party

xaerigi: foreigners

Zyand-e-Rud: literally "river of life"